The following is ... the
made by Admiral R... he

" .5 18..

My Lord,

Again I address your Lordship on th...
. My Son has lately visited the Islands
so much insisted on ... your Lordship. A...
Miss Colleton au... Mrs Fullford
and this Power of ... is a Forgery —
similies of the hand writing.

I have therefore to request your Lordshi...
pretended Power of Attorney from my ...
home immediately & its authenticity pu...
...ip may be enabled to produce it withou...
...nor to give sufficient notice of my inten...
...d for in the House of Commons, en the gr...
... establish a right which has been too ...

THE SPITE OF FORTUNE

THE SPITE OF FORTUNE

The Fabulous Story of
an 18th-Century Heiress

KISHANDA FULFORD

ASHGROVE PUBLISHING
London

Contents

*

Contents

Notes on the Text

*

Quotations from letters and documents are presented in their original form.

Converting sums of money from the 18th and 19th centuries to the present day is a matter of controversy, but at a rough estimate one can multiply a sum x200 to give an approximate value. During Louisa and Richard's lifetimes, travel was hugely expensive, as were clothes and food. Their servants, however, cost little, as did labour. Richard's income of £200 a year from the Admiralty was not 'paltry', as he would claim, it is today nearly £26,000, but it was not enough to live as a 'gentleman'.

As significant sums of money appear in this manuscript, I give below, in date order, an approximation of the sums as they would be today:

1729 – payment for the Sovereign Rights to the Bahamas, £17,000,000
1746 – award for the 'Heritable Jurisdictions', £23,000,000
1759 – loan to Sir John Colleton, £50,000
1777 – value of Fairlawn, £25,000,000
1780 – damage to Devil's Elbow, £1,000,000
1785 – value of offer for share in Bahamas, £500,000
1789 – claim for Fairlawn, £2,000,000
1793 – new carriage, £12,000
1808 – Samuel Colleton Graves overspending his allowance, £80,000
1817 – value of Fairlawn and Devil's Elbow £15,000,000
1828 – award to Duke of Atholl for the Sovereign Rights to the Isle of Man £33,000,000

To my husband, Francis,

and our children, Arthur, Matilda, Humphrey and Edmund

Prologue

*

Great Fulford, Devon

HISTORY hangs heavy at Great Fulford which has been the home of my husband's family, the Fulfords, for over eight hundred years. Trunks and boxes are stuffed with deeds and letters, and portraits of the family line the walls. The library shelves groan with row upon row of leather-bound books. It was fate that one day I pulled down a slim volume and opening it read: *Desultory Thoughts, on various subjects, by Louisa Carolina, wife of Rear Admiral Richard Graves of Hembury Fort, Devonshire, and daughter of Sir John Colleton, Baronet. Born Baroness of Fairlawn, Landgravine of Colleton and Sovereign Proprietress of the Isles of Bahama.* Who could fail to be intrigued by someone with such titles?

I hastily turned the pages to find part of Louisa's book was filled with her poems. She wrote, in a vain manner, that by the time she had been 'dust a hundred years', her 'compositions' would be highly prized by her biographer. It was not, however, her charming verses which grabbed my attention but her adventurous life. She was born in 1763, a year before Horace Walpole was to publish *The Castle of Otranto* which began the vogue for Gothic novels and the role of tragic heroines. Having read *Desultory Thoughts…* I rapidly came to the conclusion that there could surely be no more tragic a heroine as Louisa, whose life seemed to have stepped straight out of such a novel.

There was obviously more to Louisa's story than she revealed in her book, and insatiable curiosity led me on a merry dance. To quote Dr Samuel Johnson, 'one inquiry only gave occasion to another'. Louisa herself left what amounted to tantalising clues. I give as an example, a short poem about a pair of pigs she fell in love with, written, she said, while aboard the *Indian Chief.* There was no clue as to *when* she was on this ship, or *why.*

Biographers often mention they are captured by their subjects, and I certainly was. I trawled archives on two sides of the Atlantic, as Louisa inherited land and property both in America and England. I was blessed to find letters that illuminated Louisa's character and that of her husband,

Richard Graves, a naval officer. The history books will tell you that he was one of seven Admirals in his direct family, which could not be matched by any other in the kingdom. The Graves family wrote copious letters, which were mostly concerned with winning the lottery, ensnaring heiresses, deaths and illnesses, the expense of supporting spinster sisters, a dislike of each other, and a dislike of the major players at the Admiralty. The First Lord of the Admiralty, the Earl of Sandwich, notably being referred to as 'that blockhead', by Richard's brother. Whilst Richard and Louisa were living in Devon, their affairs were also the subject of endless gossip. Their neighbour, the spinster bluestocking Miss Mary Anne Burges, liberally sprinkled her letters with the latest news of the 'goings on' at Hembury Fort.

Visitors to Great Fulford very often complain about ghosts; they see a shadowy figure on the stairs or hear the swish of a dress and footsteps outside their bedrooms. Could one be Louisa? She spent much of her childhood at Great Fulford. As I trace her footsteps, I often pass her portrait which hangs in the drawing room. Louisa gazes at me from her oval frame, and I can now look back and say, here is your tale, and tales you did not tell.

CHAPTER 1

The Sovereign Lords Proprietors

*

LOUISA began her memoirs with a brief summary of her 'illustrious' paternal ancestors, the Colletons. Most though sadly is myth or folklore as until the 17th century the Colletons failed to leave any mark in the history books or in the learned county histories compiled in the late 16th and 17th centuries in which Devon is particularly rich. But this did not deter Louisa from weaving a romantic pedigree of the Colletons beginning with one who came over with William the Conqueror in 1066. The truth is that the family sometime in the 12/13th century took their surname from a manor or farm called Colleton where they lived. In Anglo Saxon, Colleton translates as 'Coles Farm' and as Cole was a popular name among Saxon Devonions, there are a number of different places from which Louisa's ancestors could have originated.

Whatever their origins, the Colletons had by the 17th century become established as merchants in Exeter and by the start of the Civil War in 1642 John Colleton, the head of the family, was one of the richest amongst them. While most of the citizens of Exeter chose the side of Parliament, he, together with some of other of the more notable citizens, declared for the king thus ending up on the losing side and paying greatly for it.

At the end of the civil war, Colleton was fined for his 'delinquency in having opposed Parliament' and had his estates confiscated. Impoverished, Colleton left England after the execution of Charles I in 1649, to seek his fortune on the island of Barbados. The island was booming due to Europe's insatiable demand for sugar, and Barbados had both the ideal climate and rich and fertile soil which produced enormous yields of sugar cane.

Five years later, out of fear that his Barbadian property might be confiscated by the Puritans, Colleton feigned allegiance to Oliver Cromwell, the 'Protector'. Consequently, he was able to secure his holdings in the West Indies and was also given back his English estates. Colleton became the third largest landowner on the island and built a house, called Colleton Great House (which still stands today), in the north of the island. A contemporary visitor there noted, 'The gentry here doth Hue [appear] far better than ours do in England: they have most of them 100 or 2 or

3 of slave apes who they command as they please,… This Island is inhabited with all sorts: with English, French, Dutch, Scots, Irish, Spaniards they being Jews: with Indians and miserable Negroes borne to perpetual slavery they and their seed: these Negroes they do allow as many wives as they will have, some will have 3 or 4, according as they find their body able: our English here doth think a negro child the first day it is born to be worth £5, they cost them nothing the bringing up, they go all ways naked: some planters will have 30 more or less about 4 or 5 years old: they sell them from one to the other as we do sheep.'

In 1660 the momentous news reached Barbados that the monarchy was to be restored, and Colleton immediately took a ship for England. He, like every other old cavalier who had served the king's father at great personal cost, was heading for London in the hope of reaping some reward for their loyalty. Most of them it has to be said were probably hoping for estates lost to be restored or some form of monetary compensation in the form of a pension or perhaps a lucrative sinecure. There were also titles to be had, which cost the relatively impecunious Charles II nothing but the expense of the parchment and sealing wax. Colleton was granted a baronetcy for his 'attachment to his beloved and ill-fated sovereign', and became 'Sir John Colleton of London'.

Sir John had ambitions far beyond a baronetcy, and the slave trade, in which he was now heavily involved having established 'The Royal Adventurers in Africa' with the king's flamboyant nephew, Prince Rupert of the Rhine. The new baronet had left four sons in Barbados, where the soil had worn thin, and there was barely a tree left standing. His ship had though, by chance, been blown by a hurricane down the East coast of America. While sheltering in an estuary, he saw from the deck a 'land ripe for planting and trees of great girth'. The area, south of Virginia, was claimed by England but had yet to be colonised. Sir John turned to his kinsman, the gallant Captain General George Monck, now Duke of Albemarle, who had been primarily responsible for Charles II gaining his throne. Together they lobbied the king for a charter to exploit the land.

For the king, it was a means of preventing encroachment from rival foreign powers, and a means to reward his loyal supporters. On March 24th 1663, he granted eight men, known as the 'Sovereign Lords Proprietors', which included Sir John Colleton and the Duke of Albermarle, 'the parts of America not yet cultivated or planted, and only inhabited by some barbarous people, who have no knowledge of Almighty God.'

'Carolana', named in honour of the king, encompassed more than 840,000 square miles of land south of Virginia and north of Spanish Florida stretching from the Atlantic to Pacific Oceans. The Sovereign Lords Proprietors, and their heirs in perpetuity, were given almost sovereign rights and immense powers, including that of waging war.

In September, with the Royal Charter in their possession, the Lords Proprietors held their first meeting in the 'cock pitt', a suite of rooms in the palace of Whitehall that covered Henry VIII's cock fighting pit, and which had once been used by Oliver Cromwell as an office. Alongside Sir John Colleton and the Duke of Albermarle, were six other 'well beloved' and 'trusty' subjects of the king, and included the enigmatic Antony Ashley Cooper, 'The Lord Ashley', Chancellor of the Exchequer; Sir John Colleton's old commanding officer, Lord John Berkeley and his brother Sir William Berkeley, the Governor of Virginia. The grandfather of Charles II's first illegitimate son, Sir George Carteret, knight and baronet, 'vice chamberlain of our household' had also been rewarded as had 'Edward Earl of Clarendon, our High Chancellor of England', and the veteran soldier 'William, Lord Craven', who had bankrolled the king and his aunt, Elizabeth of Bohemia, when in exile.

Just three years after the charter was granted, Sir John Colleton was on his deathbed when he received the news that the first settlers in Carolina had left for want of supplies. He died of malaria, probably contracted in Barbados, in the winter of 1666/7. His ambitious eldest son, Peter, now thirty-three, became the second baronet and was, according to a contemporary, a 'chip off the block.' On his father's death, Sir Peter sailed for London and would establish himself in a brand-new house in Golden Square, St James's, from where he bankrolled one of the king's pet projects. Sir Peter also took his hereditary place as Lord Proprietor of Carolina.

The Lords Proprietors commissioned John Locke, the noted philosopher, to draw up a 'Grand Model' for the governance of the new colony, which promised freedom of worship as well as the prospect of a title that the Lords Proprietors could bestow as long as they differed from those in England. 'Landgraves' would own four 'Baronies', each barony containing 12,000 acres (18.75 square miles). Below them were 'Cassiques' who would own two baronies, while 'Lords of the Manor' would hold a single barony. Hence Louisa's titles, 'Landgravine of Colleton' and 'Baroness of Fairlawn' inscribed on the flyleaf of her memoirs. The historian Edward

McCrady wrote of the Lords Proprietors' feudal ambitions: 'This was a most extraordinary scheme of forming an aristocratic government in a colony of adventurers in the wild woods.'

The Lords Proprietors wanted wealthy settlers, including established and experienced colonials from Barbados, Virginia and New England because as Lord Ashley wrote, money was needed to stock Carolina with 'Negroes, Cattle and other Necessarys.' Every Tuesday, the Lords Proprietors or their agents were to be found in the Carolina Coffee House, in the City of London, to be on hand to encourage settlers to go to Carolina, where they boasted that land was a tenth of the price in England, and twice as productive.

In 1669, three ships the Lords Proprietors had purchased, the *Albermarle*, the *Port Royal* and the *Carolina*, set sail for Carolina on August 1st. On board were about one hundred and forty passengers, which comprised of nineteen families with their servants, thirteen lone settlers and the Lord Proprietors' servants, who were tasked to carry out experiments on crops. Only one, the *Carolina*, completed the voyage and having landed at Port Royal in March 1670 the settlers were advised by local Indians to move further north, to Albermarle Point. There, they discovered miles of virgin forest filled with game, clear rivers and streams, and an abundance of oysters and clams on the seashore.

It soon became of concern to the Lords Proprietors that the Bahamas, a straggling collection of mostly uninhabited islands lying off the coast of Florida, might be taken by the Spanish and used as a base to strangle trade to and from the new colony. To counter this threat, in 1670, Charles II granted Sir Peter Colleton and five of the original Lords Proprietors, (two were then out of favour) a charter for the Bahamas on similar terms to those for Carolina. Louisa would, in time, become a 'Sovereign Proprietress' of the islands, and it was a title of which she would be inordinately proud, but one which would cast a long and profound shadow over her life.

By then, Charles Town had been established on land where two great rivers, the Ashley and the Cooper, converge. The rivers were named after Anthony Ashley Cooper, and his fellow proprietors too stamped their names on counties, bays, and rivers across the colony. In 1675, Lord Ashley, who was now the Earl of Shaftsbury, was granted a 12,000-acre tract on the River Ashley, and the second notable grant by the Lords Proprietors, in 1678, was to Sir Peter Colleton who took possession of 'Fairlawne', which covered 12,000 acres adjacent to the River Cooper.

Sir Peter's younger brothers, Thomas and James were also granted great swathes of land: John, the third of the brothers, had by then died of injuries sustained in a duel. Thomas, a 'landgrave', second only in seniority to a Proprietor in their feudal rankings and entitled to 48,000 acres, was granted the Barony of Cypress, on the headwaters of the eastern branch of the River Cooper. While James, also a landgrave, had laid out for him, amongst other blocks, the Barony of Wadboo on the opposite bank of the River Cooper to 'Fair-lawne'.

The problem for the Lords Proprietors was recruiting reliable Governors and officials who would carry out their instructions and rule the colony in their best interests. Eventually, after a number of failures, in 1686 they asked James Colleton to take the post. Initially this was a success. Carolina was then plagued by pirates many of whom sheltered in the Bahamas. As one Captain had written: ' as surely as spiders abound where there are nooks and crannies, so have pirates sprung up whenever there is a nest of islands offering creeks and shallows, headlands, rocks and reefs - facilities in short, for lurking, for surprise, for attack, for escape'. James however soon sent word to London to say he had 'stamped out the sea robbers'. While the antics of the pirates were of concern to the Proprietors, so was the continuing illegal slave trading of the indigenous Indians in Carolina. Sir Peter Colleton ordered James to put a stop to the trade: 'These poor people have done us no injury... We are determined to break this barbarous practice.' The Proprietors could foresee that there would come a time when the Indians would rise up against the colonists as they had done to previous French and Spanish settlers. James however ignored his brother, and made a deal with the leader of the Yamasee tribe who agreed to send three hundred of his tribe to work at Wadboo for the next seven years.

In 1690, James, who was renowned for his bad temper, and having declared martial law, was ousted as Governor of Carolina and ordered to London to face charges. He chose to ignore the edict and with his posse of Indian slaves began to experiment with growing rice at Wadboo. James was more successful as a farmer than Governor: an observer wrote that he grew rice in both savannah and swamp, and 'without any weeding or howing he has a most glorious and hopefull crop of Rice beyond any field of corne I ev'r saw in Europ'. While James was planting rice and ignoring his brother's orders it was reported that Sir Peter was 'dangerously ill of asthma', and he subsequently died on March 4th 1694.

Sir Peter's heir, Sir John, the 3rd baronet, was only fourteen when he inherited his father's considerable estates in England, Barbados and Carolina. He came of age in 1700, and attended his first meeting as Lord Proprietor in 1702. He would never travel to Carolina, which in 1712 was divided into North and South Carolina. But in 1726, after great dissent among settlers against the Lords Proprietor's rule, Sir John anticipated that the charter for Carolina, would by some means, be revoked. The baronet then owned about 27,000 acres in South Carolina, and decided to send his two sons to the colony to take possession of the land. John the eldest, at the age of twenty-six, was given Fairlawn, a barony on the western branch of the River Cooper, some thirty miles from Charles Town that had been granted to his grandfather, Sir Peter Colleton, nearly fifty years before. Peter, John's younger brother, was given the remote barony of Devil's Elbow, near Port Royal. His father had won the barony in a lottery held between the Proprietors for land that had been captured from the Yamasee Indians after a bloody war. Louisa would later inherit both plantations.

In 1729, as Sir John had anticipated, the British government compelled the Lord Proprietors to sell their charters back to the crown. One, John Carteret, 2nd Baron Carteret, later 2nd Earl of Granville, refused to sell and was given land in North Carolina in lieu which remained in the family until American Independence. The condition of the grant mandated the baronet would have no say in political matters there. The other seven Lords Proprietors were however paid £12,500 for their rights over Carolina, and an additional sum of £5,000 for rents due.

When John and his brother Peter arrived in South Carolina in 1726, the colony, then sixty-three years old, was booming. This was due, principally, to the exportation of significant quantities of tar, pitch, turpentine, rice, and deer skins. The brothers soon made their fortunes by following in the footsteps of their great-uncle, James Colleton, and grew rice. Both Devil's Elbow and Fairlawn provided ideal conditions for its cultivation.

John decided to settle in the colony and on the proceeds of 'Carolina gold', as rice was known, he set about building a house at Fairlawn that would not look out of place in the English countryside. Louisa would later write: 'This mansion, as it was for a family residence was of course very magnificent.' In those days of prosperity, Charles Town could compete with any sophisticated European city. The cellars at Fairlawn were filled with the finest claret, and the ladies of the colony had no need to order dresses from Paris or London. John would not deign to marry a colonist so went to England for 'wigs and wife', and in 1730 married his first cousin, Susannah Snell. They returned to South Carolina, and after John was appointed to the Royal Council* in 1736 he became widely known as the 'Honourable John Colleton'.

His father, the hermit-like 3rd baronet, had by now left London to live at Rill Manor on the coast at Exmouth, in Devon, near to his English estates. There, he and his wife were attended to by a retinue of both American Indian and black slaves which the Honourable John had brought with him from Carolina on his rare visits to England. He had also brought with him native plants, which Sir John tended to in his large glasshouse. Soon the brick walls which surrounded his garden were adorned with exotic flowers that had for the most part never before been seen in England. His prized specimen was a magnolia he named *magnolia grandiflora exonia*. The gardens attracted many visitors, including the famous naturalist, Mark Catesby. As the baronet pottered in his glasshouse, generously dispatching cuttings to friends, he remained largely detached from the lives of his two sons in South Carolina.

While John and Peter steadfastly improved their plantations, James Colleton, the son of Sir Peter Colleton's illegitimate son Charles, had clashed with Indians. Charles had been harshly treated by his father in his will, for siding against the Lords Proprietors, and had been left only Fairlight, a plantation of five hundred acres to the northwest of Fairlawn. It was at Fairlight that James was 'killed by a blow from a hatchet thrown into the verandah of the house by an Indian Chief, who came with his gang to demand spirits according to their custom.' His orphaned daughter, Anne, had been brought to England and was later married off to the 3rd baronet's youngest son, Robert.

Robert suddenly became the owner of Devil's Elbow after his elder brother, Peter, drowned on a voyage to England in 1748. Robert was a soldier, scholar, linguist and inveterate traveller with no desire to manage

---

* The Royal Council consisted of twelve men who served as advisors to the Governor, and upheld British policy. The Honourable John's appointment would have been approved of in London by the Board of Trade. Members of the Royal Council were the Carolina equivalent of the British House of Lords, presiding over a Court of Appeals and approving legislature. Unpaid, they met only when called on by the Governor. The Commons House of Assembly was the lower house of provincial legislature – equivalent to the British House of Commons – whose members were elected.

the plantation and he made a gentleman's agreement with his brother, the Honourable John, to receive profits from part of Fairlawn, in exchange for Devil's Elbow. It was not the only death in the family that year. The Honourable John's eldest son, who had been sent to England at the age of ten to be educated under the watchful eye of his grandfather, also died in 1748, at Rill Manor, aged eighteen. So did his younger sister, Hannah, at Fairlawn. She was most likely a victim of the yellow fever epidemic that year. Dr John Lining, then working in Charles Town, described his patients vomiting blood, and hemorrhaging from the nose, eyes, and ears; liver failure would follow and victims would be dead within seven to ten days of being infected.

Disaster again struck the family four years later when the Honourable John, at fifty-two and one of the richest men in the colony, died at Fairlawn in August 1752. An inventory of Fairlawn showed that he owned more than two hundred slaves. His wife, Susannah, a month after giving birth to a daughter, followed her husband to the graveyard that December. This left their surviving son, John, (later Louisa's father), then fourteen, and his two sisters, one-year-old Elizabeth, and the infant Susannah without any close family on the continent.

For reasons unknown, the 3rd baronet did not bring his orphaned grandchildren back to England. It might have been expected that the heir to the baronet's title, young John, would be brought back to England to be educated, as had been the case with his brother. Instead, the elderly baronet, now seventy-three and a widower, wrote to his lawyers in the colony giving them authority to manage the plantations and take charge of his grandchildren. He stipulated that all the carriages and horses were to be sold, 'except what is absolutely necessary for plantation use.' The lawyers were ordered to take everything of value into their custody, including the silver and plate, with the exception of a 'little silver boat for feeding young children', and six silver spoons. These items were to be delivered to 'Mrs Jones' at Fairlawn, who was to give a receipt for them: she no doubt had charge of the children as well. However, the children's fate would soon be in the hands of their grandfather's lawyer, William Field.

The 3rd baronet died in September 1754. He had left as his executors his son, Robert, and his housekeeper, Miss Collins. Such was Robert's distrust of Miss Collins that after receiving news his father was dying, he had rushed from London, (suffering a crashing fall from his horse on the way) to Rill Manor to sweep up as many of his father's papers as he could find. Four months later, Robert was dead from his injuries, but before his untimely death he had deposited the 3rd baronet's papers with William Field, together with his own. Miss Collins, the spinster daughter of a vicar, had been well provided for in the will of the old baronet; she had been left the use of Rill Manor for her life, together with a generous annuity. But this was insufficient reward for her so she sold most of the contents of the house and, pocketing the money, left it to look after itself. Miss Collins, however, had not dared to sell the baronet's books, which she later told the court were 'in storage', or his magnificent jewels which Louisa would later wear with great effect and delight.

The housekeeper then colluded with William Field, who had been appointed as guardian to the Colleton children in South Carolina, to defraud young John, now the 4th Colleton baronet.

It was not until the late winter of 1755, more than a year after their grandfather's death, that Field decided to bring the now seventeen-year-old Sir John Colleton and his sisters back to England, and place them in Rill Manor. On arrival there, Sir John was horrified at the state of the manor, and the once much-vaunted garden was full of holes as neighbours had raided the rare and desirable plants; in particular the magnolias. The glasshouse was littered with pots of desiccated plants and, thanks to Miss Collins, the house was almost empty of the 3rd baronet's possessions.

Sir John wrote to Field demanding that monies be made available so that he and his sisters could live in the state to which they were accustomed, only to be fobbed off with the excuse that there were no funds. Now, the young man showed his mettle. In early 1756 he managed, with the help of his relation, the 4th Earl of Rochford, to take both Field and Miss Collins to court and triumph. In Field's stead, the court appointed the Earl of Rochford, and other relations as Sir John's guardians who ensured sufficient monies were made available for the young Colletons' living expenses and education. Oddly, even though Field had been found unfit by the court, Sir John's new guardians did not challenge Field for the Colleton family papers. This was to prove a crucial mistake for the whole family, including, many years later, Louisa herself.

In 1759, after the successful court case, Sir John and his sisters left Rill Manor and went to live in the Colleton family house in Exeter. There, he was swept into the narrow channels of English high society.

CHAPTER 2

Tell Mama

*

IN the spring of 1763, Sir John's wife, the twenty-year-old Lady Colleton lay in a darkened room at Fairlawn, awaiting the birth of her fourth child. The air was heavy with the scent of wild jasmine abounding in the gardens around the house, and the haunting calls of mourning doves floated into her room. The young girl would have had little hope that her child would live long; in the preceding three years a son and two daughters had not survived the ever-present diseases lurking in the swamps of Carolina's countryside.

Before her marriage to the 4th baronet, Sir John Colleton, in Exeter on a cold February day in 1759, the then sixteen-year-old Ann Fulford would not have previously entertained the thought that she would soon be leaving England to live in America. The scribbles on the endpapers of one of her precious leather-bound books, dated only a year before her wedding, clearly reveal a naïve teenager. Her father, Francis Fulford, scion of an ancient landed family in Devon, had died when Ann was six. Ann, her three brothers and mother had continued to live at Great Fulford, a large four-square Tudor mansion set around a courtyard and commonly agreed to be one of the most imposing houses in the west of England. It was set in an estate of more than 4,000 acres some ten miles west of Exeter on the edge of Dartmoor. Ann probably had little say in the matter of her marriage to the twenty-year-old baronet. Her mother, considered Sir John a good match; the baronet had property not only in South Carolina but also in Devon, Dorset, Hertfordshire and the City of London.

On reaching his majority in August 1759, Sir John finally came into his estate. He discovered that the income from his English estates was insufficient to cover his considerable debts in South Carolina that had accumulated during his minority due to mismanagement of his plantations. He decided that it was imperative that he return to South Carolina and put his plantations at Fairlawn and Devil's Elbow in order. Ann began packing their bags for what she assumed would be a temporary visit, and that, once Sir John had sorted out his affairs, they would return to England leaving their colonial property in the hands of local agents and lawyers.

Sir John decided to leave his two young sisters with their paternal aunt, Mary. Her husband, Wenman Nutt, had the lucrative occupation of collecting customs duty on the River Thames and the children were duly delivered to the Nutt's lodgings in the Tower of London. There was also the matter of funding the journey to America and Sir John, out of necessity, went to the rogue William Field for a loan. The funds that Field subsequently lent him, about £400, was money he had siphoned from the Colleton estate.

At the beginning of October 1759, Sir John and Ann left England on board one of several merchant ships sailing under the protection of the warship, HMS *Mermaid* – the Seven Years' War with France was then in its third year. Some six weeks later, on November 17th, the convoy was guided across the ever-shifting sandbars into Charles Town harbour. With some difficulty in the driving rain, the ships dropped anchor among a mêlée of nearly a hundred vessels filling the port. The passengers disembarked and joined the 8,000 people then living in Charles Town, of which approximately half were white, and the remainder slaves. After a devastating hurricane in 1752 that destroyed nearly five hundred houses, the city now appeared almost newly built. But despite the new houses and the traffic in the harbour, one of the richest American colonies was at a low point – the war had greatly disrupted exports and smallpox raged in the city, sending people to their graves every day.

Had it not been for the smallpox epidemic, the Colletons would have recovered from their taxing Atlantic crossing at Sir John's townhouse in the city. Instead, they immediately made their way by schooner up the River Cooper to Fairlawn. On both sides of the river, set back from the banks, plantation houses rose against the background of woodland. Spreading out in front of the houses were formal gardens and meadows leading down to the river where great live oaks dipped their roots in the brackish and inky water. Lurking amongst the banks were alligators: their flared nostrils, armoured backs, and great tails just visible above the waterline when the tide ebbed. Ann had been transported into another world, far from the library at Great Fulford where such beasts were only to be seen illustrated in books.

Nearly thirty miles from Charles Town, the River Cooper divides and Sir John's schooner took the western branch. News of their arrival had already reached Fairlawn's 'patroon', Haman, who as well as being in charge of the schooners belonging to the plantation, was also responsible for sounding the horn as soon as he caught sight of his approaching master. Indeed, when Sir John and Ann landed at the pier, a carriage emblazoned with the Colleton coat of arms awaited them. As they left the river behind them, they passed by a village of wooden shacks which provided meagre living quarters for nearly two hundred slaves working on the plantation. Some of them were descended from those purchased by Sir John's great-grandfather, Sir Peter Colleton, after he had taken possession of the barony in 1678.

During the mile's drive on a straight sandy track from the river to the house, Ann saw only a glimpse of the 12,000 acres of Fairlawn. The plantation was a mixture of rice fields, forests, watery swamps, marshland, and other land, now bare but which would be planted in the spring with cereal and rice crops. The terrain was gently rolling near the river, but a mile back was almost flat, rarely rising.

When they arrived at Fairlawn, household slaves dressed in fine livery adorned with silver buttons and stamped with the Colleton crest stood on an impressive flight of steps leading to the main entrance. At just seventeen, Ann was now chatelaine of what was arguably the grandest house in South Carolina, only rivalled by Drayton Hall, thirty-five miles from Fairlawn on the River Ashley. The new Lady Colleton was shown into a handsome, cedar-panelled hall hung with English landscapes, where she warmed herself by the fire – it was unseasonably cold and wet winter.

In the middle of the hall stood a mahogany dining table on which were laid out three pairs of silver-plated candlesticks and a large silver punch bowl and ladle: 'well-stuffed' chairs, covered in the finest French green brocade were placed on either side of the doorways that led to the everyday domestic rooms. The parlour would become Ann's domain, and was well-furnished with expensive looking-glasses, a mahogany breakfast table and a small kettle and stand for making hot drinks.

Behind the hall, a sweeping mahogany staircase rose to the 'Long Room', which ran almost the entire length of the first floor. Off the Long Room was the Colleton's bedroom, the 'Blue Chamber', which had its own commodious closet. The room was furnished with a four-poster bed, several chests of drawers, a 'toilet table and washstand' and half-a-dozen chairs. On the floor, at the foot of the bed, was a large iron chest in which were stored letters, jewellery, deeds, and the family Bible. Along one wall stretched a bureau bookcase containing more than a hundred volumes. Also off the Long Room was the drawing room, decorated with plaster-work, and furnished with pier glasses, card tables, and sofas. Silk curtains framed the windows, and on the floor was a large Wilton carpet imported from England. There were several further bedrooms off the Long Room, all of which had adjacent closets. In another wing, was the kitchen, quarters for the household slaves, and offices. There was also a secure storeroom in which ornate pieces of silver, pistols, swords, sugar, damask tablecloths, maps of Carolina and valuable charts of the waters off the Carolina coast were locked away.

The house had views over gardens and landscaped ponds created by the Honourable John, and roaming in the paddocks were horses, working oxen, a large number of cattle, sheep and pigs. There were several outbuildings; some were used to store crops, another for the blacksmith's anvil and bellows, stables, and housing for the carriages. The overseer lived in his own house nearby.

Sir John and Ann had arrived in the winter and in South Carolina that time of year heralded the new 'season'. Plantation owners would leave the country for their townhouses in Charles Town. There were balls to enjoy, evenings at the theatre, and afternoons spent in leisure in the well-stocked town library or at William's Coffee House where the men met to discuss current affairs, politics and commerce. However, the continuing smallpox epidemic prevented the elite from gathering in Charles Town for their normal festivities, so at Fairlawn the carriages gathered dust.

Ann felt isolated at Fairlawn and soon became dreadfully homesick. She could not understand the slaves, who spoke in their common language, gullah, and they were her only company apart from her husband. The Colletons had few neighbours, and these lived at some distance from Fairlawn. The nearest, had he been in residence, would have been Sir John's cousin, Colonel Colleton, who owned the nearby Baronies of Mepkin and Mesphew, and Wadboo, also on the River Cooper. But he lived in London and his family had not even visited Carolina since 1694 when his grandfather, Governor James Colleton, was banished from the province. The Broughtons, at the relatively nearby plantation of Mulberry, were most often in Charles Town. The Colleton's only visitor, that dreary and cold winter, was Colonel Colleton's agent, Robert Raper, who had called into Fairlawn on his way back to Charles Town from Wadboo. After his visit to Fairlawn, Raper wrote to the Colonel, and said of Sir John: 'I understand he finds affairs very bad he told me he must borrow money to pay his estates' debts.'

South Carolina also faced the terrors of an Indian uprising. The Cherokees had been on a war footing after they had been attacked by settlers in Virginia in the late winter of 1758. By February 1760, groups of marauding Cherokees were only fifty miles from Fairlawn. The widespread tales of Indians scalping and torturing captives were not exaggerated. The *South Carolina Gazette* reported: 'A hundred-and-fifty settlers were attacked by a hundred Cherokees on horseback: After the massacre, many of the children were found helplessly wandering in the woods. One man alone carried to Augusta no less than nine of the pitiful innocents, some horribly mutilated with the tomahawk, others scalped, and all yet alive.' As Robert Raper wrote at the time, 'No war is so bad as an Indian war.'

The Americans called upon the British for military assistance to help defeat the Indians, but it was not until the summer of 1761 that the war came to an end, and the smallpox epidemic waned. Ann's hopes of returning to England were dashed by the arrival, in December, of the new governor, Sir John's cousin, Thomas Boone. The following year Sir John was duly elected to the Commons House of Assembly, where more than half the members were descended from the original seventeenth-century settlers. Colony business meant that the Colletons now spent part of their time in Charles Town where vultures swayed on currents in search of carrion above gabled houses, taverns, and 'houses of correction' built for errant slaves.

The city proved more entertaining for Ann than being at Fairlawn. The Surgeon General, George Milligen-Johnston, wrote at the time: 'The Men and Women who have a Right to the Class of Gentry (who are more numerous here than any other Colony in *North America*) dress with elegance and neatness.' He recounted that the 'Ladies' were genteel and slender, with fair complexions, and that they were 'fond of Dancing, an Exercise they perform very gracefully.' And, he boasted they 'could not be excelled in social virtues necessary for the Happiness of the other Sex, as Daughters, Wives, or Mothers'. The assembled women often had the humiliation of being served by the half-caste offspring of their husbands who rather than being sent to work in the fields became household slaves. The 'gentlemen of the province', Milligen–Johnston wrote, drank copious amounts of claret, port and Madeira while the ladies mostly drank water, which was then particularly unpleasant in Charles Town, having a mixture of sand and earth in it. The gentlemen would hunt when it was cool enough, and raced their horses. The South Carolina Jockey Club had been established in 1758, and races, now held on the New Market course, were the highlight of the social season.

As Fairlawn was then in order, Sir John turned his attention to Devil's Elbow, which took its name from a bend in the River Okatee which formed one of the boundaries of the plantation. The barony boasted the deepest natural channel south of Norfolk, Virginia. Sprawling salt marshes were fed by tributaries which coiled their way down to the estuary, and the land behind served well for the raising of cattle. Two years before his death in 1750, Sir John's father made an agreement with a planter, Morgan Saab, to develop the plantation. This would last for seven years and both men shared the cost of 114 slaves: a further fifty had been sent to the plantation by Sir John's mother shortly before she died. Under the agreement Morgan Saab was to, 'clear and cultivate and make plantations and work & labour upon the said Barony by improving and breeding flocks planting rice corn and other grain sawing timber making pitch tar turpentine Indigo & other commodities thereon.' Indigo, a plant that rendered a valuable blue dye, was then a relatively new crop in the colony, but one that could be grown on land above the rice fields. Having seen for himself that indigo flourished at Devil's Elbow, Sir John set more land over to the crop. When in production, which required skilled and intense labour, it would attract swarms of flies, and the pervasive odour from the vats was apparent over more than a quarter of a mile's distance. It is unlikely that Ann ever travelled to Devil's Elbow as there were no suitable living quarters.

In 1762, the Colletons had new neighbours on the River Cooper. Sir John's cousin, Colonel Colleton, a very extravagant man, had sold his three-thousand-acre plantation of Mepkin to Henry Laurens for £8,000. Henry's father, of Huguenot descent, had been one of the most successful saddlers in the colony, and made enough money to send Henry to London as an intern with a company of merchants. On his return to Charles Town, Henry set himself up as a merchant in commodities, and also became a slave trader. It is estimated he and his partners sold nearly ten thousand slaves. They also exported rice, indigo and skins whilst importing necessities such as frying pans, lead paint, rope, Cheshire cheese, blankets and cider. Out of the proceeds of his lucrative trading activities, Henry built a substantial townhouse in Charles Town, set in four acres of productive garden, which boasted an English head gardener. A fellow Huguenot descendant, Mrs Ravenel, admired the garden and wrote that besides shrubs and flowers, the garden was filled with 'oranges, sugar cane, figs, olives, and numerous rare and beautiful plants gathered from distant lands.' But, Henry had long aspired to join the higher echelons of land-owner and planter.

Henry largely shunned social occasions, preferring to work, and his wife, Eleanor, and the 'high faluting' Lady Colleton had little in common except that both their families hailed from the same English county. Eleanor's family, the Balls, came of peasant stock from North Devon. Eleanor had been brought up on a plantation where the only book in the house was a copy of the Bible. She spent her days not only caring for her many children, but for her slave as well: dispensing medicine and making clothes for newborn babies. Ann, in contrast, is known to have not shown the slightest interest in or concern for the welfare of her slaves.

Despite the disparity between the two women, they had one common bond which was the loss of their children in infancy. There is no account as to why Ann's three children died, but perfectly healthy children, such as Henry Laurens son, 'as fine and promising a boy as was ever born under my roof', contracted 'purple thrush' at two weeks old and was dead in three days. His daughter, Martha, was more fortunate. As an infant she caught smallpox and believed to be dead, 'was actually laid out prepara-tory to her burial'. Martha was only saved because her physician later returned to the room and saw in her a sign of life. Mrs Manigault, the wife of one of the richest men in the colony at the time, wrote a diary in which she frequently comments on the illnesses and numerous deaths in her family and acquaintances. They suffered from fevers, boils, smallpox, measles, whooping cough and deadly sore throats.

Now, in the spring of 1763, Ann lay in confinement at Fairlawn awaiting the birth of her fourth child. On March 14th she was delivered of a daugh-ter, Louisa Carolina, who was destined to survive. She was born on a Mon-day and, as predicted by the old nursery rhyme, she would indeed be 'fair of face'. Ann sent word to her family in England of Louisa's safe arrival, and added that she 'hated the Carolinas, and pined for England'.

A few months after Louisa was born, the Seven Years' War ended. Under the terms of the peace treaty between England and France, the British took possession of Quebec, Florida, Minorca, most of India and large parts of the West Indies – 'A vast Empire', the diplomat George Macartney observed, 'on which the sun never sets'. The end of the war stimulated trade with the American colonies and for the next two years

Sir John Colleton's plantations began to make substantial profits. He was now renowned for growing indigo considered as 'equal in quality to the best French', and had also turned more land at Fairlawn over to rice. Aside from the ever-present tensions between the local Royal Assembly and the Royal Governor, South Carolina continued to prosper.

But in 1765 the British Government passed the 'Stamp Act' to raise money from the colonies to defray the costs of the Seven Years' War and the war against the Cherokees. This levied a tax on items made of paper, including newspapers, legal documents and playing cards. The colonists were furious at this internal tax, created in Parliament where they had no representation. By October that year, there were widespread protests and riots. Shipping was disrupted – Robert Raper reported to Colonel Colleton in London that 'the port is shut up still and will continue so without the Stamp Act is repealed or some orders from the ministry to let ships load and depart'. Raper later informed the Colonel that he was at a loss as to what to do with the crops, 'I cannot sell it nor can I ship it.'

Because of the fierce opposition in the colonies to the Stamp Act, it was repealed in May of 1766. This had a salubrious effect on trade; the price achieved for rice was soon higher than it had ever been, even higher, adjusted for inflation, than it had been during the Honourable John's time. Sir John now resigned from the Royal Assembly and accepted in June an appointment to the Royal Council. The Board of Trade in England had instructed the new Lieutenant Governor, William Bull, to appoint 'men of good life and well affected to our government and of good estates and abilities'. They wanted English gentlemen, such as Sir John, who owned swathes of land, or rich merchants and lawyers to keep the increasingly powerful members of the Assembly in check. Sir John was duly sworn in and took his seat alongside forty-eight of the richest men and most influential men in the colony. Ann's dream of returning to England became ever more distant.

Sir John was now often in Charles Town, the seat of power, and was there when word reached him from Fairlawn that his only surviving child, then four years old, was ill and in danger of dying. He rushed back to the plantation. Louisa later wrote, 'my life was despaired of, the European doctors having given me over.' It was then that her attendant nurses 'who recollecting that there was an African on the barony, said to be well skilled in magic and herbs, entreated my parents to permit him to be called in; to which they readily consented; for, although they had no confidence in his magic, they were well aware that the African doctors were skilled in medicinal herbs.' With hope receding, the African was allowed into the nursery where he stayed with Louisa all night. At dawn, he asked Sir John for permission to collect plants from the woods before the sun got to them. Before he left, he placed a Bible under Louisa's head. He then, according to Louisa, returned with a juice he had pressed from 'potent herbs' that would save her life.

When Louisa was strong enough, she was sent with her nurse to a boarding school in Charles Town for the sea air. The school was probably also attended by Henry Lauren's daughter, Martha. She was a few years older than Louisa and later recounted that she had been in class one day when, in a 'moment of irritation', her teacher threw her precious doll out of the window. She was, according to Martha, a 'waspish person'. Louisa suffered too. She wrote: 'The benefit in the change of air was counteracted by the conduct of the Governess, who chose to confine me during the school hours, equally with her pupils. I remember one day my nurse came to the door of the school room, and beckoned me to her, tired of confinement, I gladly ran over to her but was obliged to return; my nurse exclaimed on her interference that I was only sent there for a change of air, for the benefit of my health, which would be injured by sitting still so long.'

Louisa's nurse remonstrated with the governess in vain until the appearance of Haman, Fairlawn's patron, followed by two of his sailors – 'all three bearing large baskets on their heads, filled with the produce of the plantations consisting of green corn which in that country is deemed a great delicacy, fruits of various sorts etc. etc. which they laid at my feet; when the patroon asked what he should say to my parents respecting my health since I had been in town? "Tell mamma I wish she would fetch me directly: I can't stay here any longer; they will not let me go to my nurse when I want to play, but make me sit still." I am quite sick and tired.'

Louisa's message to her parents prompted them to collect her and when back at Fairlawn, 'finding I had not derived any benefit from the change of air, it was determined that my mother should immediately take me to England…'

CHAPTER 3

Spurious Issue

*

AFTER eight years in South Carolina, it was without regret that Lady Colleton stood on the deck of the ship and watched the coastline fade into the distance. The journey to England must have been exciting for four-year-old Louisa, who soon became a favourite of crew and passengers. But for most, weeks spent on board a damp, creaking 'wooden kingdom' was taxing. And, even for some hardened sailors, sea sickness would take its toll. There were no antidotes, but at the time beef stock or rum were considered the most effective remedies. Some passengers spent all day in bed and only ventured out onto the deck in calm weather. As the ship rolled and lurched on the long swells, books remained closed and chess sets firmly shut. The passengers could no more than stoically wait out the voyage.

Their ship sailed with the prevailing winds and currents of the Atlantic Ocean. Finally, the lush volcanic island of Madeira could be seen, shrouded in cloud. Once in the harbour the passengers disembarked to lodge on the island for a few days, while the ship was resupplied with fresh water and provisions. It was not until the latter end of November 1767 that Ann and Louisa arrived in Bristol, from where they travelled to Exeter and then by post-chaise to Ann's ancestral home, Great Fulford. The ten-mile journey from Exeter took them along rough, rutted lanes enclosed by thick hedges and through small hamlets of whitewashed thatched cottages before they arrived at a grand set of gates. The carriage then clattered on the neatly cobbled drive under an avenue of beech trees until the road turned a sharp corner, and through the window Louisa caught first sight of her mother's old home.

The exterior of the house had not altered in the eight years since Ann had left England. Great Fulford had once been described as 'a large and stately pile standing pleasantly on a gentle ascent in open but somewhat coarse country'. However, significant alterations had been made by Ann's eldest brother, John Fulford, to the surrounding 'coarse country'. He had indulged in the new fashion of landscape gardening and the results were dramatic. In front of the house where once a stream had run through the valley, there lay a great expanse of water. The old stables had been knocked down and a large red-brick building stood in their place. John's wife, Elizabeth, had taken a hand in transforming the interior of the house, unaltered for nearly a hundred years. Old Tudor walls had been knocked down to provide larger rooms which she lavishly re-decorated.

After such a long absence, Ann was warmly welcomed home by her family, as was Louisa, then heiress to her uncle's estates. Louisa's grandmother summoned her children's nursery maid out of retirement to look after the child. Louisa soon wore out this faithful servant with her 'playfulness', but the servant eventually retaliated, exclaiming to her: 'At your age, I could read a chapter in the Bible and you can't tell great A from round O, tho you are a great lady and I am only a poor servant.' After this encounter, Louisa says she was 'so forcibly struck with her words, which were indeed most true, for I did not know a single letter, that my amusements lost their charm, my toys dropped from my hand'. Ann found her once playful child 'was now sad' and asked why 'I cannot read', Louisa exclaimed, 'I do not know even a great A from a round O.'

Only three weeks after Ann and Louisa had arrived at Great Fulford, Ann left for London. From the events that followed, it would seem that she had recklessly embarked upon an affair. Louisa would later write of her mother, that after their arrival from South Carolina, 'I soon had the misfortune of being deprived of her maternal care. I then wept as a child, and have since shed many an unavailing tear.' When her mother deserted her, Louisa was not yet five years old.

Her grandmother, no doubt to distract her inconsolable granddaughter, employed a governess and her sister to take care of her. Louisa recalled that they would argue as to how she should be taught. At the time it was against prevailing theory to allow a child to read at such a young age, but the governess insisted that Louisa should not be left to tiresomely repeat sounds all day, but be allowed to see words on a page.

Ann had gone to live in the Royal Navy dockyard at Deptford, with a servant, Abigail Fryer – presumably Ann's lover was attached to the Navy in some form or manner. To keep up appearances, Ann went often to the Tower of London, some three miles away, to visit Sir John's aunt Mary, her husband Wenman Nutt and Sir John's only surviving sister, fifteen-year-old Elizabeth. In July the following year, 1768, Ann moved to lodgings in Church Lane, Kensington. Wenman Nutt would later testify that after Ann moved to Kensington, he and his family did not see her again until the week running up to Christmas when to the astonishment of all, she was 'very big with child'. Displaying her adulterous behaviour was a calculated move. Allowing Sir John's family to witness her condition would ensure that Ann would never have to return to her husband; or to South Carolina. However, Ann would have been aware that Sir John had the law on his side and the means to prevent her from ever seeing Louisa again. Such was Ann's seeming lack of maternal feelings towards her daughter, that she was prepared to accept that almost certain outcome.

The family's reaction to her appearance, as Ann had no doubt anticipated, was swift. Wenman Nutt immediately put pen to paper and dispatched a letter with the news to Sir John in Carolina. On February 7th 1769, Ann called a midwife, Elizabeth Lucas, who lived in the same lane. It was not, however, until two weeks later, on February 21st, that the midwife was again sent for and Ann was delivered of a son 'about ten minutes after three o'clock in the afternoon'. On March 17th, Mrs Jane Fergus, who kept the lodging house, saw a carriage arrive and Ann and Mrs Lucas, carrying the baby, left for St Paul's, Hammersmith to have the child baptised, after his uncle, as 'John Fulford'. In the records there is no mention of his parentage. The baby was then taken away to a wet nurse as was then the fashion in the upper classes.*

Wenman Nutt again wrote to his nephew informing him of the child's birth and by return Sir John wrote of his intention to divorce his wife. He could do little else – if he did not divorce Ann, her illegitimate son would, legally, be deemed his heir.

Divorce then was very rare, and a lengthy and expensive procedure that could only be obtained through an Act of Parliament. In anticipation of the costs involved, and perhaps to settle his accounts before he left Carolina, Sir John sold nearly three thousand acres of land at Fairlawn. He also arranged for the sale of eighty horses, as well as members of his household which included, a 'young Mullato Wench, that is a good seam-stress, and House-wench, with her Child; and a Mullato Boy, that is a tolerable Cook'.** He was no doubt anticipating that he would be in England for some time.

---

* I can find no trace of Ann's baby, 'John Fulford', after his christening, and presume he must have died as an infant.
** A 'Mullato' was the word then used for describing a person with mixed ancestry: in the main a person with one white and one black parent.

Sir John left Charles Town on August 18th 1769 on the *Queen Charlotte* sailing for Dover. On arrival, he first went to the Tower of London to see his uncle, aunt and his sister, Elizabeth; but only a few days later, and with no warning, he appeared at Great Fulford. Louisa's grandmother was unaware that Sir John had arrived in the country, and was distraught when he told her that he was immediately removing the now six-year-old Louisa from Great Fulford. She had no legal claim over the child and was obliged to ask her servants to pack Louisa's bags. It was then that Sir John first caught sight of Jane Mutter, the Fulford's very young and alluring laundry maid, who was most likely dispatched to do the task. When this was done, Louisa's grandmother, who had suffered the deaths of seven of her children, stood at the drawing-room window and could only watch as her beloved granddaughter was swept away in her father's carriage. Sir John maliciously ensured that she never saw Louisa again.

Louisa had not seen her father for two years. Even before she had left South Carolina with her mother, she had rarely spent much time with him, so Sir John was almost a stranger to her. In her memoir, Louisa passes over the next six years of her life, mentioning only that her father was so pleased with her progress (she could then write in blank verse) that he spared no expense to complete her education. It can be presumed, reading a later report from a solicitor in Exeter, that Louisa was first taken to Rill Manor, Sir John's old family home in Exmouth. There, she lived in the company of governesses and servants, one of whom was, likely, Jane Mutter. Louisa's grandmother was perhaps happy to lose a young laundry maid in order that her granddaughter would be attended by someone familiar to her. Sir John, consumed with the matter of divorcing his wife, left for London.

With the help of his old guardian and cousin, the 4th Earl of Rochford, then Secretary of State for the Northern Department, Sir John began divorce proceedings in earnest: he first had to prove his case in the ecclesiastical court. In the meantime, he served a lawsuit against his mother-in-law for rent due to him from land that formed part of Ann's marriage settlement.

Mrs Fulford was then living alone at Great Fulford, and could not rely on the support of her eldest son, John, as he and his wife Elizabeth had recently been forced to leave the country. They had been unable to economise on their household expenditure. It was not just the lavish redecoration of the house but their continuing extravagant lifestyle that drove them into debt. When they left for Europe an inventory was taken which revealed that under lock and key in the housekeepers' room were eleven dozen large bars of soap, and enough candles to light the whole house. In the 'new wine cellar' were over five hundred bottles of port, and various bottles of wine, cherry brandy, raspberry brandy, liqueurs, and rum. A local rector to Great Fulford told his brother: 'We have lately lost our nearest neighbour, Mr Fulford, who was the only Gentleman besides the Clergy that was near us. Poor man. He came into his estate young and imprudently lived above it. The consequence now, though not much above thirty, he is obliged to leave his ancient family seat, which is one of the best, if not the very best in the County and go to France where he proposes to live at less expense than he has done at his own seat'. In John Fulford's absence, the onus of foiling the Baronet's numerous lawsuits fell to his younger brother, Francis, a curate.

In October 1770, Sir John served another lawsuit against his mother-in-law, in which he stated that Ann was 'kept so mean and scanty even in necessary apparel as not to have more than one gown fit or proper to appear in and that she was equally bare of linen both as to quality and quantity'. He accused his mother-in-law of neglecting her daughter's education, 'which it was for many reasons incumbent on the complainant to have done and was the principal cause of the misfortunes which have since happened to the said Dame Anne Colleton.' Sir John demanded a hundred pounds from Mrs Fulford which, he said, had been promised him so he could buy clothes for his wife. He also demanded his mother-in-law hand over to him a pair of diamond earrings, which he claimed belonged to Ann and therefore belonged to him. By November 1770, Sir John had not received the back rent from Ann's estates, and he had his mother-in-law arrested and incarcerated in Dorset, where she was staying at the time. Ann's brother, Francis, hurriedly raised a bond of £1,000 and his mother was released from prison. The court later ruled in Sir John's favour and ordered Mrs Fulford to pay him £573.19.9.

After this debacle, Ann wrote to Sir John in January 1771 and apologized profusely for the manner which she and her family had treated him. The sincerity of this letter is doubtful and was penned in the vain hope that Sir John would drop his expensive lawsuits against her family. Having received Ann's grovelling letter, Sir John would only concede to the Fulford's lawyers that he may have offered to give John Fulford a hundred pounds for Ann to buy her trousseau.

Sir John, still in full control of his wife's affairs, sold some of her land and with the proceeds purchased Shewte Manor, an estate near Bovey Tracey on the wilds of Dartmoor. Under the complicated strictures of their marriage settlement, the estate was also held in Ann's name, as Sir John could not deprive her of the capital sum she brought into the marriage. On the estate was a charming 17th-century manor house, where Sir John installed his new mistress, Jane Mutter. It was perhaps because of his domestic arrangements, and his lengthy absence from the colony, that in late October 1771, Sir John resigned from South Carolina's Royal Council.

As could have been expected, Sir John's case to divorce his wife came before the House of Lords nearly two years after he had arrived in England. In the proceedings, Sir John accused his wife of entering into 'a criminal Intercourse and adulterous conversation with some person or persons unknown to your said subject', and of having a 'male bastard child'. Sir John stated, that since October 1767, he had not 'cohabited nor had any intercourse conversation or communication' with his wife. He later claimed that he was liable to have 'spurious issue' imposed on him to succeed to his estates and fortune unless his marriage be declared 'void and nulled' by Parliament. He demanded Lady Colleton's 'male child' be officially declared a 'bastard', and that any other children she may have would not be considered his 'lawful' issue. Should the divorce be granted, another clause would ensure, that should Sir John remarry, the 'children of that union would be deemed lawful'.

Witnesses were called to the House of Lords, among them Sir John's aunt, her husband, his sister, several servants, including Ann's servant Abigail Fryer who had no doubt been bribed, and American friends of Sir John's who were in England at the time, and all testified against Ann. Ann had by then fled to Calais, where she lived in penury.

The final motion for Sir John's petition was not heard in the House of Lords until April 1st 1772. By chance, Sir John's Carolina neighbour, Henry Laurens, was then in England arranging his children's schooling and attended the House of Lords that same day. Laurens wrote that a friend had visited him, insisting that he take his carriage to see 'the King of England on his throne': 'I went and was highly entertained.' He continued: 'His Majesty assented to a vast number of Public and private bills not less than 20 at the head of which was the very unpopular Bill for regulating the future Marriages of the Royal Family. Wits say such Bill should not have been passed any day but this of All Fools. Sir John Colleton's was the 2nd private Bill among four for Divorces, these People's Practices made me think in the House of Lords of our Negroes throwing away one Wife and taking another.' Had Laurens known that the baronet's mistress, Jane Mutter, was daily expected to be delivered of a child he might have added a further comment to his letter. Within a month of the divorce being granted, 'John Colliton, son of John Colliton by Jane Mutters, Plow Court Fetter Lane' was christened on April 29th in the City of London.

With the matter of his divorce settled, the astute Sir John now turned his attention to the Bahamas. The islands had a troubled history; when the 12-year War of the Spanish Succession ended in 1714, hundreds of British privateers sailing under 'Letters of Marque' issued by the British government no longer had the quasi-sovereign authority to plunder enemy ships. Nearly 1,400 of these sailors and adventurers retreated to the Bahamas and set up a 'Pirate's Republic' at Nassau, in New Providence. While some pirates, such as Edward Teach, known as Blackbeard, terrorised ships off the coast of Charles Town, others lurked in the Bahamas to prey on passing ships. Anarchy in the Bahamas and the losses in shipping caused uproar in England. In 1717, the British government sent notice to the Lords Proprietors that they were taking over control of civil matters, and of the military.

Since then, the government had repeatedly tried to buy the islands from the Lords Proprietors, but had been blocked at every attempt. This was due to the charter having been granted to the Lords Proprietors and 'their heirs in perpetuity', which inevitably involved minors. Under the law, their future interests had to be protected and this proved a stumbling block for the government's solicitors, who could find no way around it.

When Sir John called the five other Lords Proprietors together in 1772 for their first meeting in ten years, their deeds and maps had mouldered and they had not even bothered to collect their quit rents – the taxes payable to a feudal superior for land grants. Sir John's fellow Proprietors, however, only owned shares in the 'soil' after their predecessors had sold their shares of the Sovereign Rights to his grandfather, in 1729, when they were all but worthless. This gave the family ownership of the mineral rights, the 'fishing of all sorts, whales, sturgeons, and all other royal fishes', and customs dues. With little persuasion, the Lords Proprietors, who had no ambitions to deal with the Bahamas themselves, signed a deed giving

Sir John 'full and absolute power over the said islands'. He now had authority to sell any amount of land or grant leases in the Bahamas, as he saw fit. The Proprietors also agreed that their respective shares in the soil, would stand as security should he incur expenses or losses in the endeavour. Even though Sir John had been given carte blanche over the Bahamas, he does not appear to have been in a hurry to return to South Carolina.

However, any ambitions he may have had to exploit the Bahamas were soon thwarted by events in America. In December 1773, the 'Boston Tea Party' had taken place, and a full-scale rebellion on the part of the colonists looked increasingly likely. This crisis might have been averted had the Earl of Rochford not cast the final decisive vote in a cabinet meeting, back in May 1769, preventing the then Prime Minister, the Duke of Grafton, from repealing 'the obnoxious American duties'. Grafton later wrote that had the vote gone his way, 'separation from America might have been avoided.' But the die was cast.

In March 1774, the Earl of Rochford wrote to the Earl of Denbigh: 'On next Thursday it will be decided whether England is master of America or America of England.' Parliament passed a bill which would close the port of Boston to all shipping until reparations were made for the loss of customs duty. This only served to instigate further insurrection on the part of the colonists, who began to prepare for war. Sir John would have known from intelligence received from Rochford, that the British were nervous of the consequences. In August, Rochford's secretary received a letter from the Earl of Denbigh stating presciently, 'I begin to be seriously afraid that the Boston business will not end without bloodshed.'

Vice Admiral Samuel Graves, the uncle of Louisa's future husband, Richard Graves, was appointed 'Commander in Chief of all His Majesty's Ships and vessels employed or to be employed in North America', and was ordered to go to America to enforce the 'Boston Port Act' which gave him the authority to blockade Boston harbour until restitution had been made.

Far away from the growing conflict, eleven-year-old Louisa was now living in Exeter at the Colleton townhouse. Her father, meanwhile, had distanced himself from London and remained at Shewte Manor in Dartmoor with Jane Mutter. When she was expecting a second child, Sir John, no doubt wishing for a legitimate heir, decided to marry her. He had learnt to his cost that 'high faluting' ladies such as Ann Fulford had no place in the colonies and it was his intention to return to America. Jane, of modest lineage, albeit a somewhat notorious one as her family were well-known smugglers in Devon would, he presumed, be more compliant. After their marriage by Special Licence in the church at Bovey Tracey, on April 21st 1774, Jane could now be brought out into society. In the early autumn, Jane was delivered of a son.

It was not until January 25th 1775, that Sir John and his wife travelled with their children to the church which served Rill Manor, St John-in-the-Wilderness, in Withycombe Raleigh, which as its name suggests was some way from Exmouth. The early Tudor church was then in such a state of dilapidation that just three years later much of it was pulled down. As the party walked through the churchyard they passed the tomb of Sir John's grandfather, and once inside the church, on the east wall, there hung the 'curious' altarpiece that Sir John's father had brought with him from Carolina. It was adorned with angels and flaming torches, and at its centre was a heart in flames over an open book. The Colleton's new baby was duly baptised 'John Snell Colleton' and noted in the parish register as being the son of Sir John and Lady Colleton. John Snell's elder brother was also taken to the font that day, and christened once more. The three-year-old was demoted to bastard status, and re-named 'William Colleton Mutter'. While Jane was noted in the records as being William's mother, there was no mention of his paternity. She presumably did not object to this, as she was now the mother of the future Colleton baronet.

At the time of the double christening, Sir John had decided to leave for America in spite of news of the growing rebellion. Rill Manor had by then been let with all the furniture, and the contents of Shewte Manor were shrouded in dust sheets. At the Colleton townhouse in Exeter, the family began packing their most wanted possessions for their forthcoming journey to America. On April 17th 1775, servants transported the family's luggage to the quayside in Exeter. A New York ship, the brigantine *Rebecca*, was waiting to sail for Charles Town. Louisa later wrote briefly of this moment: 'Just as I completed my twelfth year, my father returned to America, with his family.'

Louisa made no mention of her stepmother, Jane, who had once washed her sheets, and indeed would never write of her. Neither did she say anything of her two half-brothers or Eliza Janverin, a strikingly pretty girl of twenty-one, who had been employed as her governess and companion.

Although Eliza was the daughter of a prosperous shipbuilder in South-ampton, she was one of nineteen children, which perhaps would explain why she had accepted Sir John's offer of employment so far from home. Eliza, along with two other servants employed to care for the boys, too, boarded the *Rebecca*.

On April 19th, two days after the Colleton party had set sail for South Carolina, Admiral Samuel Graves and his nephews were helping to transport British troops across the waters of Charles River to fight at the battles of Lexington and Concord. There, the first shots of the American Revolution were fired and the war began in earnest.

CHAPTER 4

Blue Gold

*

THE *Rebecca* sailed swiftly and arrived in Charles Town on May 26th 1775. On his arrival, Sir John was put under enormous pressure to resume his seat on the Royal Council. However, he steadfastly refused and openly stated that he wished to remain neutral in the hostilities. *The South Carolina Historical and Genealogical Magazine* in October 1900 characterised Sir John as: 'If not in sympathy with the Revolutionary movement to the extent of severing ties which bound the Colony to the Crown; he was in sympathy with the resistance to the unjust course of Great Britain in seeking to make and enforce laws in the Colonies enacted without their representation or assent.'

On June 1st, Henry Laurens, who had been appointed to the Provincial Congress of South Carolina in January, was elected president. Within days, the Congress voted to raise an army of fifteen hundred men to protect themselves from English forces. The rebels' imminent fear was that local Loyalists would incite the Indians to attack them and persuade slaves to aid the British. Citizens were obliged to sign allegiance to the new state or be banished from the city, but by then Sir John had left Charles Town for Fairlawn. A few months later, on September 15th, the Royal Governor of South Carolina, Sir William Campbell, dissolved the last Royal Assembly. He took refuge on board an English warship in Charles Town harbour and weakly left the Loyalists to their own fate.

Meanwhile, at Fairlawn, Jane, who for some time had been kept in the shadows at the remote Shewte Manor, was revelling in her newfound status in a society where humble lineage was of little hindrance. The now grand Lady Colleton often ordered the carriage to take her to nearby Moncks Corner, where some of Charleston's finest shops had outposts. This was not only an opportunity to arrive in such style and buy one of the last available bolts of silk or household goods as blockades took effect, but also an excuse to continue her flirtation with Othniel Giles whose father ran a large general store in the town.

As the rebellion intensified, necessities such as pins and shoes were in short supply. Sir John was daily pressed by his overseers to send his schooner, *Success*, to the Bahamas to fetch supplies including much-needed salt. Louisa, however, would write that her father dared not, for fear his coveted ship would be captured and confiscated. On Louisa's thirteenth birthday, March 14th 1776, Henry Laurens had written a gloomy letter to his daughter, Martha, then in France: 'The sound of war increases, and the danger seems to be drawing nearer and nearer.' He added: 'Our friends should prepare themselves for learning that we are numbered amongst the dead.'

It was not long, as Laurens had feared, before a British fleet of eleven ships carrying nearly three thousand men swept into Charles Town harbour on a hot humid day at the end of June. Three of their frigates were grounded on the notorious shifting sandbars which guarded the entrance to the city. Admiral Parker, who led the force, had his breeches blown off and the American Patriots sent the British packing. Five days later, on July 4th 1776, the thirteen American colonies declared independence. It was now inevitable that South Carolina, as one of the richest colonies, would become the ground of intensified armed conflict. Indeed, more battles and skirmishes in the Revolutionary War would be fought there than in any other colony. But, for now, the intolerable summer weather, which heralded the 'sicklie season', provided a calm before the storm.

There was no such calm at Fairlawn, for Sir John's marriage of little more than two years had disintegrated. What occurred between him and Jane can only be a matter of conjecture, but Sir John, seemingly consumed by jealousy and anger, had confined his wife to the back quarters of the house. He also believed that their two sons were not his, and refused to have either of them in his sight, so they, too, were banished with their mother. In the middle of July, the baronet sat down to write a vitriolic will. It appears that he was not aware of Jane's attachment to Othniel Giles, as the will was witnessed by Othniel's father and brother.

It might have been difficult to explain to a child as young as Louisa, why her stepmother and half-brothers were suddenly forbidden to enter the main part of Fairlawn. But Louisa, at best indifferent to her stepmother, was probably relieved that she no longer had to engage with her. Louisa's governess, the beguiling Eliza Janverin who always took her meals with the family, soon took advantage of Jane's absence and became mistress of Fairlawn, and of the baronet.

Louisa later wrote that in the autumn of 1776, after she had sufficiently recovered from a bout of 'Autumnal fever to render it needless for any person to sit up with me', that she was woken by a loud crash in the middle of the night. Her father had left for Charles Town that day and Louisa 'concluded that the negroes had taken that opportunity to rise, and that the noise I heard was occasioned by their approaching my chamber to murder me. At this time, agents were believed to have been employed by the British to stimulate both the Indians and negroes to rise and murder the white inhabitants! Aroused by this idea, I derived courage from despair, and getting up put on my slippers and dressing gown, resolved to brave my fate rather than await it; I threw open the door, all was dark and silent: I proceeded to the apartments of a lady, who was so confined to her bed by a fever, and was so ill that she had two women attending her'. Louisa did not reveal who the 'lady' was but it is unlikely that the Colletons had visitors at the time, so it can be presumed that the 'lady' was either Jane or Eliza.

When Louisa reached the room, she saw through a window that one wing of the house was on fire. The flames, she wrote, 'were raging dreadfully; and, had I not been awakened by the crackling of the fire, as it ran along the roof of the piazza, in all probability the catastrophe would have been most awful. This sight awakened apprehensions most alarming, as I knew that there ought to be three watchmen every night on duty walking the rounds of the house, gardens and stables, who passed under my father's window every hour to give the watchword, "all's well", or, in case of danger, to alarm. Their not having given the alarm, led to the suspicion of the house having been purposely set on fire. I sent one of the nurses to call the servants; the lady was much alarmed; I told her I would return to her as soon as I had given the orders necessary on the occasion, and begged her to be composed, as she was sufficiently remote to be out of danger for the present, and I ordered the nurses not to leave her before I returned.'

Louisa ran along the passage and down the front stairs leading into the cedar-panelled hall. Here, on top of the mahogany dining table amongst the candelabra and silver punch bowl, were several conch shells, 'which when well sounded, can be heard at a considerable distance. ' The conch shells, Louisa wrote, 'were kept for the purpose of giving alarm in the case of danger, either from the Indians, who, at that time, were continually passing in great parties, to and from Charles Town, owing to the Civil War then raging, in case of fire etc. etc.'

'Judge my dismay at seeing the servant to whom I gave the conch instead of sounding the alarm walk away with it!' With no time to lose, Louisa and another servant ran through the double hall doors, into the garden and up the gravel path to where the alarm bells were housed. Thirteen-year-old Louisa impressively re-established her authority: observing her errant servant she commanded him to sound the alarm although 'determined to exert my utmost efforts to ring them myself, should he refuse; but he immediately obeyed my orders. The overseers with men from the plantations quickly arrived and the fire was speedily extinguished without any lives being lost'. The fire, it was later discovered, had started in the kitchen, where some of the household slaves taking advantage of the master's absence had been drinking.

When Sir John heard of the fire, he returned post haste to Fairlawn. Louisa told her father of the events during that night, and she later wrote he was 'greatly affected; he folded me to his heart, and hung over me in silence; at length he said, "I am glad I was not at home, my child, as it has given me an opportunity of knowing what a great mind you possess; may your lot through life be fortunate; for with a mind so highly awakened as yours, you will acutely feel either happiness or misery." Louisa was overwhelmed by her father's 'tenderness' towards her, and after the fire she rarely left his side. She now spent much of her time with her father in his office where she wrote, and copied his letters.

But, shortly after Louisa's fourteenth birthday, Sir John contracted a serious case of malaria. 'My beloved father,' she remembered, ' who aware of his enfeebled state of health, with true parental affection ever awake for the welfare of his child, in order to save me from the dangers in which I might be involved at his death, both from my youth (being then only fourteen) being unsupported by the ties of blood with any person on the continent of America and also from the state of the country; determined to send me to England, where I should at least be exempt from the horrors attendant on a civil war, and be near both paternal and maternal relatives, amongst whom he no doubt trusted his child would find a friend.' Eliza Janverin, she failed to mention, would accompany her to England.

Sir John arranged for a consignment of indigo, or 'blue gold' as the valuable dye was known, to be packed into barrels and stored at his wharf in Charles Town. The blockade of the rebellious colonies by the Royal Navy had caused the price of the best quality indigo to soar in France. He planned that its sale would provide Louisa with funds to allow her to travel through France in style and on to England, and leave her with a sufficient amount to support her during her minority. Sir John was understandably anxious over the dangers his daughter might face on what was already her third journey across the Atlantic – his uncle, and many others he once knew, had perished. There was also the peril of being captured either by the Royal Navy or one of the privateers who 'infested' the ocean carrying Letters of Marque. Sir John, however, had found passage for Louisa and Eliza on the *Three Sisters*, a brigantine, designed for both speed and manoeuverability, that could easily outrun and out-sail any threatening vessel. The ship, of one hundred tons, was bound for Nantes at the mouth of the Loire.

By the first week of April 1777, preparations for the departure of Sir John's precious daughter were well underway. John Hazard, the master of the *Three Sisters* then docked in Charles Town harbour, stood on the deck overseeing the loading of his cargo. Over the next few days, he signed bills of lading for 660 casks of rice, 190 half barrels and numerous casks of indigo, 25 of which were marked with the stamp of 'Sir John Colleton'.

At Fairlawn, word came from Charles Town that the *Three Sisters* was nearly ready to sail. The carriage was ordered and Sir John, Louisa and Eliza set off for the city. There, the quay was crowded with loyalist merchants, planters, and members of the clergy all endeavouring to find passage out of the country. On April 26th, Sir John walked his sad but brave daughter up the gangplank of the brigantine. It was then that he discreetly handed a copy of his will to Eliza Janverin, the keeper of his secrets, and ordered her to keep it on 'her person' at all times. It is likely that the will was sealed, but Eliza undoubtedly knew of its contents. When her father left the ship, Louisa must have feared, given the state of his health, that it was unlikely she would ever see him again. It is hard to fathom what she felt as the ship was guided away from the wharf and over the bar until it reached the open sea.

Once out in the ocean, such was the fear of attack by opportunist privateers that the ship's windows were covered in sailcloth and lights kept low to ensure that she would not be seen during the night. At the helm John Hazard, part-owner of the ship and a native of New York, commanded a crew of eight men: four Danes, a Pole, an Englishman, a Scotsman and an American. There were nine passengers including Louisa, Eliza and their three servants. Amongst them was 30-year-old Reverend Alexander Macauly, a Scot who for the past three-and-a-half years had divided his time between Charles Town and Scotland. The reverend was in daily attendance to the extremely unwell Archibald Baird, recently Collector of Customs in George Town. Baird, who had refused to sign allegiance to the new regime in America, had fled South Carolina and was now being closely cared for by his African slave.

One of the passengers' great fears at sea was that in rough weather they would be tossed out of their beds when asleep and break their bones, so to avoid this they strapped themselves to their beds. The only rare pleasure for the ladies was bathing in a large cask on deck when weather allowed. This was a 'solemn affair', according to another young girl who crossed the Atlantic shortly after Louisa, and the ladies would bathe in peace while everyone else remained below deck. These journeys across the Atlantic made for 'heavy' hours, but the days were enlivened by the occasional sight of schools of porpoises and flying fish swimming alongside the ship. At night, passengers would stand on deck to see the twinkling lights of the phosphorous plankton. Much of their time on board was, however, spent trying to find something agreeable to eat and ensuring the cabin stove was kept alight.

On May 19th, the elderly Archibald Baird believed he was dying and wrote to his merchants in London, giving his position at sea (The *Three Sisters* was then in the middle of the Atlantic near the latitude of Lisbon) as his address. Baird stated that he had entrusted all his possessions to Reverend Macauly and asked that his nine barrels of indigo on board, containing 1642 lbs, be sold in either in France or in London. Baird had left his wife behind in South Carolina and intended, he wrote, to continue trading in indigo 'in order to withdraw my property from a Country from which I am banished'. He made no provision for his wife, whom he had abandoned, and clearly attached more importance to the fate of his slave. She was 'so valuable a property' that he did not want to risk sending her back to America in such times, and requested that she should be sent to his sister in Scotland in the event of his death.

The natural pattern of winds took the *Three Sisters* off the coast of Madeira. There, on Friday, June 13th, disaster struck. The ship was sighted by the *Elizabeth*, a privately owned merchant ship carrying a Letter of Marque. Usually, the *Three Sisters* would have been able to out-sail the *Elizabeth*, but she had been taking on water and this slowed her down considerably. The *Elizabeth* gave chase and fired a shot across the bows of the *Three Sisters*. She had no option but to heave to. Benjamin Hughes, commander of the *Elizabeth*, boarded their ship, ordering master John

Hazard and all the crew off before removing all the papers he could find. Peter Hannan, the *Elizabeth*'s second mate, was left on the ship with five men and was ordered by Hughes to take her to the nearest English port, preferably Plymouth. Hannan quickly discovered the source of the leak and set all hands to the pump, only to find that sodden rice was coming up with the water.

Their troubles were not yet over. A few days later, as the *Three Sisters* rounded Ushant off the coast of Brittany, they were sighted at noon by HMS *Valiant*, a third-rate ship of the line of seventy-four guns, commanded by Captain the Hon. John Leveson-Gower. And then began another dramatic chase. When the *Valiant* came close enough to fire a shot across the bows of the *Three Sisters*, she once more heaved to. Captain Leweson-Gower sent an officer on board to take possession of the ship, only to discover she had already been taken and so, reluctantly, allowed her to continue on her voyage to Plymouth.

The adventures of the *Three Sisters* had not come to an end. On June 18th, a third vessel, HMS *Ceres*, a sloop of war under the command of Captain Samuel Warren, sighted the *Three Sisters* off Plymouth Sound and ordered her to heave to. Warren found the Prize Master had no proof of a Letter of Marque and duly led her into the port. To Warren's fury, and that of his crew given the value of the prize, the owners of the *Elizabeth* were later able to prove they had a valid Letter of Marque and therefore the *Three Sisters* and her cargo were theirs by right.

After five eventful days since the *Three Sisters* was captured by the *Elizabeth*, Louisa and Eliza finally came ashore and found lodgings at an inn. Louisa immediately wrote to her father that the ship was taken but that they were safe. Some of their fellow passengers petitioned Admiralty officers at a nearby inn and were allowed to keep some or all of their cargo. However, at no point were Louisa or Eliza interviewed by the Admiralty, and they had no one to intervene on their behalf. When the investigation was completed, the ship and the rest of the cargo, which included Sir John's indigo, were sent to London and officially deemed a prize. When the ship reached London, it was found that the rice on board was contaminated, and thus valueless, but the indigo had survived the journey. Louisa later wrote that she still had the original bill of lading for her father's indigo and that the bricks of 'blue gold' had been valued at £1,000.

Louisa's letter to her father reached him, 'and relieved him from the anxiety he had felt, both on account of the dangers of the sea, and of the enemy.' She was later told by her father's attendants that her letter 'was a great consolation to him; he would not suffer it to be taken off his bed, but continually perused it, but was too weak to write after the letter he had addressed to his steward in Exeter, directing him to provide a supply necessary for my support'. This landed on the desk of Sir John's trusted lawyer, Joseph Burrows, who then rescued Louisa and Eliza from Plymouth, and brought them to Exeter where he had opened up the old family house on Fore Street. No one had lived in the gabled house, which the Colletons had built in 1619, since the family had left for South Carolina some two years before, and Louisa found herself once again in the familiar dark oak-panelled parlour on the first floor.

At Fairlawn during the early months of 1777, Sir John had rallied a little and was well enough in May to turn his attention back to his business affairs, including issuing a notice in the *South Carolina Gazette* stating that he could not be held accountable for any damage to freight on his schooners. He may have then been hoping to follow Louisa and his mistress to England, as a month later he placed a further notice: 'Any persons having claims on Sir John Colleton are desired to present their accounts and all those indebted to him to make immediate payment.' He also put blocks of land up for sale at both Fairlawn and Devil's Elbow.

But, Sir John's health was waning, and in his misery had turned to the bottle. He died, aged thirty-nine, on a hot day in September of 1777 and was buried across the river from Fairlawn, at Biggin Church, which stood on land donated to the parish by the Colleton family.

CHAPTER 5

Mournful Event

*

LOUISA was grief-stricken when the news of her father's death reached England. She later wrote that she now considered herself to be orphaned although, of course, her mother was alive and well. While Eliza comforted her charge, she also revealed to Joseph Burrows that she had in her possession the baronet's will. Burrows immediately sent word to Louisa's uncle, John Fulford, for whom, conveniently, he also acted as lawyer, to suggest they meet at the Colleton's townhouse in Exeter. Burrows then opened the will which Eliza had handed him. The document was crumpled and virtually illegible in places. It later transpired, Sir John's estranged wife, Jane, had somehow got hold of the will and had violently scored through several lines. Fortunately, though her actions came to nothing as a master copy was lodged with lawyers in Charles Town.

The will itself began innocuously enough. The 4th baronet declared he was of sound mind and that he wished to be buried in a very 'plain manner' at the 'usual burial place belonging to the parish where I may happen to die'. The next fourteen lines were obliterated and unknown to the assembled company, underneath was written: 'I give and bequeath unto Dame Jane Colleton, my unhappy wife, if she should survive me a clear annuity of £60 sterling per annum' which was to be paid quarterly on the usual feast days 'so long as she remains my chaste widow'. Sir John also left his wife 'the sum of fifty pounds sterling to pay her expenses to that part of the world she may choose to retire to for I do not choose that she should live in any place that belonged to me and likewise I give her the watch that she used to wear that she may make notice of how time passes and earnestly entreat her to make better use of time to come than she has of time past.'

The next words, however, could be read: 'I give and bequeath to Miss Eliza Janverin, in consideration of the extraordinary care in the education of my daughter Louisa Carolina Colleton, on condition she still supports the conduct and duration of my daughter, who I leave entirely under her care till she arrives to the age of twenty one years or is married, the sum of one hundred pounds sterling per annum.'

Eliza, Sir John wrote, was also to have possession of the house and its contents on his plantation, Fairlawn, in South Carolina, unless she married. One hundred acres of pasture around the house was to be marked out for her benefit, and the plantation should provide Eliza with sufficient timber and firewood. All the carriages were to be at her disposal, and she could choose any of the 'saddle horses' for her own riding. It continued, 'likewise all the house negroes and, the benefit of the dairy and poultry and sheep and, use of the wool and carcase of the sheep as long as she remains single and unmarried and no longer.' He added as an afterthought that the 'house negroes were to be clothed and fed at the estate's expense'.

The next few lines were scrawled through in places, but it was clear enough for Burrows to read that Sir John left to 'William Colleton Mutter my wife's son before I was married to her and which I have not the least reason to believe to be mine one shilling'. An angry pen again obscured the text until it could be read, 'John Snell Colleton born of the body of Jane Colleton after I was married to her I have no right to believe him mine although his mother had when child of him art enough to make me believe so which was the reason of my marrying her.' The following lines were defaced and crossed through with a bold 'X'. In between, it was possible to decipher the words, 'I would have him brought up to reading writing and accs [accounts] and... some trade. I bequeath to the said John Snell Colleton one shilling in lieu of what he might further claim.'

Having left his two sons the sum of one shilling each, Sir John ended his will by leaving all his estates, 'real and personal wheresoever situated lying or being whether in America or Great Britain' to his 'dear daughter Louisa Carolina Colleton'.

Eliza Janverin at the age of twenty-three was legally Louisa's guardian; however, the Fulford family, not only on account of Eliza's age but the fact that she had clearly been Sir John's mistress, deemed her a most unsuitable person to care for Louisa. Eliza agreed to hand Louisa over to them and mindful of her annuity, Eliza went to London to try to unravel Sir John's affairs. There, she confronted William Field but the young girl proved no match for one of the sharpest lawyers in the Inner Temple.

Louisa did not elaborate on Eliza's dismissal and merely wrote: 'On the mournful event of my father's death being announced I was conducted to the seat of my maternal ancestors by my maternal uncle Mr Fulford of Great Fulford in Devonshire.'

Fourteen-year-old Louisa was lucky that her uncle John, and his wife Elizabeth, were in the country. They had only just returned from a seven-year exile on the continent, brought about by John's inability to live within his income. After the death of his mother, he had let Great Fulford and sold their Dorset estate and anything else that was not protected by entailment. Life on the continent, though, had not been much of a hardship as it was estimated that ten pounds bought you in France and Italy what would cost a hundred in England.

While the Fulfords had been in Europe, they flitted about the usual watering holes of the impoverished English gentry. In November 1773, they were in Florence where Elizabeth fell under the eye of the inveterate letter writer and snob, Lady Mary Coke: 'There is an English lady here, a Mrs Fulford, who I saw four years ago in the South of France. I thought she was a little vulgar and foreign countries have not polished her.' A few weeks later, Lady Mary complained that Elizabeth was surrounded by admirers and Lady Mary 'determined to make her no more morning visits'. Nevertheless, by early January 1774, Lady Mary had to admit that everyone far preferred Elizabeth's company to her own.

Lady Mary Coke was no doubt jealous of Elizabeth, who by all accounts was vivacious, accomplished, attractive and extremely intelligent. She had met John in Bath in 1762, while she was still on crutches after a traumatic riding accident in the Peak District. She had accepted the offer of an elderly Dean to ride before him on his horse, up a steep peak. Near the summit, on a narrow track, the horse lost its footing and they fell down a precipice. Elizabeth's fall was broken when her hair became entangled in a gorse bush, and she lay on the ground for three hours before being rescued. She was blind for two days, her face lacerated, and she was horribly bruised. The Dean never recovered consciousness, and died the next afternoon: the horse remarkably survived the fall. Elizabeth told her mother at the time: 'My face mends very fast; they say I shall not be disfigured.'

After a lightning romance, John and Elizabeth were married by the Archbishop of Canterbury in Lambeth Palace in 1762. Elizabeth, then 31, was six years older than John. She was also a woman of independent means, which may have been the reason that she had not married before. Elizabeth, her brother, Sir James Laroche, and her four sisters had inherited an equal share of the fourth Earl of Radnor's considerable Cornish estates where her father had been employed as steward. The Fulfords had no children, and as Elizabeth was forty-six when Louisa arrived at Great Fulford, it could be presumed that she never would. Louisa, however, was no longer heiress to the Fulford estates as John's younger brother had had a son, Baldwin, some two years before. Although in an era of high infant mortality, it was not inconceivable that Louisa might, one day, still inherit her uncle's estates.

The Fulfords gave refuge not only to Louisa but also to Elizabeth's youngest sister, Frances, a spinster of gentle disposition. Both she and Louisa were given grand rooms in the East wing of the house. Louisa was thoughtfully returned to the Yellow Bedchamber with the four-poster bed in which she had slept as a child. Frances' bedroom was equally as sumptuous: her handsome domed bed was hung in crimson silk, and hanging on the wall was a three-quarter-length portrait of her father. Louisa wrote that she spent her minority 'devoting my hours to the study of history etc. etc.' and became fluent in the French language, which would later stand her in good stead. But, she would reveal that she did not spend all day incarcerated with her governesses.

Instead of the ominous bell that rang at Fairlawn calling the slaves to work, a great brass bell called the hour from the clock tower, which rose above the parapet of the house. Breakfast was served at nine in the morning and, according to a French visitor in England at the time, was 'not of a lively nature'. In the grand house, he observed: 'You come down in riding boots and a shabby coat, you sit where you like, you behave exactly as you were by yourself, no one takes any notice of you, and it is all extremely comfortable. At ten or ten-thirty everyone goes off on his own pursuit – hunting, fishing or walking.'

Elizabeth and Louisa, both of whom had no love of riding, would go on forays around the park in a coach-and-four, with grooms astride the leading horses dressed in the Fulford livery. Sometimes, Elizabeth would wear an impractical white silk suit which was one of nineteen elaborate morning dresses that hung in her dressing room. Louisa would probably have been dressed equally as extravagantly. As they returned to the heavy gates leading into the park, a very young girl recalled waiting all day for a carriage to come through and being rewarded with a few coins as she opened the gate for them. The locals nicknamed Elizabeth 'Lady Betty', an indication perhaps that they thought she acted above her station. John Fulford, probably to her chagrin, had refused the offer of a baronetcy, preferring to remain plain 'Mr Fulford of Fulford'.

After everyone had spent the morning enjoying outdoor pursuits, they would sit down to dinner. This was a far more formal affair than breakfast, eaten at about two o'clock in the afternoon, although sometimes if John and his guests had not returned from hunting or racing their horses, it would be taken as late as four o'clock. Amongst those whom Louisa often saw was John's closest friend, Montagu Parker, who lived at Whiteway, near Chudleigh, not far from Great Fulford. He shared John's passion for horse racing and adored young children. Louisa always looked forward to his visits. While his elder brother, Lord Boringdon, led a life in high society and often left Saltram, his glorious Adam house, for London, Monatgu preferred the life of an English country squire. According to his sister-in-law, Montagu 'seldom shone in conversation but in woodcock season'. And, her sister wrote of Montagu: 'He is a great a Nimrod as ever, he does nothing but hunt now, he goes out every day. They are very extraordinary hares for they breed after they are killed, for if he kills a brace by night it is generally two in the morning.' No doubt Louisa learnt the art of embellishing her stories at the feet of Montagu Parker.

While life in country houses could be monotonous when there were no visitors, it was not the case at Great Fulford. Her eccentric uncle, Louisa wrote, was the last Englishman to retain a fool dressed in 'the motley coat, as an appendage of the family establishment'. Since Elizabethan times, the Fool's colourful harlequin suit kept 'him outside the social hierarchy and therefore not subjected to class distinction', and allowed him to speak more freely. The Fool played as much a part in Louisa's education as did her governesses, and Louisa was extremely fond of him. On dull days, he would entertain Louisa with stories of the reigns of both King George I, and King George II and he not only had sound knowledge of history but also of literature and music. Being a Fool, he was also a man of sharp wit, and Elizabeth would often tell the anecdote of him at Exeter races, when, 'habited in his appropriate costume, he happened to obstruct the view of the racecourse, as the horses were coming in, from a person anxious to observe them, who with a tone of ill-humour, exclaimed: "Whose Fool are you?" to which without moving out of his way, replied: "I am Squire Fulford's Fool", whose fool are you? Enraged at this retort, the man struck him with a whip; on which the servants belonging to Great Fulford, deeming the defence of the Fool of the family incumbent on them, closed round the aggressor and returned the attack until he cried for mercy.

John Fulford was often to be found in his library where, beside the fire, he entertained Louisa with fanciful tales of their ancestors. 'Oh!' she wrote, 'for a pen of magic power to retrace through ages past my descent from Woden and Friga, the Saxon divinities, from whom are descended all the crowned heads in Christendom.' Uncle John would tell her that they were allied by blood or marriage to some of the first families in the kingdom, including the royal houses of the Tudors and of the Plantagenets. He would often put on plays which illuminated the exploits of the knights in the family, of which there were seventeen. John was very proud of the fact that his ancestors had been royalists in the Civil War and not only had himself painted as a dashing cavalier, but spent much time attempting to prove a family legend that Charles I had stayed in the house during the civil war. This he failed to do, perhaps because the story referred to the king's son, the future Charles II, rather than his father. In any event, his enthusiasm and pride in his family's history were obviously infectious as Louisa also became inordinately proud of her Fulford lineage, which stretched back to the reign of Richard the Lionheart.

They also enjoyed forays to the fashionable spa town of Bath and it was there that the now sixteen-year-old Louisa, with her hair frosted with white powder as was the fashion, sat for the noted artist Thomas Lawrence.

The diarist and novelist Fanny Burney met Lawrence that year of 1779, and wrote that he was 'a most lovely boy of ten years of age who seems to be not merely the wonder of their family, but of the times for his astonishing skill in drawing'. Despite his age, Lawrence's portrait of Louisa is one of remarkable insight into her character and disposition, a talent he was to be famed for. One of her dark chestnut eyes stares ahead, filled with light and steely determination. The eyelid on the other eye is slightly cast down and filled with sadness as if a tear were about to fall. Below rouged cheeks, her cupid lips mirror her eyes; on the left side, as you look at her picture, the corner of her mouth is turning up, almost to a dimple, while the right side of her mouth, slightly in the shadow, reflects her melancholy eye.

Although John and Elizabeth ensured that their young niece was suitably educated, entertained, and her portrait painted for posterity, they paid scant attention to her inheritance across the Atlantic. With the war still raging in America, there was little or no opportunity to do so. Sir John Colleton's instructions in his will that his former wife, Jane, leave Fairlawn had been ignored by her. She had had the advantage that Sir John's lawyer and executor, James Parsons, died shortly after Sir John, and she must have felt confident that Eliza Janverin would not risk the journey back to America in times of war to claim her right to live at Fairlawn.

In the confusion, Jane had managed to have herself appointed as 'administratrix' of Fairlawn and personally dealt with officials who, on December 30th 1777, made an inventory of the 'all the Goods Chattels Rights and Credits belonging to the estate of Sir John Colleton'. His goods and chattels, which included his slaves, were valued at £202,000. The inventory revealed that on the plantation there were 54 horses, 35 working oxen, nearly a hundred head of cattle, 70 pigs, and 31 sheep. In storerooms were vast quantities of corn, rice, and rye. Of 197 slaves, Old Primus was valued at £800, Phillis at £600, the Boatswain at £1,000; but the most valuable slave was Haman, the patroon, who was valued at £1,700. Eleven children were noted, and the least valuable of these was presumably a baby, and valued at £3: twenty older slaves were recorded as valueless. There was also a detailed account of everything in the house, which had been noted room by room. The officials, however, did not take into account Devil's Elbow or Sir John's 'chattels' on the plantation, which amounted to over two hundred slaves.

There may have been some justification for Sir John's unpleasant will: in Charles Town on January 5th 1778, not four months after her husband's death, Jane had married 28-year-old Othniel Giles. His bold signature, at more than two inches high, indicated that he was a man clearly not lacking in ego. It is not difficult to imagine the couples' delight at Fairlawn as they took charge of the house and the plantation. Jane, once a laundry maid and having been all but imprisoned in the servant's quarters when married to Sir John, was again mistress of the house. Giles, the son of a 'shopkeeper', now considered himself *de facto* owner of all he surveyed. In order to keep themselves in funds, they liberally began to liquidate what they could for cash. One advertisement in the *South Carolina Gazette* listed for sale, two surplus carriages and a 'valuable brick house' in Church Street that had served as the family's townhouse in Charles Town.

It had been two years since Louisa had left South Carolina, and as Parsons had not been replaced there had been no one to bring Jane to account. But, even if Fairlawn and Devil's Elbow had been managed on Louisa's behalf, it is unlikely that the plantations would have made a profit.

Louisa's cousin by marriage, Margaret Colleton, who inherited the nearby properties of Wadboo and Mepshew from her husband, had not received the 'smallest remittance' from her estates since 1775.

Margaret Colleton wrote to her agent, Robert Raper, to say she was 'a good deal alarmed at a report that has prevailed, that the Proprietors of Estates in Carolina without distinction, are required to appear there, within a given time upon pain of confiscation of their Property, or some other grievous Penalty'. She begged Raper to plead her case with the 'Gentlemen in Authority', for at the age of seventy-six she was far too old to travel there to save her estates. Shortly after she wrote this letter, Margaret died and the 'Authorities' soon penalised absent landlords with double taxation on their properties. As Jane was at Fairlawn, Louisa escaped such penalties.

Unfortunately, John Fulford's health began to fail. In the early summer of 1779, Elizabeth and Louisa accompanied him to Bath where he was attended to by the best physicians much to their profit but predictably with no benefit to him. On their return to Great Fulford, John, fearing he would not recover, began to put his affairs in order. He was understandably concerned for his adored niece, and with good reason. As Louisa herself wrote: 'friends', 'alas! the orphan heiress rarely meets one.' As matters stood, in the event of his death Louisa would become the ward of Eliza Janverin until she came of age. John was determined this would not be Louisa's fate, and consulted Francis Coleman, his lawyer and good friend.

Coleman advised that the best solution would be to have Louisa made a Ward of Court before John's death. However, the Lord High Chancellor had to be convinced that Louisa's inheritance was being mishandled by her current guardian. Her current guardian was of course John who had done nothing of the sort. So, Coleman had to bring a series of fictitious lawsuits against John on Louisa's behalf.

In July 1779, Coleman petitioned the court to require that John account for rents he had received from Louisa's estates and to 'apply a sufficient part for her maintenance and education'. John refused to do so without the indemnification of the court. This gave Francis Coleman the opportunity to take the matter to the Lord High Chancellor. He demanded, as was usual in such cases, that a proper guardian be appointed for Louisa and that John be issued with a subpoena to attend the court to answer directly as to where the money from Louisa's estates had gone. When

John refused to appear in court, as he and Coleman had planned, Louisa was made a Ward of Court.

It was no doubt on the order of the court, that in December, Sir John Colleton's will was registered in Southampton by Eliza Janverin, who was living there with her family. In her deposition, duly sworn, Eliza stated that four months before she left South Carolina, Sir John had given her the will and that she had then seen several alterations and the will appeared 'in the same plight and condition in every respect' as when she received it. Now that Louisa was a Ward of Court, John and Coleman had ensured that Eliza, Louisa's legal guardian, could not interfere in Louisa's affairs, financial or otherwise, although she still had the right to her annuity from Sir John and the right to live at Fairlawn until she married.

It was not quite three years after Louisa arrived at Great Fulford that John died, in early January 1780, at the age of 44, having 'suffered a long and painful illness with fortitude and resignation to the will of the Supreme Disposer'. His wife erected a monument to him which reads as a paean of praise to an adored husband by an adoring wife: 'He was brave, affable, generous and charitable never opprest anyone, gentle in his manner, true to his word, sincere in his friendship.' It seems John possessed every virtue save that of financial acumen. A cousin wrote to John's heir, his nephew Baldwin Fulford, stating: 'The late Mr Fulford, (I have been told) was inattentive to pecuniary matters.' John, who sold much of the Fulford's outlying estates, was afterwards known by the family as 'Red Ruin', as in his portrait he wears a cerise silk coat. For Louisa, who was not yet seventeen, the death of her amiable, loving, protective and entertaining uncle was a severe blow.

CHAPTER 6

It is all Over

*

BEFORE John Fulford's death, Louisa had received news of the destruction of her plantation at Devil's Elbow. In late April 1779, a British force led by Major General Provost, and accompanied by American loyalists and bands of Indians, crossed the Savannah River with the goal of capturing Charles Town. The attempt failed and the forces retreated to Beaufort, where nearby Devil's Elbow provided a much-needed larder. By the end of the year, there was not a building, crop, or beast left standing, and most of the slaves had been captured or lured away through false hopes of freedom.

William Bull, the former lieutenant governor of South Carolina, wrote that his plantation at Ashley Hall on the Ashley River, 'Had been plundered and greatly damaged by the irregular and great swarm of Negroes that followed Gen'l Prevost's Army in May 1779 where I had left a quantity of bottled wine and rum.' Part of his library was carried away along with his papers, and title deeds torn up and 'scattered in the pasture'. Bull had sought compensation from the British army for the damage done to his plantation, as did Louisa's agent. Bull's petition was denied and Louisa's agent refused the offered compensation of £8,000, as being unequal to the loss, for the damage at Devil's Elbow. This was to prove a poor decision.

In spite of the destruction, Prevost's campaign in South Carolina proved unsuccessful. The Commander-in-Chief of British forces in North America, Lieutenant General Sir Henry Clinton, now assembled his forces in New York for an assault on Charles Town, considered the jewel in the crown. On Boxing Day 1779, in one of the worst winters of the 18th century, a fleet of 104 vessels, manned by 5,000 sailors and carrying 8,500 troops set sail. The usual ten-day voyage took some five weeks and substantial amounts of provisions, horses and ordinance were thrown overboard

Serving under Clinton, was the notorious and dashing cavalry officer Banestre Tarleton who commanded a cavalry detachment of dragoons, and an infantry regiment of American loyalists. Tarleton's ship was one of those driven by the wind beyond Charleston, to Savannah. After landing, 'Butcher' Tarleton, as he was later nicknamed by the rebels, set about remounting his men on requisitioned ponies and farm horses. After a brace of skirmishes, he arrived at Moncks Corner, near Fairlawn, where he proceeded to cut the rebel lines of supply to Charles Town, then under siege by the British. On the evening of April 13th 1780, he launched a night attack against rebels encamped outside the city, forcing them to scatter and abandon 42 wagons, 122 wagon horses, 82 dragoon horses, several officers' horses, all the officers' clothing and baggage, rum, sugar and tea.

As with most armies operating on foreign soil, Tarleton's dragoons relied on foraging parties for supplies. The British policy was that only abandoned plantations and farms be plundered, but in reality commanding officers had little control over their men out in the countryside. It was on one such raid, carried out the day after Tarleton's successful night attack on the rebel positions around Charles Town, that a party of his foraging dragoons approached Fairlawn.

Louisa's stepmother, Jane, was there with three companions, Miss Betsy Giles, Miss Jean Russell, and 22-year-old Ann Fassoux. The dragoons forcibly entered the house with swords drawn and accused the ladies of harbouring rebel soldiers. This was not an unwarranted accusation: Jane's husband, Othniel Giles, was serving with the rebel army and the young Ann Fassoux was married to the rebel Surgeon General, Dr Peter Fassoux.

The main protagonist was the dragoon, Henry McDonagh. One account related that rather than searching for hidden rebels, as he had claimed upon entry, he instead discovered a supply of rum. His eyes soon fell on Mrs Fassoux, whom he nearly strangled in his attempt to rape her. It was only the 'shrieks and struggles' of the other women as the dragoons tried to rape them as well, that Mrs Fassoux was released. Jane, who appears to have done everything she could to defend herself and her young guests, was flung around the room and then badly cut on the hand. Perhaps unnerved at the sight of the blood pouring from Jane's wounds and unable to deal with the screaming women, the dragoons went in search of more rum, which they found and then left the house. Other accounts suggest that Mrs Fassoux and Miss Giles were indeed raped, but to preserve their honour this was couched in euphemistic terms.

Lieutenant Anthony Allaire, an American loyalist serving with the British army, met with the ladies that night and wrote in his diary:

Friday, 14th. Remained at Monck's Corner, collecting the stores, etc. About seven o'clock at night, accidentally a store house caught fire, in which were two casks of powder; was very much alarmed by the explosion, and all got under arms. This confusion was scarcely over when three ladies came to our camp in great distress: Lady Colleton, Miss Betsy Giles, and Miss Jean Russell. They had been most shockingly abused by a plundering villain. Lady Colleton badly cut in the hand by a broadsword, and bruised very much. After my friend, Dr. Johnson, dressed her hand, he, with an officer and twelve men, went to the plantation, about one mile from camp, to protect Mrs. Fayssoux[sic], whom this infamous villain had likewise abused in the same manner. There he found a most accomplished, amiable lady in the greatest distress imaginable. After he took a little blood from her she was more composed, and next morning come to camp to testify against the cursed villain that abused them in this horrid manner. He was secured and sent to Headquarters for trial.

Saturday, 15th. The army got in motion about twelve o'clock. My friend, Dr Johnson, and myself had the happiness of escorting the ladies to their plantation. Before we got there we were met by a servant informing us that there were more plunderers in the house. This news so shocked Lady Colleton and Mrs. Fayssoux [sic], who were some distance before us, and the young ladies in a carriage, that I am not able to describe their melancholy situation, which was truly deplorable.

After their fright was a little over we passed on to their house; but the ladies fearing to stay alone, Lady Colleton and Mrs. Fayssoux got into the carriage, Miss Giles behind me, and Miss Russell on a horse, which I led for fear he should make off with my fair one; they passed on with us four miles to a plantation called Mulberry Broughton, and here we bid adieu to our fair companions with great regret, they thinking themselves out of danger of any insults.

Their assailants were sent 'Head-quarters for trial', and while the commanding officer, Lieutenant Colonel Patrick Ferguson was in favour of executing the culprit, Colonel Webster commuted the sentence to a flogging. Mulberry Castle, a fortified manor house, was built by the Broughton family in the early 18th century and, as well as being neighbours and friends of the Colletons, they had acted as their trusted lawyers for many years. It is not known how long Jane and her companions stayed there, but at the end of April 1780, Lieutenant Allaire returned to Moncks Corner where 'Dr. Johnson and myself went and dined with Lady Colleton, Miss Russell and Miss Giles, the ladies we protected in their distress when we were here the fourteenth of April'. Jane was referred to as 'Lady Colleton' in these accounts. As she was now under British protection, she no doubt believed it expedient to stress her English credentials by using her former title.

It is somewhat of a mystery that the various accounts of this time contain no mention of Louisa's half-brothers; William, then eight, and his six-year-old brother, Sir John Snell Colleton. As the latter was the only baronet in the colony, he should have warranted a comment if he had been present. Perhaps during the attack on Fairlawn, the boys were sheltering in the attics or in the outbuildings at Fairlawn, cared for by servants. They may have still been at Fairlawn whilst their mother later took refuge at Mulberry.

By May, Clinton had taken control of Charles Town and the British forces became unpopular even with loyalists who were not exempted from raids by British soldiers. In June, one of Henry Laurens' servants wrote to tell him that his townhouse had all but been destroyed: 'a shel… entered through the rouf of the Passage. Boarsted in the midst of it, threw the Mahogany stairs in flinters besides considerable other damage.' The outhouses were struck too often to be counted; the stable and kitchen were entirely down, the garden entirely destroyed, one house seized as barracks for Hessians and the residence 'hardly worth repairing'. Laurens was not in South Carolina at the time. Whilst on a diplomatic mission to Holland he was captured by the British, who charged him with treason. Incarcerated in the Tower of London, he claimed he was held 'under insulting conditions'. Laurens is the only American ever to have been held captive within its 11th-century walls.

Both armies continued to plunder the countryside around Charles Town. In July 1780, the heir to Wadboo, James Edward Colleton, received unpleasant news from his agent, William Ancrum. Ancrum, who was managing the plantation, reported that Wadboo had been plundered by both armies: many of the slaves had absconded and smallpox was spreading among those that remained. He asked for money and more urgently 'Winter Clothing out for the Negroes and Broad Hoes for plantation use as the produce of the Estate this year will not be more than sufficient for provisions, with regard to the Clothing no time is to be lost for Winter will be advanced before it can arrive if not speedily shipped'. He added: 'I have given Orders to the Overseers to be sparing and frugal as possible in regard to the distribution thereof.' James Edward was sanguine after receiving this letter and told a cousin: 'We must Expect to bear our Share of the Calamities of a Country that has been the scene of War.'

Louisa learnt some months later that her former stepmother, Jane, 'most barbarously treated during the sacking of Fairlawn, by the Troops' during the evening of April 14th, had 'died in consequence'. Her death, soon after the assault, left her sons, William and Sir John Snell, 'unsupported by the ties of blood with any person on the continent of America', just as their father had feared might happen to his only daughter.

At the beginning of December, a new inventory was taken of Fairlawn. Since Sir John's death in 1777, more than two-thirds of his books went missing and much of the silver had gone. Many items were noted as being broken, and there was no mention of Sir John's strongbox. In an earlier inventory, this was recorded as being in the Blue Chamber, and contained his jewels, among which were several diamond and emerald rings, various deeds, coin, and the family Bible.

There were, however, still a number of pictures, card tables, and backgammon tables, large looking glasses with sconces, mahogany bedsteads and great quantities of china. There was also listed a 'gold Watch', which was perhaps the very one Sir John had left Jane so 'that she may make better use of her time'. The inventory revealed that more than a quarter of the plantation's slaves were missing. At the time of Sir John's death there had been 228 at Fairlawn, but only 159 remained; of these eight were old or disabled and classified as an expense, two were children and 'Cate without a nose' appraised as almost valueless. 'Charles', a mulatto, was noted as being worth fifty pounds. Seven slaves were listed as absent.

In the three years to December 1780, livestock numbers on the plantation had plummeted. More than half the working oxen had gone, so had a third of the cows, and of 54 horses noted at Sir John's death, there remained only 'Cricket, Pigeon, Chesnut, Snip, and Brig, a mare' and eleven others which were unbroken. There were 24 sheep, compared to 100 in 1777, and the pig population suffered in the same proportion.

The agent, William Ancrum, had also informed James Edward Colleton that: 'Provision has been exceeding scarce in the Country and particularly about Wadboo, we were obliged to buy and send thirty Miles for Rice for the Negroes, owing to the dryness of the Season last Year.' Fairlawn suffered the same fate: there were '11 small cocks of Rice, supposed to contain 88 bushels', and 300 bushels of corn compared to the 1200 recorded in 1777. The slaves must have been reduced to eating roots and 'pease', of which there were 30 bushels remaining of each and these were stored along with '33 old Rat eaten hides'. There is no mention of the carriages; however, two of the plantation's schooners, the *Nancy* and the *Success*, remained. Presumably, the schooners at Fairlawn, designed to carry crops, were of no use to the armies.

At the beginning of 1781, the rebel army was vulnerable. The British held New York, and General Lord Cornwallis' army was running loose throughout the South. By May, the British had taken control of the River Cooper and lines of communication to Charles Town. Louisa later dismally wrote: 'The Barony of Fairlawn unfortunately for me was particularly well situated for the British troops, the river Cooper, being navigable for their armed vessels, as far as my landing.' It was indeed unfortunate. The British took possession of Fairlawn and Lieutenant Colonel Archibald McArthur who was given command of the plantation, forced Fairlawn's slaves to fell the mile-long avenue of cedar trees stretching from the house to the King's highway. Many of the cedars, planted some fifty years before, towered nearly fort feet tall. With the timber, McArthur built a strong fort above the river, half a mile from the house. The house itself was encircled with an abbatis,* and became a base for troops, a hospital, and provided a secure place for the British to store their munitions.

It was during this turmoil at Fairlawn that Major Othniel Giles, as he was by then, appeared on the plantation in early September. It seems that the British did not question where his loyalties lay and he managed to gain entrance to the house. With the help of Fairlawn's slaves, he moved everything of value to the attics. Louisa was later convinced that the British stole her father's strongbox after they captured the house, but since there was no mention of the box in the detailed inventory of Fairlawn taken in December 1780, it had probably been removed long before,

---

* An 'abbatis' is a field fortification of trees laid in a row, the tops of which, facing outwards, are sharpened.

most likely by Giles, before or after Jane's death. Giles seems to have had an eye on the future as on September 4th 1781, he applied to the court in Charles Town for letters of administration over Fairlawn, in the right of his late wife. He may have believed that the war was turning in the favour of the rebels and that they in due course would grant him legal possession of the plantation.

The war was, indeed, turning in the favour of the rebels. On September 5th 1781, after a series of blunders and mixed intelligence reports, Rear Admiral Thomas Graves' fleet was caught by the French fleet under the command of de Grasse, in the mouth of the Chesapeake. The British admiral, a close cousin of Admiral Samuel Graves, later explained to Lord Sandwich: 'The mutilated state of the squadron prevented my keeping wind of the enemy, as well as several shifts of wind in their favour'. Tom Graves, later Louisa's brother-in-law, commanding HMS *Bedford* on the day, believed that had a different flag been hoisted they would have beaten the French. In his log book he criticised Rear Admiral Samuel Hood, second in command of the fleet, 'for not bearing down and engaging with the enemy, which was his duty; but kept his wind, by which means a most glorious victory was lost, and with it the loss of Lord Cornwallis's army in Virginia.' Michael Lewis, the naval historian, wrote: 'It was one of the decisive battles of the World. Before it, the creation of the United States of America was possible; after it was certain.'

Three days later, on September 8th, a bloody battle was fought at Eutaw Springs, about thirty miles north of Fairlawn. There were roughly 1,000 rebels under the command of General Nathanael Greene, facing approximately 1,200 British troops led by Lieutenant Colonel Alexander Stewart. Both sides later claimed victory but the battle was indecisive. Stewart was forced to leave his dead and wounded on the battlefield and five hundred of his men were taken prisoner. The Americans, delighted by the comparative luxuries they found in the deserted British camp, temporarily gave up pursuit of their foes.

Lieutenant Colonel Stewart was now on his way to Fairlawn and summoned Lieutenant Colonel McArthur from the plantation to cover his retreat. General Francis Marion, known as the 'Swamp Fox' for his highly successful harassment of British forces through guerrilla tactics, heard that the British intended to move their sick and wounded from Fairlawn Fort to Charles Town. He went to attack the fort, but withdrew after realising it was too heavily defended. Three days later, General Nathanael

Greene reported to 'His Excellency George Washington', from his head-quarters at 'Martin's Tavern, Near Ferguson's Swamp', that the British had vacated the fort at Fairlawn, but still occupied the fortified house.

Just more than a month later, on October 19th 1781, Lord Cornwallis surrendered his force of 8,000 soldiers at Yorktown. When the news of the defeat reached London, the Prime Minister, Lord North, exclaimed: 'Oh God! It is all over.'

News of the surrender at Yorktown notwithstanding, the conflict continued in South Carolina. A British captain, Murdock MacLaine, had re-enforced the fort at Fairlawn with fifty men and transported fifty of the most seriously ill patients from the house to Charles Town. On November 17th, General Marion dispatched a cavalry force to draw out the newly promoted General Stewart and his men from their camp at Wantoot, lying halfway between Fairlawn and the battlefield at Eutaw Springs. As there was great sickness in his camp, Stewart could only counter with a small cavalry detachment. They set out on the heels of the rebel cavalry of 180 men under the command of Colonel Hezekiah Maham, 'a despotic, high tempered man', who headed for Fairlawn, as did another 200 men under the command of Colonel Shelby. Captain MacLaine's scouts alerted him as to their movements and he withdrew soldiers from the house to the fort.

The historian William Johnson wrote: 'The landing place was covered by a fort of too much strength to be carried by assault, with such troops as Shelby's and Mayham's; but at the distance of half a mile, was a strong brick house, built at a very early period, and known to have been calculated for defence, as well as comfort. This had been inclosed by strong abbatis; and being on the route from Charles Town to Monck's Corner, had been used as a stage for their troops and convoys, in passing from post to post. It was sufficiently capacious to cover a party of considerable magnitude, and was unassailable by cavalry, the only force from which sudden incursions could be apprehended. It was also a convenient depot in transportation of negroes, stock, &c. taken above the British posts, and moving to Charleston, and had been used as a hospital.'

Mayham and his men rode up to the house where: 'A party of the riflemen were ordered to dismount, and, approaching the abbatis, appear and act as infantry, while the residue of that corps advanced boldly into the field and demanded a surrender. The idea of resistance was abandoned, and the place surrendered at discretion. In it were found three-hundred stand of arms, many stores of value, some sick, and eighty convalescents, able to have fought from the house windows. The medical men, officers, and the sick were paroled; and the convalescents carried off on horseback behind Mayham's men. But the house, with its contents and the abbatis was committed to flames.' MacLaine, at a distance, and without enough men could not interfere. It was strongly rumoured that Mayham ordered the house be set alight as his soldiers had found quantities of liquor, and this was the only way to bring them into order.

General Stewart was outraged by the rebel's behaviour at Fairlawn. He wrote to General Francis Marion: 'The burning of a hospital and dragging away a number of dying people to expire in swamps is a species of barbarity hitherto unknown in civilised nations – especially when the hospital has been left without a guard for its defence – that could justify an attack upon the defenceless inhabitants.' The complaint from General Stewart was passed to General Greene, who in turn demanded an explanation of Marion. General Greene wrote in defence: 'I have not the least doubt that the burning of the hospital was to destroy the stores, which could not be effected in any other way.'

In February 1782, the newly formed Congress of the Confederation passed an act authorising confiscation of land and property owned by British subjects in South Carolina. Lists were drawn up, and Thomas Boone, the unpopular Governor of South Carolina, had his estates confiscated and sold. The only woman named on the 'Number One' list was Margaret Colleton, as owner of Wadboo, even though she had died and her plantation now belonged to James Edward Colleton. As Sir John Colleton's will had not yet been proved in South Carolina, Louisa's estates under her father's name were also on the list. When the 'Number One' list was drawn up, all that was left at Fairlawn was 'The Schooner Nancy with her tackle, ditto the Success', and seventeen slaves, one of whom was Haman, the patroon, and another just a child.

Further afield, in the Bahamas, rebel privateers were raiding for gunpowder and ammunition. The British Governor fought back and reported that he had captured 127 rebel ships lying at anchor in the harbours, but unable to feed his prisoners, he had to let them go. On May 6th 1782, two American frigates and 40 accompanying ships under the overall command of the Governor of Cuba arrived at the capital Nassau and demanded that the Governor, John Maxwell, surrender. As he did not have the men or means to defend the islands, Maxwell capitulated the next day. With the help of the Americans, the Spanish soon took possession of the islands.

During the final days of the American Revolutionary War, on August 28th 1782, Henry Laurens' eldest son, John, the apple of his eye, was killed at the Battle of Combahee River, in Beaufort, South Carolina. John had earlier served as an aide-de-camp to General George Washington. The 'battle' was described General Nathanael Greene as a 'paltry little skirmish' with a foraging party. The news of his son's death would not reach Laurens for months, but his daughter Martha later revealed to her husband that she had 'sat up in bed one night, knowing John was dead'. After the Battle of Brandywine, which had taken place early in the hostilities, the French General, the Marquise de Lafayette, had remarked of John: 'It was not his fault he was not killed or wounded... he did everything that was necessary to procure one or the other.'

John, educated in England and Switzerland, had very strong opinions on slavery. He wrote: 'We have sunk the Africans & all their descendants below the Standard of Humanity, and almost rendered them incapable of that Blessing which Heaven bestow'd upon us all.' He advocated that slaves be released to fight for the rebel cause; a few were, but the idea of releasing greater numbers was repeatedly rejected by Congress. Whilst Henry Laurens agreed with his son's views on slavery in principle, it was not one he ever upheld, even though he had written in 1777, that slavery was not compatible with the concept of a 'free' America.

The day after John Laurens was killed, one of the last clashes in America between the rebels and British forces took place at Wadboo. The plantation had become the headquarters of the 'Swamp Fox', who learnt that the British intended to raid the plantation and take a valuable 'head of thirty cattle'. On August 29th, Marion reputedly hid his men in the stately cedar trees which formed an avenue leading to the house, their festoons of Spanish moss concealing his snipers. Here, they lay in wait for the British. Marion's ambush proved successful; the British lost nine men killed, and others wounded.

Shortly after this victorious skirmish, the substantial house James Colleton had built at Wadboo when governor of the colony, was set on fire. It is not known whether General Marion's men or British forces were responsible. The South Carolina state geologist wrote in a report, published in 1848, that they had found the ruins of a dwelling house of considerable size: 'Of the house little more remained than the dilapidated foundation, but there was an outhouse, or office in a pretty good state of preservation. It is evident the walls were of stone, and at first sight I reminded of Portland Stone, which I supposed had been imported in those early times.' In fact, the house had been made of local marl. 'The stone was well dressed and coursed, the window jambs well cut; and within the building, the fireplace was decorated with a tasteful mantle, handsomely moulded, with angles quite sharp, and all composed of the same stone. Even where the wall was exposed to the weather, the marks of the tools were so well defined as if they had been impressed yesterday.'

During those few years from 1779 to the autumn of 1782, the Colleton family's South Carolina property was reduced to ruins, their remaining slaves left hungry and unshod, and their lands untended. The American Congress had doubled taxation on absentee landlords and warned that they had every intention of confiscating their property. For Louisa, on her own account, the Spanish had taken possession of the Bahamas. At Fairlawn, her half-brothers, William, now ten, and his younger brother John Snell, had been left to fend for themselves.

CHAPTER 7

Perfectly Fruitless

*

IN 1782, Louisa was nineteen, still underage, and frustrated at being unable to manage her affairs. Meanwhile, her cousin, 30-year-old James Nassau Colleton, was desperately trying to save Wadboo from confiscation, which his childless cousin, James Edward Colleton, proposed to hand over to him.

James Nassau had had his share of misfortune. After his father, Robert, died, lawyer William Field purloined his money. The family had also not received an income from Fairlawn, promised under the agreement between Robert and his brother, the Honourable John. James Nasssau and his family were rendered almost destitute. The Earl of Rochford, however, found employment for James Nassau and his brothers. The eldest, John, was placed as a cadet in the India Service. But, on his arrival in India, the twelve-year-old fell between the ship and a boat; he was seized by a shark and drowned. Charles Sackville the youngest of three brothers, and a promising lieutenant in the army, had recently drowned in Lake Ontario. The Earl, (when Secretary of State) had placed James Nassau, at the age of eleven, under his patronage in what was now the Home Office.

In August, James Nassau, who twenty years later still worked for the Home Office, wrote to Wadboo's agent, the lawyer William Ancrum in Charles Town and asked whether the best way of safeguarding the plantation from confiscation by the victorious American revolutionaries would be for him to at once set sail for America, and settle in the country. Ancrum replied that he could not help: his own estates had been confiscated, and he was to be banished from South Carolina. At the end of November 1782, James Nassau sought the help of Benjamin Franklin in Paris, one of the American peace commissioners there, who sent word via a friend that he would do everything he could to help.

Franklin was present when a preliminary peace treaty, signed in Paris on January 20th 1783, ended hostilities between Great Britain and America and allied nations, the Netherlands, France and Spain. Under its terms, Spain would cede the Bahamas back to the British in exchange for Florida, which Spain had lost in the Seven Years' War. One British newspaper later commented on the bargain: 'The Bahamas are an expensive Nothing', and argued that the British had given away possessions 'without any equivalent whatever'. Had it been generally known that whilst the British government had civil and military control of the islands, they did not own the 'soil', the press would have had further reason to be critical. It was, however, very welcome news for Louisa, for not only was she a Lord Proprietor of the Bahamas, but she also owned land in her own name, including Long Island which alone amounted to 230 square miles.

In February, after Wadboo had been formally signed over to James Nassau by his cousin, he determined to sail for South Carolina with his wife on the 'first safe conveyance'. They found passage on one of the government packets, medium-sized ships employed to take mail, passengers and freight to the colonies and sailed on a scheduled service. James Nassau embarked in Falmouth, taking with him dispatches 'containing the preliminaries for peace' for the Governor of Florida, General Patrick Tonyn, at St Augustine, which included the plea that British subjects should not have their lands confiscated. James Nassau had been instructed by the British Government, 'to endeavour by all possible means to prevent the Sale of the confiscated Estates, settled on him and his Heirs male, in order to spare this Country from any further claims for remuneration'. The British Government was clearly worried that if the new Government of America carried out its threat to dispossess British subjects of their property it would be overwhelmed by costly demands for compensation.

James Nassau's son would later write that his father and pregnant mother crossed 'at very great risk in an open boat, the notable bar of St Augustine, (whereon 13 vessels were wrecked in one morning)' and having completed his duty here, proceeded with his lady and a female servant, who had been saved from one of the wrecks, in an open canoe, by the Inland Navigation (as it was termed) among the islands, to Charles Town, where after a perilous passage of 400 hundred miles, he arrived just in time to see his Estates advertised for sale on the following day'.

James Nassau immediately petitioned the Commissioners of Forfeited Estates to prevent the sale of Wadboo proceeding. He was unsuccessful and the twelve-thousand-acre plantation, split into twenty-eight tracts, was sold on June 1783. Under the terms of the sale, raising just over £26,000, the buyers had up to five years to pay, in gold or silver. Benjamin Franklin had been unable to offer any effective assistance.

No slaves remained at Wadboo: between 200-300 had been dispersed, or carried off by British troops and sent to Florida. James Nassau was appalled to learn that forty of them had drowned on the journey. While Wadboo was now gone, the authorities had failed to consider Epsom, which the family wrote was '3 or 400 acres of nearly uninhabitable bad swamps' north of Moncks Corner, and where a few of his older, less valuable slaves were still living. James Nassau then decided to take an oath to become an American citizen in the hope that Wadboo might be returned to him.

He also planned to wrest Devil's Elbow back from Louisa, and went to the plantation only to find it 'abandoned'. James Nassau, nonetheless, made a claim for Devil's Elbow on the basis it had been left to his father by his father's elder brother. But, James Nassau's son, James Roupell, would later write: 'The decision was in favour of those in possession, and their long possession considered as giving right.'

In early June 1783, a volcanic fissure in the South of Iceland erupted with catastrophic global consequences. Weather patterns were severely affected and the 'poison' blew across Europe. At Great Fulford, the once verdant park was scorched dry and the Fulford family moved quarters to the lofty Marble Hall in an attempt to escape the heat. During this eerie summer, Louisa did not know of James Nassau's attempt to claim Devil's Elbow, but had the welcome news that her name had been temporarily removed from the 'Number One List' because she was a minor, and 'a girl'. This gave her some chance of avoiding confiscation of her properties in South Carolina.

The future of the loyalists who had fled to Florida during the revolution was now uncertain, as the territory was to be returned to Spain. Initially, they were offered sanctuary and land in British-held territory in Canada and Nova Scotia, but there were many for whom the chilly Northern climate held little appeal and wished instead to settle in the Bahamas.

In late July, General Sir Guy Carleton, Commander-in-Chief of the British forces, then in New York, ordered Lieutenant Wilson, the acting engineer at St Augustine, to survey the Bahamas. Brigadier General McArthur, his commanding officer, then in rough-shod offices in St Augustine, was charged with overseeing the evacuation of the loyalists. He had a thousand people waiting to sail to the Abaco Islands in the Northern Bahamas. On August 22nd, Carleton told McArthur that some refugees in New York had already left of their own volition for the Bahamas, and had settled on the Abaco islands and Cat Island. Carleton admitted, that he was 'unacquainted with the tenure of lands in all the Bahama Islands, and whether the King has any to grant or not, I could give them no encouragement.' Carleton did not know at the time, that the purchase of the islands from the Lords Proprietors was already in motion in London. On August 6th 1783, the Leader of the House of Lords, Lord Sydney, wrote to John Maxwell, Governor of the Bahamas, informing him that Parliament had voted for funds to be made available to buy the 'soil' from the Lords Proprietors and that land grants would soon be possible. There was, interestingly, no mention in Parliament of the Sovereign Rights to the islands.

It is unlikely the Treasury Solicitors informed Louisa of their potential purchase of the Islands. They also had made little effort on her behalf to save her American estates, so Louisa took charge. She, herself, prepared a statement appealing to the American Congress to have her estates in South Carolina formally restored to her.

Towards the end of August 1783, Louisa learnt that her agent in Charleston (as it was now named) had died. With no one to look after her affairs in America, she wrote to Henry Laurens for advice. He had been released by the British from the Tower of London at the end of 1781, in their attempt to obtain the parole of Lord Cornwallis. Laurens was in Bath at the time where he had on occasion met with Louisa and her aunt. He replied in a letter dated September 4th, apologising for not answering more swiftly: 'you will excuse me I am sure when I tell you business of a very important nature had engaged my whole attention.' Laurens had just returned from France where he had been a signatory to the treaty that brought a formal end to the American Revolution. He gave Louisa a list of six merchants who could act as her agent, any of whom he said he would entrust with his own estates. A few days later, as tremendous thunderstorms raged across England, Louisa again wrote to Laurens, her letter chasing him to London. She was desperate to know if her appeal to Congress had arrived in America, but he did not know. He was then, he informed her, on his way to France to see his dying brother and rescue his sister and daughter, Polly. Laurens grumbled that he would have to go back to Bath to recover from the journey and that he was suffering from terrible gout. He added that he thought it unlikely that he and his family would return to America that year.

The British government, meanwhile, was inundated by refugees request-ing sanctuary in the Bahamas. In early September, McArthur received a letter from Sir Guy Carleton, offering him the role of presiding over the Court of Chancery in the Bahamas. McArthur had doubts of the honour and wrote in reply that he was, 'a plain soldier who has only made his own profession his study'. Nevertheless, he told Carleton that he would sail for Providence as soon as all the refugees had been transported out of Florida.

McArthur added at the end of this letter, written on September 12th 1783: 'The Colleton family of South Carolina are said to have a claim on all the lands of the Bahama's, which government does not admit; as few people have settled thereof last year, such as become settlers, set down where they thought proper without any grants, this account I have from many people who have been there; and without recourse to their records not better can be had.' As McArthur had been ensconced at Fairlawn for part of the war, he may have learnt then of the Colleton's connection to the islands. He informed 'His Excellency' that he would send Lieutenant Wilson once more to the Bahamas to make a more detailed report as to their suitability as a sanctuary, and to search the government records to see if the claim about the Colleton family was valid.

Lieutenant Wilson soon submitted a report listing the various islands and the crops grown at the time, among which were corn, beans, yams, plantains, cassava, pumpkins and cabbages. Wilson thought that cotton, indigo, salt, and dye woods could be managed and exported. There were several valuable trees such as mahogany, boxwood, tamarinds and pines and a variety of shrubs such as wild sage, aloe vera and bamboos. Wilson also trawled through official documents in Nassau to find evidence of the Colletons claim to the Bahamas, and found an original deed of sale of the Sovereign Rights to the Bahamas from the Lords Proprietors to Louisa's great-grandfather, the 3rd baronet. The deed was passed to a superior officer, perhaps McArthur or Carleton, whereupon it was sent to England.

However, the matter of the Sovereign Rights to the Bahamas was of little importance to the British Government when faced with the re-settlement of so many loyalists. Title to the land was now their main concern and George II signed a Royal proclamation of the Crown's intention to purchase the 'soil' of the Bahamas from the Lords Proprietors. The government declared they would distribute the land to new colonists in the following proportions: the head of every family was to receive 40 acres, with an additional 20 acres for every member of their family and slaves at an annual ground rent of 20 shillings per hundred acres. Loyalists were to be given land free of charge and had only to pay a quit rent ten years after the land had been granted.

Louisa, still a minor and tucked up in the distant English countryside, was not aware that her fellow Lords Proprietors had recently taken steps to assert their authority over the Bahamas. They had informed Officials there that only they, as Lord Proprietors, could grant land before a sale to the Crown was agreed. The Chief Justice of the Bahamas, Thomas Atwood, acceded to the Lords Proprietors' demand, but was admonished by the government in London. In October, Atwood wrote an obsequious letter to Lord North, then Home Secretary, which began: 'It is impossible to express the distress I feel upon the information of having incurred your Lordship's displeasure.' Atwood assured Lord North that he would relinquish every idea of acting under 'some' of the Proprietors.

There is no record of exactly how many people evacuated Florida to the Bahamas between 1783 and March 1st 1785 when the last British convoy left for the islands, but estimates range from 6,000 to 9,000. One of the British naval officers involved in the evacuation was Captain Richard Graves, who sailed hundreds of loyalists and their slaves to the Islands. There they were given grants of land, even on Long Island, which unbeknownst to him, and regardless of her Sovereignty over the Islands, belonged to his future wife, Louisa Carolina Colleton.

Colleton Great House, Barbados, built by Sir John Colleton, 1st Bart. c.1655

Great Fulford, Devonshire

Map from 1690 showing part of Carolina, and the port of Charleston

Obverse of the Lords Proprietors' seal, with the motto, Domitus Scultiribus Orbis, (*The taming makes the land*).

Rear-Admiral Thomas Graves, 1667–1755 (National Maritime Museum, Greenwich, London)

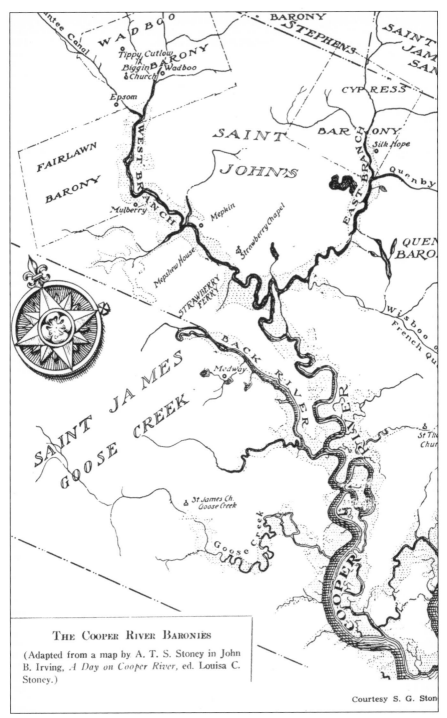

The Carolina Baronies of Fairlawn, Wadboo and Cypress

'Rice Hope' plantation on the River Cooper, c.1803, by Charles Fraser
(Gibbes Museum of Art, Charleston, South Carolina)

*Ann Fulford, Louisa's grandmother,
by Thomas Hudson*

*Elizabeth Fulford,
by William Hoare of Bath*

John Fulford, by William Hoare of Bath

*Sir John Colleton, 4th Bart.
as a young man, by Jeremiah Theus*

Cottages at Gittsham, by Alfred Leyman

Ann Fulford, Lady Colleton,
by Jeremiah Theus

Sir John Colleton, 4th Bart.,
English School

Eliza Janverin, Mrs E. Taylor, by George
Romney (National Portrait Gallery of Ireland)

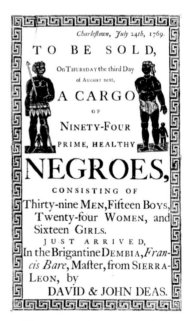

Newspaper advertisement for a
Charles Town slave auction, July 1769

Mepkin, the seat of Henry Laurens, by Charles Fraser, c.1796
(Gibbes Museum of Art, Charleston, South Carolina)

*Slave houses at Mulberry Plantation, with the house in the background,
by Thomas Coram, c.1800* (Gibbes Museum of Art, Charleston, South Carolina)

Drayton Hall, built c.1738. Watercolour, c.1765, by Pierre Eugene du Simitiere

*Admiral Thomas Graves, 1st Baron
Graves, known as the man who 'lost
America', by Thomas Gainsborough*

*Rear-Admiral Richard Graves,
by William Beechey*

*Miniature of Sir Thomas Graves, K.B.
as a young officer*

Miniature of Rear-Admiral 'Sam' Graves

The 'Yellow Portrait' of Louisa, by an unknown artist, c.1787/88

Henry Laurens, painted in 1782 by John Singleton Copley
(National Portrait Gallery, Smithsonian Institution, Washington, D.C.)

The Old Plantation, anonymous folk painting, American slaves dancing to banjo and percussion, c.1780s

Hembury Fort House

Admiral Samuel Graves by James Northcote

William Pitt the Younger

Exmouth c.1829

Sidmouth c.1800

Battle of Virginia Capes, (Battle of the Chesapeake), 1781,
19th century painting by V. Zveg (Hampton Roads Naval Museum Collection)

Rear-Admiral Sir Thomas Graves, K.B. by James Northcote (National Maritime Museum)

Charlestown harbour, engraving, 1774

*Ann, mother of Mary Anne Burges,
by Francis Cote*

Elizabeth Simcoe by Mary Anne Burges
(Library and Archives, Canada)

Mary Graves

*Elizabeth Bonaparte by Gilbert Stuart,
1804* (Metropolitan Museum of Art, New York)

Painting of *Exeter* (*detail*) *by William Turner. c.1827, showing Colleton Crescent*

Richard Graves,
artist unknown, c.1781

Sketch of Mrs Admiral, by Mary Anne
Burges (Devon Record Office)

King William II of the Netherlands, Queen Anna Paulowna
and family, by Jan Baptist van der Hulst, 1832 (Dutch Royal Collection)

CHAPTER 8

Hands of Kings

*

THE market town of Honiton in Devon nestles in the beautiful open
Otter Valley, some nine miles from the sea. A traveller, approaching the
view, wrote that it was the 'sweetest scene of cultivation I ever held', and
declared: 'This may be called the garden of Devon.' The main thorough-
fare of Honiton in the 18th century ran for nearly a mile through this
coaching town, and could be covered in an all-enveloping dust, or in wet
weather knee-deep in mud. The road was lined with thatched houses and
a small stream ran down a gully on one side. In the middle of the wide
highway stood a large open-fronted, ramshackle building, known as the
Shambles, where a daily market was held and where in times of rebellion
bodies had been strung up from its pitched roof. Nearby was the
renowned hostelry the Golden Lion, just one of the many inns that
served the endless stream of travellers passing through; some on their
way to the all-important Devon dockyards. The finest lace in England
was made there and on sunny days the women labouring over this intricate work could be seen sitting outside taking advantage of the light.
They were only disturbed by the rumble of coaches, which ran on a reg-
imented timetable and could be heard as they approached the town. Dis-
embarking from these coaches were heiresses, spinsters, curates,
ne'er-do-wells and on occasion, Admiral Samuel Graves and his wife,
known to all as 'Mrs Admiral' in deference to her husband's rank.

The couple lived across the valley from the town, where the land rose
steeply to a wooded escarpment, at the southern end of which were the
remains of an iron-age hill fort. A hundred feet or so below it stood the
admiral's house, Hembury Fort, a large white stuccoed building, with
pediment wings and a recently added fashionable Doric porch. On a clear
day, the admiral could, from his vantage point high above the valley,
catch the sea glinting in the distance. He was now in his seventieth year
and his seafaring days were over.

The Graves were an Anglo-Irish family who during the course of the
18th and early 19th centuries were to furnish the Royal Navy with a
wealth of officers, of which no fewer than seven were to reach flag rank.

Admiral Samuel himself had been born in 1713 and joined the navy in 1732, serving his uncle, Captain Thomas Graves, in the frigate *Norfolk* as a midshipman together with his elder brother, John, who served as ship's chaplain. Admiral Samuel's naval career was distinguished, and in 1774 he had been appointed to command the North American Station.

However, when war broke out the following year, he was recalled to England for failing to bring the 'daring rebellion' under control. The Admiralty knew he was not to blame for the situation, and as a douceur, had promised him command of the Mediterranean. The admiralty reneged on their offer, and instead offered the admiral the post of commander-in-chief of the naval base at Plymouth which he refused, stating that he was determined 'never to hold any employment in the time of war, except of the most active kind against the enemies of this country'.

Now in bitter retirement, Admiral Samuel avidly scanned the newspapers for news of the war and in particular for any account of the doings of his four nephews, Samuel, Thomas, John and Richard Graves, the sons of his brother John, now rector of a parish in Ireland. Admiral Samuel had reason to be proud of them. All four were to end the American War of Independence as Post Captains and all distinguished themselves, not though without some cost to their health. Tom had been badly burnt early in the war when defending his ship, a 120-ton schooner, HMS *Diana*.

After she became stranded on a riverbank as the tide turned, rebels set it on fire. For the rest of his life, his injuries would remain visible to all. John, serving in another ship, had gone to his aid and was also burnt. Sam, the eldest, was the most unfortunate. At the age of sixteen, he had lost an eye fighting in a battle against the French off Ushant, and Tom had reported to his mother in April 1776 that Sam had now lost an arm: 'By a very late letter from himself to my Uncle (Admiral Samuel), we find that he is quite well, though it is true with the loss of his left arm. A loss we are now and then glad to compound for, and which you have some reason to thank God is no worse than the loss of arm to one of the many sons you have exposed to accidents of that, or a worst nature, at a time when the officers of the Army and Navy have bled so profusely.'

Captain Richard Graves, at 25, the youngest of Admiral Samuel's nephews, had also been 'severely wounded' during the war. His cousin, Admiral Thomas Graves, Commander-in-Chief of the North American Squadron, had written a dispatch to the Admiralty, from Sandy Hook, dated August 20th 1781: 'The Swift brigantine Captain Richard Graves of 14 guns and 60 men on board, coming with dispatches from the Chesapeake proved so leaky that in order to bail at the Hatchways, they had taken their lumber and stores upon deck, in so distrustful a situation they found themselves attacked by the Holket privateer carrying 10 guns and full of men. It was impossible to stand a cannonade; they therefore with great spirit boarded the enemy twice, but the privateer having greatly the advantage in sailing disentangled and made away leaving their enemy to pump and bail or drown, fortunately she arrived and was hauled on shore. She had two men killed and wounded.' Admiral Thomas Graves did not mention that Richard was one of those wounded: he had been hit hard in the thigh by a shard of wood, and although he had recovered, the wound would always plague him.

Richard returned to England in the middle of November 1783 and was then expected at Hembury Fort where he had often stayed when on leave. The government of the day was keen to reap 'the peace dividend' and cut taxation. One method of doing so was to immediately reduce the Royal Navy to a fraction of its wartime strength, lay-up ships and pay off the crews. The officers could not be so easily disposed of as they held the King's commission, and those who no longer had a ship to serve on were 'put on the beach'. Richard's ship was duly paid off and as with many other officers, he was 'obliged to retire from active duties of a profession in which he had so highly distinguished himself'. Unless they had private means, officers had to eke out an existence on half-pay. Richard had no private means and for many years had been relying on marriage to Mrs Admiral's niece to secure his future.

The subject of his marriage had first been raised in 1775, the year the Revolutionary War began. Richard, then seventeen, had been sent from Norfolk, Virginia, to Boston with an express to John Burgoyne, the commanding general, and to his uncle, Vice-Admiral Samuel. His fellow officers gave odds of 500-1 against him completing the mission. Nevertheless, his small schooner duly limped into the port and he boarded the admiral's flagship, HMS *Preston*. Here in the admiral's cabin he found not only the admiral but also his wife, as it was not unusual then for wives to sail with their serving husbands. Mrs Admiral, who ruled her husband 'absolutely' according to the admiral's nephews, had married the widower admiral when he was 56 and she 42. *The Naval Chronicle*, a fount of intelligence on such matters, noted in admiration that the former Margaret Spinkes came into the marriage with a fortune of £30,000.

Whilst on board HMS *Preston*, Richard wrote to his parents, whom he had not seen since he was fifteen, in Ireland: 'Since I began this letter my Uncle told me what he intended for me which is marriage between me and my Aunt's Niece.' Elizabeth Gwillam, whose middle name was Posthuma to indicate that she was born after her father died, was baptised on the same day her mother was buried. At the time of Richard's letter, the orphaned Elizabeth was thirteen years old and had often stayed at Hembury Fort. Richard wrote of her: 'She is a very accomplished girl and has a fortune of upwards of thirty thousand pounds, and an estate of eight hundred per annum.' He said he believed the best way of ensuring the marriage took place was to keep on the 'best of terms with my Aunt.'

Two years later, in 1777, Richard informed his mother that he had received a letter from his uncle 'explaining to me his intentions with regard to my Aunt's Niece and myself, and I believe there is nothing that would prevent it taking place but her youth, and my promotion, and I have every reason to believe that if nothing intervenes it will be finally settled on my return from the Mediterranean.'

But the plan backfired after the Admiral invited his godson, Colonel John Graves Simcoe, to stay at Hembury Fort in 1782. The pudgy-faced 30-year-old Simcoe was still recovering from wounds incurred during the war. The plain and diminutive Elizabeth Gwillim soon grew fond of him and when he proposed to her, the admiral and his wife did not object to the marriage. In part, they thought it unlikely Simcoe would squander her fortune. The wedding had taken place the year before Richard returned to Hembury Fort. Elizabeth, in fact, had never even considered Richard as a potential husband. They had met often at Hembury Fort, and Elizabeth thought him a 'tease and a bully', and when he came to stay, she would do everything she could to avoid him.

The admiral and Mrs Admiral, however, remained intent on finding Richard another heiress, and 'showed' him around the county. His brother, Tom Graves, wrote they also meant to 'show' Richard at Bath, 'where I hope he will pick up a woman of fortune as he has been imprudent to spend all the money he has made in the war except £2000 which I hope he will have sense to take care of, as times of peace are not likely to put money in any of our pockets.' In late November 1783, Richard was sent on ahead to Bath from Hembury Fort to arrange accommodation for his aunt and uncle.

Meanwhile, at Great Fulford, Louisa, her aunt and Frances Laroche were packing in anticipation of spending much of the winter in Bath.

This may have been as much to do with the weather as with Mrs Fulford's desire to find a suitable husband for her niece. The aftermath of the volcanic eruption in Iceland had led to a boiling hot summer, but it turned bitterly cold during the winter of 1783-1784. When the party left for Bath, the windows at Great Fulford were glazed in ice both inside and out and the lake was frozen solid.

It was noted in the *Bath Chronicle* that Mrs Fulford, Miss Colleton and Miss Laroche arrived there on December 10th. The card tables in the Assembly Rooms abounded with tittle-tattle on the arrival of the notable American heiress. Louisa, then a slight girl of twenty, with a clear skin and enchanting eyes, later wrote of these days in Bath: 'It would be a waste my dear children both of your time and mine, to enumerate how many sought to win the hand, they deemed so wealthy.' She was, however, under no illusions: 'The heiress is ever the object of attraction, however destitute of merit either mental or personal: the very cause that renders her an heiress leaves her an isolated being and assuredly the mark of interest or envy to aim at; she is fortunate if she has understanding enough to resist being the dupe of the insidious flattery she will receive.'

Richard Graves was but one of many fortune seekers on the prowl in the city . It was to his advantage that he was by all accounts exceptionally handsome and cut a fine figure in the Assembly Rooms. His subsequent pursuit of Louisa was likened by his brother Tom to that of a naval campaign, and the Graves family advised Richard on an almost daily basis as to how he should proceed with the courtship. At first, Louisa rejected his advances with the most 'Sovereign contempt'. One can presume by this comment that she had ensured the Graves family knew of her titles, as indeed did everyone else in Bath.

Louisa's attitude towards Richard appears to have altered considerably when she heard that Admiral Samuel had revealed his intention to make Richard, his favourite nephew, his heir. This was due to Mrs Admiral's influence, as she had no time for Sam, the eldest of her husband's nephews, and had always heartily disliked John, even once refusing him entry to her house. As John commented of his aunt: 'She is one of those ladies that does not stop saying anything of a person she has taken a dislike to.' Tom had married an heiress, which left Richard alone to inherit his uncle's estates.

Descendants of the Graves family today also believe that there was another reason for the admiral choosing Richard over his elder brothers.

Whilst he did not like their wives, he found Louisa captivating. However, the romance did not reach a conclusion and after the season Louisa returned home to Great Fulford.

Word had by then reached the Colleton family in England, in late November 1783, that James Nassau's voyage to Charleston 'promises to be perfectly fruitless.' The news also arrived that his wife had been safely delivered of a son they named James Roupell Colleton. The family was still in Charleston at the beginning of 1784, but James Nassau had contracted swamp fever. He was, however, able to prepare a 'memorial' – a written statement of facts, for presentation to the General Assembly. James Nassau was carried into the chamber on a stretcher and from this, he delivered his speech. The Assembly was purportedly moved by his outpourings and one of its members made the appeal: 'Let not the descendant of one of the first founders of our country, (to the exertions of whose ancestor at least we are indisputably indebted for the very lands we now enjoy,) go forth from this Assembly *destitute*'. He added that now they had achieved independence, they could well afford to be generous.

At first, it seemed that James Nassau's gesture had, to an extent, paid off. The General Assembly voted for Wadboo to be taken off the list of confiscated estates. However, the purchasers of the twenty-eight tracts refused to relinquish their titles. It was then agreed that James Nassau should be given the proceeds of the sale of Wadboo, but there was not enough silver or gold in the country for him to be paid. The Assembly subsequently voted that the purchasers of the twenty-eight tracts of Wadboo be allowed to pay in discounted 'State Paper', thirty dollars of which brought a one-dollar silver piece. James Nassau, increasingly unwell, had not only run out of money, but his leave of absence from the Home Office in England had come to an end. He submitted a further petition, asking for permission to bring his slaves back from Florida. He added that he now had to leave Charleston with his wife and child, as he had been made 'a beggar by the people of the very country which his ancestors had wrested from the wilderness and made habitable for future generations'.

James Nassau, with his wife and son, left South Carolina shortly after, and before he left he appointed an agent to collect the money due to him from the sale of Wadboo. He was unlucky in his choice. The man he employed was, it turned out, heavily in debt. This agent soon sold the 'State Paper' belonging to James Nassau, which had a nominal value of £22,000, 'in the market for £2,200', and 'having secured this sum to his own purposes, he put a pistol to his head and thus settled all accounts'. James Nassau's wife would later maintain that the agent had not shot himself, but had cut his throat.

Whilst these dramas played out in South Carolina, Louisa celebrated her twenty-first birthday and her coming of age. This fell on March 14th 1784 and was heralded by the arrival of an unexpected packet. Inside, she found a miniature of her mother whom she had not seen or heard from for seventeen years. Louisa merely wrapped up the miniature and is said to have put it aside, without a word. Years later Louisa wrote of her twenty-first birthday: 'At length, the hour, the important hour arrived which gave the heiress uncontrolled command of her splendid fortune both in the New and the Old World.'

However, 'her splendid fortune' was in disarray. Regardless, she undoubtedly did believe that she was now a great heiress. Her life until then had consisted of drifting between a great plantation house in Carolina, to the stately beauty of her uncle's house in Devon, with intermittent stays at various grand townhouses both in Exeter and London, not to mention extended holidays in Bath. She believed that she was fabulously wealthy as did her prospective lover, the gallant Captain Richard Graves. This belief was mistaken. As Louisa would later admit, her baronies in South Carolina had been desolated by the war and her property in England 'drained for the re-establishment, thus might my envied wealth be said to have taken wings and flown away'.

Nevertheless, Louisa now had 'uncontrolled command' of what was left of her fortune and the Treasury Solicitors, Messrs Chamberlayne and White, who had acted for her while she was a minor, were at her bidding. Some eleven days after her birthday she ensured they submitted a memorial on her behalf to the Commissioners appointed to look into the claims of American loyalists. It stated that her father owned very large estates in South Carolina, a 'Capital mansion house called Fairlawn' and a large number of 'Negroes or Slaves'. Louisa, they wrote, was an 'infant of tender years' when she had been sent to England at the 'breaking out of the troubles'. The house was 'totally burnt together with all the furniture therein and great numbers of negroes destroyed, driven away, or carried off from the said estates'. She had received no income from the plantations for more than six years and was not sure of the amounts involved or the losses sustained. The lawyers asked that her case be considered and that in the meantime Louisa would try to assess her losses.

On the romantic front, Richard had made faltering progress with his courtship but on March 29th, Tom Graves reported: 'Richard has met with a slight repulse in his attack upon Miss Colliton for want of generalship only, he is not equal to his friend Colonel Simcoe in this respect.' Simcoe had been much admired by the Graves brothers for his quasi-military tactics in winning over his wife, Elizabeth. 'However,' Tom wrote of his brother's romance, 'the matter is again renewed with an absolute certainty of success. His person has done everything for him, as he has not shown the smallest degree of address or cleverness in any part of the attack.' Richard had, seemingly, won Louisa's heart on his looks alone.

Tom added at the bottom of his letter that their eldest brother, Sam, had won a prize off the Cape of Good Hope, of which his share would be £6,000, 'So,' wrote Tom, 'you will find him richer than all his brothers except if Richard is married to Miss Colliton before he arrives'.

The general presumption must have been that Richard and Louisa would soon marry. But Louisa told Richard that she had no intention of doing so before she had crossed the seas to investigate her 'transatlantic concerns'. Richard would have found it almost impossible to obtain full leave from the Admiralty to travel with her, and he could not prevent her from going. Mrs Admiral, who had been so instrumental in the match between them, now thought Louisa 'rather odd'. It was 'odd' at the time that an unescorted, unmarried woman would consider such a journey. However, for the willful heiress, neither the potential danger of an Atlantic crossing, nor the discomforts involved would prevent her from trying to salvage her inheritance from a rapacious British Government on the one hand, and on the other, the newly victorious American rebels. To Richard's further consternation, it would be another year before Louisa planned to make the journey.

It was not until early April 1785 that Louisa left Great Fulford with her aunt for London, from where she would sail to the Bahamas. Initially, the most pressing matter for her was to obtain probate on her father's will, which she was duly granted on April 9th. Elizabeth Fulford was then distracted not only by Louisa's imminent departure to the Bahamas but also by the affairs of her sister, Susannah. She was addicted to gambling on cards which was then an endemic pastime amongst the bored upper classes. On her death in 1806, aged forty-eight, Georgiana, the Duchess of Devonshire, left gambling debts of nearly £50,000. While Susannah had not racked up debts of such magnitude, they were nonetheless considerable and she had by then 'spent every penny of her fortune'. Susannah had recently turned to her brother-in-law, the extremely rich Mr Berners, but he had refused to bail her out yet again.

Elizabeth was thus summoned to St James's Square by the notoriously formidable Lady Falmouth with whom Susannah lived as a companion. And although Louisa was about to cross the Atlantic without a chaperone, Elizabeth, as protocol demanded, took her niece in tow. Louisa witnessed the terrible scene when Lady Falmouth bullied her aunt into signing a bond over to her for £600, to prevent her sister's ruin. This, however, did not even begin to cover Susannah's debts: it was later discovered that she also owed her bank £4,000.

Louisa, however, had her own pressing affairs, as it was only a matter of days before she was due to sail. With probate granted on her father's will, she met with Mr Chamberlayne of the Treasury Solicitors, whom she continued to engage. He had, he said, a power of attorney for her to sign which would enable Mrs Fulford to deal with Louisa's estates in Exeter, while she was abroad. This included the Friars, a large block of land in Exeter above the River Exe. It seems that it was by chance that Joseph Burrows, called upon Louisa whilst Chamberlayne was there, and seeing papers on the table asked Louisa, 'Are these papers for you to sign?'

Burrows asked to read the documents. Louisa wrote: 'I acquiesced from the deference I felt for him, on account of his well known integrity, and also from his having been my father's steward and confidential legal advisor, from my childhood and also mine ever since the death of my father; we therefore resumed our seats while he looked over the papers, during which he made the following remarks to me: "pretty papers you were going to sign – umph! lucky for you that I had business that brought me to town. At length, he threw the papers on the table, exclaiming: "you will not sign these papers; I will draw up the power of attorney that is proper for you to sign." Mr Chamberlayne said not one word, but folded the papers up and carried them away with him and I never heard any more of them; neither did I enquire, as I took it for granted that a lawyer in London did not understand about the mode of leasing in the western counties.' Burrows, true to his word, returned to Louisa on April 20th with a power of attorney, which she duly signed.

But, Chamberlayne once again called on Louisa, this time when Richard Graves was present. Chamberlayne bore an offer from the Crown in the sum of £2000, for her sixth-part share of the Bahama Islands.

Some months before, on September 3rd 1784, a King's Warrant had been signed by the Prime Minister, Judge Buller and a Mr Aubrey, in which they had authorized that a sum of £7,800 should be paid to 'perfect the purchase' of the Bahamas, and to 'Support the Civil Establishment of the said Islands'. The money to pay for this was to be raised by duties on rum and cider, and also 'by a land tax granted to his Majesty'. A portion of the money raised was to pay for the Treasury Solicitors to prepare 'An Abstract of Title to the several Proprietors to their several shares in the Bahama Islands.' This document ran to 23 pages and revealed how each of the six present-day Lords Proprietors came to own their share. Of the six, four were a matter of simple descent from the six men created Sovereign Lords Proprietors of the Bahamas in 1670. The Colleton share was owned by Louisa; the Craven share by William, 1st Earl of Craven; the Berkeley share by Sophia Woodehouse, a Berkeley niece and the Carteret share by three men, Henry Frederick Carteret Thynne, Thomas, Lord Viscount Weymouth and thirdly the 6th Earl of Coventry. The Albermarle share had devolved upon Henry, 5th Duke of Beaufort by marriage in the 18th century. The remaining share, that of the Ashley Cooper family, had been sold on May 13th 1725 to Sir John Tyrell. His two granddaughters, Mary and Elizabeth, who were of a similar age to Louisa, had inherited his share. The Treasury Solicitors also wrote a short rendition as to why the Crown had been unsuccessful over the years in their attempts to buy the islands from the Proprietors.

The British Government was now under increasing pressure from refugee loyalists in the Bahamas to purchase the islands and grant land. It was not only the settlement of displaced loyalists on the islands at stake, there were also claims from individuals such as one Dennis Rolle, who hailed from Bicton in Devon and wanted title to Exhuma Island in the archipelago as compensation for having spent £2,300 establishing a plantation in Florida, which now belonged to Spain.

Louisa rebuffed the offer brought by Chamberlayne, and 'declined accepting, both on account of the inadequacy of the sum, and because I did not wish to part from them'. Richard intervened and told Chamberlayne that he had a friend, a refugee from Florida, who would willingly pay £20,000 for Long Island alone, which Louisa owned outright. Chamberlayne then threatened Louisa and told her that if she did not take the sum offered by the government that they would 'seize them as an escheat to the Crown, for they were determined to have them'. Louisa replied that though the government could forcibly take the islands, they could not escheat them, because the islands had been given for services to the crown, and in compensation for 'a large sum of money expended and property confiscated', which, she added, 'were at the time they were granted very inadequate to the loss'.

According to Louisa, 'Mr Chamberlayne smiled at the unavailing energy of youth unbroken by calamity', and warned her: 'The hands of kings are long and strong, that might would overcome right'. He urged Louisa to accept the offer, otherwise the islands would be taken anyway, and she would receive nothing 'as the government was determined to have them, and as proof, they had already taken possession'.

What Louisa did not know was that her fellow Proprietors had been colluding to sell their rights. Earlier, in March 1784, they had met to discuss 'some scheme for settling the sale of the Bahama Islands', with the Treasury minister, George Rose, a close friend and ardent supporter of the Prime Minister, William Pitt. Also unknown to Louisa, the duplicitous William Chamberlayne had attended the meeting purportedly on her behalf, and would later sign numerous proprietary documents also on her behalf without Louisa's authority, and in the full knowledge that she had refused to sell her share of the islands.

CHAPTER 9

'Our Little Queen'

*

ELIZABETH would not leave Louisa's side until the last possible moment, so together they travelled to Gravesend, on the Thames Estuary, where the *Sally* was lying at anchor. On April 29th 1785, Louisa parted from her aunt 'with the greatest affection', and set sail for the Bahamas.

The 45-year-old captain of the *Sally*, John Crosskill, a seasoned mariner who had sailed the Atlantic on numerous occasions, had settled in the Bahamas after the Revolutionary war. It was fortuitous that the 200-ton merchant vessel had been overhauled just three years earlier, for the voyage would last for nearly three months. Louisa wrote: 'It was not only long but most distressing; it commenced very alarmingly.' The *Sally* had not even left the choppy English Channel when there was a disturbance on board following an altercation between the captain and the crew. The crew then hailed a passing man-of-war and offered themselves up for service. The man-of-war declined to take them aboard, whereupon the crew went on strike. For two days the 'gentlemen' passengers assisted the captain and the cabin boy in running the ship.

Louisa described how a menacing sailor, 'holding his knife horizontally wished for a breeze that would turn the edge of it, and then, exclaimed, 'we shall see what these fair-weather jacks will do'. It was at this point, Louisa later wrote, that one of the passengers, a Mr Tattnall, 'who was a great coward at sea, was greatly shocked at the expression', and remonstrated with the crew. He told them that they were "wicked", and were endangering the lives of the passengers with their conduct. He asked them to return to their duties, as the fault, whatever it may be, did not lie with the passengers. Mr Tattnalls's outburst, along with the fact that the crew were unlikely to be able to jump ship at this point, sent the men reluctantly back to work.'

Later conversations revealed that Tattnall had recently been appointed Surveyor-General of the Bahama Islands. Also on board was the newly appointed Attorney-General for the islands, Mr Wegg. She remarked imperiously of the government officials, 'They sailed in the *very* same ship that I sailed in.' Louisa would barely contain her fury, often reminding both men that, as she had not 'treated with government', and that her signature was 'requisite to give validity to their appointment'. A month after Louisa set sail, Chamberlayne, on behalf of all the Lords Proprietors and their agents, gave Lord Craven's agent, Mr Hill, authority to sell the Bahamas to the Government. This was provided 'that the contract is completed this session of Parliament'. Perhaps the other Proprietors wanted the sale to be completed before Louisa returned to England, thus creating a *fait accompli* that would be difficult to reverse.

As the voyage dragged on, the atmosphere on board the *Sally* sorely tried the passengers and crew. The unseemly spats between Louisa and the government officials continued until the *Sally* reached the dreaded doldrums, where the trade winds converge at the Equator. There, they experienced a dead calm for six days. Only then did it become apparent why the crew had wanted to jump ship in the Channel. They knew that the *Sally* had left Gravesend with only six weeks' rations on board and this included some salted beef which had soon become tainted.

Louisa wrote: 'The atmosphere appeared thick; at this <u>time</u> we were at short allowance, the gloom of melancholy overcast every countenance; all dreaded the sequel! we were reduced to one fowl or one duck a day, between nine. Soon the pease, potatoes, and flour were exhausted and of the biscuits, nothing but what is called the broken bread was left; even the most fearful prayed for a breeze, fair or foul to relieve us from the dead calm which we fancied affected our breathing; and the heat was oppressive, the surface of the sea had an oily appearance, from the quality of blubber which rose to the surface, I suppose in consequence of the perfect calm: on the starboard quarter of the ship at the distance where the horizon bounded our view, we saw water continually spouted, which passengers were informed by sailors, was done by some whales sporting in the beams of the setting sun. At length one of those sudden and violent gusts of wind arose which are so frequent in those latitudes, the ship was nearly on her beam ends when she righted by her sails shivering to ribbons.'

For seventeen days, contrary winds blew the ship off course. By then, they were out of rations but had the fortune to sight an American ship from Philadelphia that was able to send some food across to the famished and desperate voyagers. When the *Sally* eventually sailed into the turquoise shallows of Hurricane Bay on the island of Abaco in the Northern Bahamas, the only things left to eat on board were 'three half-starved fowls'.

On the *Sally's* arrival, a planter, desperate to hear of news from England, rowed his canoe to the ship and, after hearing that those on board were starving, soon returned with limes, lemons, oranges, pineapples and a present of 'a cage of aboconian ring-doves' for Louisa. Another plantation owner, Captain Alexander Wylly, a refugee from South Carolina and once a student at Oxford, also came on board and later sent a supply of provisions and fruit from his plantation. On July 19th 1785, the lieutenant governor of the islands, James Powell, sent a report from Nassau to the Home Secretary, Lord Sydney, in London saying that he was waiting for Tattnall to arrive in Nassau with his dispatches. That evening Louisa remained on board and marvelled at the dolphins which cruised around in the phosphorescent waters, causing the sea to sparkle.

It was not until the following morning at sunrise, after nearly three months at sea, that Louisa was finally able to leave the ship for dry land and walk on the white sands. Here, she 'had the opportunity of seeing the provident skill and care with which the turtle endeavours to prevent the nest of eggs which she has deposited in the sands near the sea, from being discovered; a short walk sufficed to fatigue me in so hot a climate, and I seated myself beneath the umbrageous canopy of a large tree, laden with fruit resembling a blooming apple. On missing me, Captain Wylly looked round and perceiving me seated at the foot of the tree, eagerly called me to leave the tree directly. I ran to the party with all possible speed, and joining them ventured to look round for the cause of the danger, but not seeing anything asked why they had disturbed me? "Because," replied he, "you had seated yourself beneath the manchinello tree: the dew yet on the leaves is dangerous."' Having been saved from the burning and blistering drops of the poisonous tree by Captain Wylly, Louisa returned to the ship and continued packing her things. She later learnt that the news of her arrival had not only reached Nassau but had swiftly spread throughout the outlying islands.

That afternoon a revenue cutter belonging to Mr Tattnall's son, Murlyne, appeared alongside the *Sally* 'decked with colours and music playing' to take the passengers to New Providence island. On July 20th, Louisa arrived at the port of Nassau.

After they had disembarked from the cutter, the party was escorted by Murlyne Tattnall to his house where within less than an hour, she met the lieutenant governor of the Bahamas. She described the encounter: 'Governor Powell waited on me in full dress, a style of compliment not usual in that climate, on account of the extreme heat; Mrs Tattnall, who had arrived at the same time and was with me, took the compliment to herself, and made her acknowledgments to the governor, for the promptitude with which he paid her a visit; to which the governor made the following emphatic reply: "Permit me, madam, to set you right, this visit," bowing profoundly low to me, "is to our little Queen, I shall take another opportunity of paying my respects to you."'

Mrs Tattnall was utterly astounded by the deference the governor showed to Louisa, who after weeks at sea dreaming of such a moment, wallowed in all the bowing and scraping which at last, in her eyes, confirmed her 'Sovereign status'.

Three days later, the *Bahamas Gazette* announced that the *Sally*, 'So long looked for,' had arrived. Along with a list of the passengers, there was an advertisement for the much-wanted luxuries she brought from England. These included 'India Chints,' spices, china, shoes, stationery, ladies' fans, powder bags and puffs, pickles, nails, almonds and currants, claret, trunks, ivory syringes, backgammon tables and, games of cribbage. They also had for sale a stock of books including *Boyers French Grammar and Dictionary*, Dryden's *Virgil*, Fielding's *Tom Jones,* and *Arabian Nights*. On the same page there was a proclamation from Governor Powell calling for people to put in their claims for land in the Bahamas: this he had placed in the paper as a direct result of the dispatch from the English government brought to him by Mr Tattnall.

The proclamation was premature, no sale between the Proprietors and the government had been yet agreed. The government, nonetheless, must have been confident of reaching agreement and thus instructed Powell to issue the notice. However, the negotiations in Louisa's absence had not gone smoothly. Although her five fellow Proprietors were keen to sell the Islands, the government was balking at the price demanded, £3,000 each, a thousand pounds more than Chamberlayne had offered Louisa for her share.

On July 9th, only a few days before Louisa's arrival, Mr Hill had sent an ultimatum to the Treasury reiterating that if the sale was not agreed upon by the end of the present Parliamentary session, the Lords Proprietors would 'consider the Treaty at an end – and other dispositions would be immediately made'. A few days later, on July 19th, the government wrote again to Governor Powell in the Bahamas: 'As to purchase of the soil, great progress had been made in concluding with the present proprietors but from various unavoidable circumstances it is not yet perfected.' This letter would, of course, take some weeks to arrive.

On her arrival in Nassau, Louisa had swiftly taken her leave of the Tattnall family and moved into the house she had rented. The author Edward Shaffer claimed during a lecture in 1940 that he had been entertained at 'a certain hospitable mansion on East High Street, where the young sea adventuring heiress of the House of Colleton' lived when she was in Nassau in 1785, 'to claim the land as Sovereign Proprietress of the Bahama Isles'. He described the house as having panelled walls, 'mirror-like' floors of English oak, and a 'quaint winding' staircase.

A contemporary view of Nassau was given by the German physician and scientist David Schoepf, once chief surgeon to the Hessian troops during the Revolutionary War. He had sailed for the Bahamas in the early spring of the previous year on a sloop that was 'crammed with people and cattle, luggage and household furniture', adding that on board were 'a number of black women and children to be sold'.

Schoepf described the dwellings lining the hilly shore where Louisa's house stood. 'There is but one tolerable regular street, or line of houses, which runs next to the water.' Most of these houses, lived in the main by Royal officials and diverse merchants, were constructed of wood and in such a fashion so as to ward off the sun's rays. There were no chimneys in these houses, but there were a 'few glass windows'. Schoepf noted that numerous raccoons wandered aimlessly through the gardens. To the east were the houses of sailors and fishermen and only half a mile away stood Blackbeard's Tree, a sprawling and magnificent fig under which the infamous pirate had distributed his ill-gotten booty. Several miles further on was 'New Guinea', a village inhabited by many mulattos, and freed African slaves.

In the centre of Nassau stood the Bourse where notices were posted and public sales held. Here captains lounged under the open-sided building to discuss business. According to Schoepf, sharks seem to have been the main topic of conversation. He overheard that three days before the Battle of the Chesapeake schools of sharks had followed both the French and English fleets and had collected around the French ship of the line, *Caesar*, as some of her crew jumped overboard in fear that she was sinking. Schoepf remarked, 'in the battle itself this gruesome assemblage increased the terror.' Wreckers, who still operated across the islands and would if needed kill their competitors, were seemingly not deterred by such tales.

Many displaced loyalists were dismayed on arrival in the Islands. One noted: 'At first view of this soil, rocky and stony, or the white and dazzling sand by the shore that all notion of planting would seem to find contradiction.' Another loyalist complained: 'I now acquaint you with my safe arrival in this miserable spot, the wretched asylum for loyalty.' In 1785, eight of the islands were settled but most of the others were considered 'desolate', although some were thought of as 'being capable of being useful and inhabited'.

Even though the land initially appeared barren to the new settlers, they were able in time to grow coffee trees, cashew nuts, tamarind, pineapples, cocoa, figs, watermelons, pomegranates, and cotton. The salt ponds, a valuable and vital commodity, were another source of income. It was estimated that 43,000 bushels were raked from the Great Pond on Exhuma over ten days, and each sold for 9d a bushel, making a profit of £1,602.10. They were also cutting down hardwoods such as mahogany, boxwood and ebony to export to America. New Providence was then the most heavily populated island. By November that year, more than 5500 people lived there, of whom 817 were white. Schoepf remarked that he never saw the slaves ill-treated: they were for many of the settlers the only 'possessions' they had left, and the slaves formed the great majority.

In England, the Proprietors continued to press for an agreement with the Government. In August 1785, Mr Hill reported to the Duke of Beaufort that he had met George Rose, who was still in charge of the negotiations at the Treasury, and the recent Governor of the Bahamas, John Maxwell. He considered the 'soil of the islands of as little value' but agreed that the islands themselves be purchased on reasonable terms. Hill left the meeting believing that an agreement would 'immediately take place'. But this was not the case, and at Hill's insistence, Chamberlayne was continually dispatched to lobby George Rose on the Proprietors' behalf.

During the next few weeks, Chamberlayne's taunting words some four months before to Louisa reverberated in her head: 'The hands of kings were long and strong: might would overcome right.' The king's troops were, *de facto*, in charge of the Bahamas and the Crown was granting land to American loyalists and others, exercising rights of ownership before these had been legally secured. Josiah Tattnall, whose family had chosen the king over several thousand acres of Georgia, was amongst those rewarded. He was granted title to land on Great and Little Abaco, and substantial amounts of land on Long Island, the jewel in Louisa's crown. In September, one of the last transports arrived from Florida, carrying the 'poorer sort, which included fourteen hundred loyalists and nearly two hundred and fifty slaves'.

Louisa grasped that it would be futile to remain in the Bahamas, even though the inhabitants paid her the most 'marked attention', and continued to call her 'Our Little Queen'. Shortly before she left Nassau, Louisa, surrounded by a group of her 'Subjects', proclaimed: 'It is to be hoped that I shall not die whilst in these Islands; for although the sovereign proprietress, the British Government have taken such full possession of my rights, that they have not left me so much land as my one little foot can rest on.'

CHAPTER 10

A Stranger in My Native Land

*

SO anxious was Louisa to leave the Bahamas for Charleston that she accepted an offer from Captain Crosskill to make the voyage with him in a wrecker, which was designed to carry salvaged goods. This he intended to fill with live turtles and fruit to sell in South Carolina while the *Sally* was being turned around for her journey back to England. Louisa presumed the small wrecker, which could carry fourteen tons, was sturdy enough for the crossing, and that they would be at sea for only a few days. Louisa's fellow passenger on the journey from England, Miss Caroline Gordon, had also been trying to find passage to return to her father in Charleston and decided that she, too, could suffer the discomfort of sailing in such a vessel.

Fairlawn's faithful patroon, Haman, had now joined Louisa in the Bahamas. He had known her since she was a child and, whilst loyalty seems incompatible with slavery, Haman was indeed loyal to his mistress. She treated him with the utmost respect and it must have been a great comfort to her to be reunited with him. He could have, given his skills and the circumstances of the past few years, made a different life for himself and his family, but had chosen to remain with the Colletons. With Haman was his daughter, Tachina, who immediately attached herself to Louisa and insisted on serving Louisa as her personal maid. When the party set sail, Louisa also had with her three other 'attendants', who may also have been slaves from Fairlawn.

They embarked late in September 1785, and as the wrecker left Nassau harbour, Louisa heartily congratulated herself on having ensured there were ample supplies on board. The memory of starvation on the *Sally* was still sharp in her mind. Before they left she asked Captain Crosskill to have a dressed English ham put on board 'as not much could be cooked on board such a vessel'. Louisa also ordered bread from the baker, as she so disliked ships' biscuit.

A few hours after they left Nassau, Louisa asked Crosskill for the ham she had ordered but he admitted that he had forgotten to put it on board. The baker, Louisa later remembered, 'Considered his own interest, fortunately for us, and sent so much bread on board, that it supported us for the voyage.' As they ventured further into the Atlantic the weather became increasingly unsettled, slowing down the wrecker's progress. Before long they ran out of 'ready-made' provisions and had to 'subsist on bread and fruit except when they could dress either rice or hominy' (dried maize). The sea became ever more turbulent; waves dashed over the small vessel putting their fire out as soon as it was lit. The bread was soaked and became mouldy, 'Yet bad as it was, we feared it might be exhausted before we landed, and therefore we ate sparingly of it lest we should be reduced to the captain's bad biscuit: thus in a vessel laden with provisions we were suffering from want; for there was no eating turtle raw, and pine apples, though delicious are not wholesome to live on.'

Between the 21st and 22nd September, 'the air was suddenly darkened, and in less time than I can relate it, the tornado came up with us, with a tremendous rushing sound.' Miss Gordon and Louisa were just leaving the deck for their cabin when a brutal gust threw the ship 'on her beam-ends; the Captain, wringing his hands exclaimed "the Lord have mercy on my soul". Miss Gordon threw her arms around Louisa's neck, crying 'save me! save me!'. Tachina knelt by Louisa, clasping her hands, while Louisa 'calm from despair' silently 'commended my soul to God who gave it; in this perilous moment when we were all but lost, the whirlwind passing round us gave the vessel a stroke under her lee bow – and she righted!!! the transition from despair to joy was so great, that it threw me into strong laughing convulsions'.

It was miraculous that the wrecker did not sink during the tornado. Its tumultuous effects were reported in the *Bahamas Gazette* on September 24th: 'Upwards of thirty sloops and schooners with a number of boats are aground on the southern shore of the harbor.' The *Sally* had smashed against a wharf and was almost wrecked, whilst across the islands several of the largest trees were torn up by the roots. Reports also came from the east coast of America: 'A higher tide and severer storms were never known at this place than happened yesterday; the damages sustained thereby are immense...' Ships were driven from their moorings, warehouses carried away, and in Portsmouth vessels were 'driven into cornfield and woods'. It was 'the most tremendous gale known'.

Although the tornado had spared the wrecker, further danger came on approach to the coast of America. Louisa overheard Haman insisting to Captain Crosskill that their course would lead them onto the infamous

St Augustine sand bar off Florida. The bar was the most dangerous on the east coast as it was the 'shallowest and at the same time exposed to the total force of the ocean playing upon it'. Crosskill was contemptuous and 'insisted he was right by his charts, and asked how he should know'. Haman, who had sailed these waters for Louisa's father for many years when collecting salt and supplies from the Bahamas, replied: 'I know nothing of your charts, but I know your course is wrong, and if you persevere in it you will be dashed on the breakers of St Augustine: I don't fear for myself, I can swim; but my mistress and my daughter Tachina are on board, and they will be lost.' Crosskill ignored Haman's warning, relying instead on his chart until the 'foam of the sea dashing on the breakers became visible; Haman clapped his hands vehemently together, exclaiming: there are the breakers, we shall be dashed to pieces on them'. Crosskill suddenly saw his appalling error and asked Haman if he could save them, should he give him command of the wrecker. Haman took the helm and safely sailed away from St Augustine towards Charleston.

More than two weeks after they had left Nassau, in foul weather, the wrecker approached Palmetto fort outside the entrance to Charleston harbour. Haman advised Crosskill to take down the colours in salute. Crosskill refused, whereupon Haman told him 'they will fire on you and one shot will sink you; remember that my mistress on board'. Louisa wrote: 'Despite the heavy rain then falling I raised my head above the deck, to remonstrate with the captain on thus needlessly endangering us; he laughed at my fears; but his mirth was soon interrupted by a shot from the fort: thus convinced of his folly, he immediately brought too, and lowering his boat went on shore. ' Crosskill was later made to pay for the powder expended by the soldiers and informed that had he not taken down the colours, they would next have aimed for him.

On arrival in Charleston, Louisa found that although she was 'a stranger in my native land, I soon found myself encircled by most hospitable friends, who kindly welcomed me to shore'. The wrecker soon became an object of curiosity, 'all wondered how two ladies could have ventured to take such a voyage in such a vessel.' Haman was incensed at Captain Crosskill's behaviour on the voyage, and his fury compounded when he learned that Louisa had paid for his passage: 'pay for me! as if I was a land lubber, me who am a pilot on the coast; me who saved his life and his vessel from being lost, and brought him safe into port, and he charge for my passage?' Louisa wrote that she tried to placate Haman and offered him money for the service that he done her, which Haman refused saying 'I was born and bred up on your lands; it was my duty to save you; but I owe no duty to him'. He added furiously that Crosskill had refused to replace Louisa's turtle after one of the crew had let it slip from its rope when Haman had slung it overboard to refresh it in the sea. 'Never mind', replied Louisa, 'it was an accident: I can buy another one,' but Haman still seethed at Crosskill's charging for his passage.

By the winter of 1785, the ill feeling between those who had fought against each other during the war had dissipated; most were keen to get back to normal business. South Carolina's population now stood at approximately 225,000, including 100,000 slaves. Commerce flourished again in Charleston, albeit on credit, and among those who seemed to be growing rich were the milliners and hairdressers; the ladies also spared no expense on the latest fashions from Europe. Charleston was then considered to be an airy city; most of the houses were built of wood and many of them had backyards and gardens. Carriages ran smoothly on the sandy roads, while pedestrians walked safely on brick pavements. A visitor to Charleston at the time, a Philadelphia lawyer, Timothy Ford, noted in his diary: 'In the highest class everybody must have a vast deal of waiting upon them from the oldest to the youngest. One or more servants (in many places) plant themselves in the corner of the room where stand and upon the slightest occasion they are called. Every child must be attended, and whenever the whim takes it the servant is dispatched on its service.' Few people could be bothered to grow fruit and vegetables, so these were imported. The elite drank to excess and ladies would frolic in rice stacks to amuse themselves while the men went shooting.

Louisa, now eager to return to England, quickly made legal representations for acknowledgement as heiress to her father's lands in America. She was given yet another copy of her father's will by lawyers, and it contained a codicil granting 'freedom' to his mulatto slave 'Judy', on the condition that 'she must not come to Charles Town or within ten miles of my plantation Fairlawn'. Manumission of slaves was rare. As was noted by the gentleman traveller, Josiah Quincy junior, 'the enjoyment of a negro or mulatto woman is spoken of as quite a common thing; no reluctance delicacy or shame is made about the matter'. It would be fair to presume that 'Judy' was Sir John's favourite mistress. But she may have been a favoured and loyal household slave, and Sir John wanted to grant her freedom. His father had done so for his personal slaves, Hector and Lissey, who had travelled to England with him on every occasion, and had not left his side until his death. There is, of course, the possibility that Judy was Louisa's half-sister.

Reading her father's will again must have brought Louisa's mind back to Eliza Janverin. It was a statement of Sir John's feelings for Louisa's old governess (and his mistress) that Eliza would have the house at Fairlawn free of charge and with benefits 'so long as she continues single and unmarried and no longer' and an annuity of £100. But, fortunately, Eliza had married a rich lawyer, Edward Taylor, shortly before Louisa came of age.

Louisa set sail up the River Cooper to Fairlawn with Haman and Tachina, 'for the purpose of collecting from the wreck of what was once a noble fortune the property that had escaped the ravages of war'. As they drifted past the once fruitful plantations of her neighbours, the destruction was only too apparent. Approaching her own landing at Fairlawn, she saw that there was not a tree left standing for two miles. As Louisa walked up to where the house once stood, she carefully trod over the uneven remains of charred bricks, musket balls and glass, all of which lay under a cover of sparse weeds.

Louisa recalled: 'I was much affected at the sight of the ruins of Fairlawn: indeed they overwhelmed me with affliction. This mansion, in which I was born, had been the residence of my family, from the time it was built by my grandfather.' Not only had the house been destroyed but 'every Building including a town built on the Barony for the residence of several hundred people belonging to the estate with the granaries, mill etc., etc'. All that was left was 'an arcade' and the ruins of the dairy. As Louisa surveyed the scene, her attendants told her that hunted deer 'often took shelter amidst the ruins; from which I then turned heart struck, at finding that desolation brooded where plenty formerly had revelled in her gayest mood.'

Her thoughts turned to the losses she had had to come to terms with; her house, her furniture, pictures, books and 'a large sum of money, which was in my father's strongbox, and even my jewels were lost to me, either destroyed or plundered'. Her father's papers would, however, prove to be her greatest loss. Having acted as an amanuensis to Sir John, Louisa knew that there were many large parcels of land, aside from Fairlawn and Devil's Elbow, that she owned but could now not prove title.

Louisa left the dreadful scene behind her and walked back the River Cooper, where lying at anchor was her schooner, *Nancy* – remarkably unscathed by the war. This twenty-ton cargo vessel with a run of sails was now empty of crops, and below-deck quarters had been hastily fashioned for Louisa. She devoted herself to business, but as the heat during the day was often 'insupportable', Louisa would work late into the night. It was now that she began writing her desultory thoughts to 'beguile the tedious hours of absence, while separated from all who were near and dear to me, to soothe the anguish of an aching heart, and to relieve and unbend a mind oppressed with the weight of business'.

Adding to her shock, Louisa discovered her missing half-brothers living in a shack with the few remaining slaves on the plantation. There had been no news of them since their mother had died, and Louisa must have feared and presumed the worst. The eldest, William Mutter, was then fourteen, and Sir John Snell Colleton, the fifth baronet, twelve. Seemingly, the slaves had sheltered them for five years. Their stepfather, Othniel Giles, was living in Moncks Corner and perhaps had abandoned them, or the slaves had believed he posed a threat to his step-sons. What they had been doing for the past five years is a mystery, but it can be assumed that they had received no education. But, they were now under the protection of their half-sister, and it is more than likely that Louisa sent the pair to Charleston to begin some sort of schooling.

Louisa wrote that she was desperate to get back to Richard, and in order to save time she was not averse to 'incurring danger'. She would frequently travel alone some fifteen miles in a canoe after dark, even when the tide had turned, to get back to Fairlawn. Haman was deeply protective of her and, knowing the dangers of the river, protested strongly, but in vain. One morning, returning with Haman in a canoe after staying the night with a friend, she had a 'very narrow escape'. They crossed the River Cooper, which rose and fell five feet with the tide, where 'the river winds in some places very abruptly, we perceived a flat-bottomed boat turning one of those points of land'. The flat-bottomed boat, 'which [is] not perfectly manageable,' was drifting downstream on the very rapid outgoing tide while the canoe was being driven against it. Louisa believed the only means of saving themselves was to jump to safety upon the flat-boat. 'Stand ready,' she shouted. 'I arose myself in readiness: the sailors in the flat stood ready to assist us; we approached... we passed in silence awfully solemn! For life hung on the moment'!!! when clear of each other the sailors on both sides gave utterance to an exclamation of joy, "Qui!" exclaimed Haman in gullah, "lilimissi, lili; for nothing him have heart big mo no to much'. Louisa, for our edification, translated Haman's words thus: 'A great heart in a little body,' and she added, 'for in those days I was as slight as I was fearless.'

Amongst the neighbours, Louisa visited during this time was Henry Laurens. He had returned to America in January 1786 and was building a house at Mepkin with a barn almost as big as the house for storing crops. Although Louisa did not have the funds to build a grand new house at Fairlawn, she did often ask Laurens' advice on restoring her plantation. He strongly advocated the planting of trees: 'our whole fund of good Ship Timber is very small, every Man cuts down & wastes, no Man within my knowledge, myself excepted, has yet planted.' Laurens intended to plant 'an hundred Live Oak & as many Black Walnut Trees'. Louisa presumably heeded the advice, as to this day black walnut trees are to be found growing near the ruins of Fairlawn.

Having accomplished what she could at Fairlawn, Louisa then settled in Charleston on Church Street where the family had once lived. This was one of the grandest and gayest streets in the city, filled with mansions built by some of Charleston's richest families. Here, she was daily entertained by old family friends who took the young heiress under their wings. Much of her time was spent assisting lawyers to draw up her cases, the most important of which was to be presented to the American authorities to formally prevent them from ever confiscating her plantations. She also commissioned detailed maps of Fairlawn and Devil's Elbow.

Addressing her children later in her life, she wrote that it would no doubt surprise them, that when so young she had the 'patience and perseverance to investigate and arrange intricate points of such importance'. It was, she advocated, that 'a woman with common sense, is equal to the situations in which she may be involved; the want of this conviction often renders a woman either a dupe or a victim by making her rely on others; by common sense I mean, that intuitive perception of right, which at once enables you to decide, to act'.

Eventually, Louisa's 'patience and perseverance' paid off and she succeeded in legally retaining her lands in South Carolina. In England, however, her fellow Lords Proprietors of the Bahamas were becoming increasingly frustrated. On December 2nd 1785, Mr Hill had written to the Duke of Beaufort to inform him that the lawyer Chamberlayne had again been trying to get the Treasury to commit to the purchase of the

Islands. In the same letter, Mr Hill noted that a meeting of the Lords Proprietors was due to be held two days hence, to decide what action to take, and that 'Mr Chamberlayne will be present & concur on the part of Miss Colleton'.

Louisa had no knowledge of the manoeuvrings in London and was then concerned only with the state of her plantations. Recovering nearly a hundred of Fairlawn's slaves who had either been taken by the British or generally dispersed, she set them to planting. Templates were taken of their feet and thick leather shoes ordered from England, along with glass, locks, nails, lamp oil, glue, paint and seeds; items then in short supply in South Carolina.

During Louisa's stay at Fairlawn, she visited Biggin Church near Moncks Corner, a ruin after British forces had burned it down in 1781. The Colleton family vault was there and its entrance still discernible. Louisa commissioned a white marble slab to be placed over her father's tomb, carved with the memorial:

> To the memory of Sir John Colleton Bart of Devonshire in England and of Fairlawn South Carolina whose mortal remains rest here in the hopes of a Blessed Resurrection Descended from Sir John Colleton formerly Proprietor of this State he lived to witness the Independence of the United States. This stone is erected in respect to his memory as a mark of her affection by his only daughter Louisa Carolina Graves.

Since Louisa had not yet married Richard Graves, the surname seems rather presumptuous, but it signified that she had every intention of marrying him when she returned to England.

Towards the end of 1786, Louisa put an advertisement in the *Charleston Morning Post*: 'All persons having any demands against the estate of the late Sir John Colleton, Baronet, deceased' were requested to send their claims, on or before January 10th of the following year. And, she asked that anyone indebted to the estate was requested to settle as soon as possible. Having 'established the plantations on the Barony of Fairlawn in proper order', Louisa wrote, she then travelled to Devil's Elbow.

The Barony, then covered over 7,000 acres. In 1670, a servant of one of the Lords Proprietors described the soil as being a 'fatt blacke mould', and noted 'plenty of corn, pumpions, water- mellons, musk mellons,...

they have two or three good crops a year …the ayre is clean and sweet, the country very pleasant and delightful'. The woods, he wrote, were 'stored with an abundance of Deer and Turkies everywhere …also Partridges great store, cranes abundanance, conies which we saw in several places; we heard several wolves howling and in the woods great flocks of Parrakeetos …oaks of four or five sorts …in bigness… almost four fathoms.' Not only was the soil naturally productive, but the Barony marked the 'northern limit of several species of a more southern type of flora'.

But only four years earlier, a member of the clergy in the district observed: 'Every field, every plantation shows marks of ruin and devastation… No garden, no enclosure, no mulberry, no fruit trees, nothing but wild fennel, bushes, underwood, briars to be seen… a very ruinous habitation.' Louisa was overwhelmed by what she witnessed at Devil's Elbow, and rarely ventured from her carriage, so fearful she was of the 'direful Mocasin', a snake whose bite, she wrote, was 'death'. It was very hot and airless, and the 'noisome vapour' of the marshes, filled with 'numerous deadly reptiles' all hastened Louisa's return to Charleston.

She later wrote of Devil's Elbow being 'of magnitude beyond my attempt; I therefore left that barony in the ruinous state to which the British Army had reduced it when they made a sweep of livestock, for which eight thousand pounds had been offered on the death of my father, and which were refused by the manager as unequal to the value'.

In the middle of July 1787, almost 27 months after she had left England, Louisa, with her half-brothers in her care, set sail for home.

CHAPTER 11

A Poor Match

*

WHILST Louisa was away in America, Richard's financial situation had grown ever more insecure. He had occupied himself by intermittently living in the north of France, with his elder brother, Tom, learning French, as this was considered an advantage for naval officers to be able to converse with their prisoners and read the language. It also gave them the opportunity to inspect the French ports. The brothers had later fallen out after Richard inherited from his father the valuable patronage of his parish in Ireland. His father intended that his bequest be not only for Richard's benefit, but also to provide his three spinster sisters with an income. Richard, however, sold the patronage without consulting the family. At the time, Tom told his brother, John, that he thought Richard's conduct was neither 'just nor honourable' and that although he would always regard Richard as an affectionate brother and sincere friend, Richard, he wrote, 'Most undoubtedly loves his own dear self better and would sacrifice the whole world to his own vanity and gratifications.'

Clearly annoyed at being berated, Richard wrote a letter to Tom that began 'Dear Sir'. He stated: 'It is my undoubted right to appropriate any part of my own property to any use I please.' He asked if any of his brothers had provided more, financially, for their unmarried sisters, and defended his behaviour by protesting that 'avarice' was not a leading feature in his character. Tom had complained to John of Richard's 'many shifts and windings', and that it was 'difficult to keep him to any fixed point'. He declared it was impossible to get the truth from him 'as he wraps himself up in mystery and self importance'. Tom added, in contradiction to his earlier letter, that had they not been brothers, they would never have been friends. Their youngest brother, William, had even stronger views on Richard, and wrote of him: 'I think him the same senseless, savage, unjust, sordid ruffian I ever did.'

Richard had rashly banked not only on Louisa's fortune but also that of his uncle, Admiral Samuel Graves. However, after the admiral's death in March 1787, Richard had been shocked to find out that his uncle's bequest, which included Hembury Fort, two thousand acres of land in Devon, and land and property in London and Nova Scotia, was left to Mrs Admiral for her lifetime, and only her death would release his inheritance.

Since October 1786, Richard had expected Louisa's imminent return to England, but it was not until September 16th 1787 that they were reunited in London. Despite the animosity between Richard and his brothers, he at once wrote to Tom to say that he and Louisa were to marry 'as soon as her health permits'. At great expense, Richard, whom Louisa always referred to as 'Graves', applied for a Special Licence to wed within the week. On Sunday, September 23rd, Louisa, thin and still a little unsteady on her feet after weeks at sea, climbed the steps of the fashionable church of St George's, Hanover Square, London. Richard was waiting at the altar, dashing and handsome in his full-dress captain's uniform. After the ceremony, the couple signed the registry, and at the stroke of a pen Louisa gave up control of all her worldly goods. After all her troublesome adventures it may have come as a relief that she was no longer responsible for her inheritance. By law, she became a *femme covert*; she could not own property nor enjoy her own income. Richard's control was absolute and he now wielded the purse.

Oddly, no members of either family attended the wedding, but the news soon reached Richard's brother, Tom. The following Thursday he hastily wrote to his brother, John, to say little more than 'Our brother Rd was married last Sunday without settlement'. To marry without previous negotiations between lawyers was then extremely rare within the upper classes. It was with some alacrity that Richard, wanting to get access to Louisa's funds, sent a letter to Elizabeth Fulford, telling her of the marriage and asking for Louisa's papers.

Immediately after the wedding, the Graveses went to Hembury Fort. Mrs Admiral had by then left to live with her niece, Elizabeth Simcoe, at her new house which lay across the valley from Hembury Fort. The Simcoe's had knocked down an ordinary one-storey house and had built in its place 'Wolford Lodge', which had forty rooms and far-reaching views to the seaside resort of Sidmouth. Mrs Admiral had informed Richard, that he and Louisa could have Hembury Fort, without the onus of paying rent. This was a gracious offer, as under the Admiral's will the house still belonged to her. Richard's only income was what he considered to be the 'paltry' £200 a year that he received from the Admiralty as his Captain's half-pay; he had of course, as Tom had feared, already squandered the £2,000 prize money he had accumulated during the war.

Elizabeth Fulford had, meanwhile, replied to Richard's letter. She herself kept meticulous household accounts after John's death and had no doubt paid the same attention to Louisa's affairs. In her summing up of Louisa's accounts, Elizabeth wrote that she had been 'summoned to London to execute a deed in the presence of the Lord Chief Justice' and claimed expenses for her journey and the cost of staying in London. Louisa, who by then was aware that the Bahamas had been sold in March that year, was, however, 'ignorant of the particulars of that transaction.' It was a mystery to Louisa as to how her aunt could have signed the deed of sale, as she did not have the legal authority to do so.

The only power of attorney Louisa had signed was the one drawn up by Joseph Burrows some three years before, and allowed her aunt to deal only with Louisa's estates in Devon. The trusted Burrows had taken the precaution of formally registering the document in Exeter Court. Richard wrote to Elizabeth again, and asked for the 'papers omitted to be delivered up'. Elizabeth revealed that she had given them to the Treasury Solicitors, among which, Louisa later wrote, were papers pertaining to the Bahamas. Elizabeth, knowing full well that Louisa did not want to sell her share of the islands, had compounded the problem by handing over Louisa's precious documents.

This revelation did not alter Louisa's desire to see her aunt to whom, as Louisa often wrote, she was 'tied by the closest affection'. Elizabeth, however, did not answer her letters and in despair Louisa travelled to Great Fulford. There, the butler welcomed her into the house and while asking the old retainer for news of her friends and acquaintances, she was told that her beloved Fool, who was then of a great age, had been run over by a recklessly driven post-chaise. He was left on the road with both legs broken. The Fulford servants found him two days later, after which he soon died of his injuries. As Louisa heard the sad news, she happened to glance out of the window, only to see Elizabeth driving away in her carriage. This would not be the last time, as Louisa would later write, that her aunt fled the house on her appearance to 'avoid a meeting'.

Apart from their own expenses, the Graveses were also encumbered with the care of Louisa's half-brothers. Sir John had stipulated in his will that young John Snell should be brought up to reading, writing and accounts and Louisa, whether or not she believed he was the son of her father, took care to carry out his instructions. The same did not apply to the elder of the brothers, William, as Sir John had written that he should be educated 'for as little expense as possible'. William remained at home with Louisa, while the young baronet was put under the care of a kindly vicar and his curate in the isolated moorland town of Moretonhampstead, on the edge of Dartmoor. This was not far from Great Fulford, and amongst the pupils was Louisa's first cousin, Baldwin Fulford who, since his birth in 1775, was heir to the Fulford estates. The father of one of John's contemporaries later wrote: 'Another of Edward's school companions was Sir John Collyton, whose father, whilst he was a babe in the cradle, took so strange a dislike to the poor boy, that he would not see him, and cut him off with a shilling, leaving all his property to his sister.'

Word of his fate reached the heirs of the childless lawyer, William Field, who had died in 1783. One was his nephew, Richard Savage-Lloyd, himself a lawyer, who had once been a Member of Parliament. He lived at the grand Hintlesham Hall in Suffolk. This had been purchased by his father, at one time Solicitor General, with the proceeds of a great fortune he had, surprisingly, inherited from an heiress for whom he acted as lawyer and executor. The other, was the Reverend Willian, the brother of Field's deceased mistress. They still had possession of the deeds to Sir John Colleton's property in London and Suffolk, among other papers. In an attempt to defraud Louisa of the Colleton properties, Savage-Lloyd and the vicar claimed Sir John Colleton's will was invalid and lodged a lawsuit on behalf of thirteen-year-old Sir John Snell to have it overturned in his favour.

Having to defend such a case would put even more pressure on the Graves' stretched finances. In November 1787, the Graves family began to voice concerns about Richard living beyond his means and unfairly blamed Louisa for Richard's financial predicament. Tom considered his marriage to her to be a 'poor match in every light'. 'The Master says our brother has not more than two hundred pounds a year to live upon, it therefore behoves him either to do this or retrench very much his mode of living which I suppose must be at least eight or nine hundred pounds a year, so that if the widow [referring to Mrs Admiral] is not polite enough to walk aside he must soon be totally done up.' There was little chance that Mrs Admiral would be 'polite enough' to hand over the admiral's estates to Richard before her death, even though she was rich enough in her own right to do so.

Richard could only hope that Mrs Admiral would die, or that he would once again be employed by the Admiralty.

The situation was even worse by December that year. As Tom pointed out, Richard did not have the necessary social skills to procure patronage from his naval superiors. He was chastised by Tom for not having 'sense enough to make a single acquaintance that could or would be of modest use to him'. Tom strongly recommended that Richard, who remained unemployed, should 'remove his negroes from South Carolina to the Bahama Islands where he will lay the foundation of a good fortune and that after the first year be able to live there genteelly, by this means he will reap some advantage from his negroes without involving himself in lawsuits with his wife's brother with respect to the Carolina Estate, to which I believe he has no right to, & be out of the expense of living and spending away foolishly at Hembury Fort & in the course of a few years be able to return to this country in a respectable manner & have some remittance from that country - if he can get a ship on that station so much the better, but at all events set off in the Spring'.

Richard took no notice of his brother's advice, and he and Louisa left Devon shortly before Christmas for Bath, and then went on to London. As the New Year of 1789 began, Tom proposed to Richard that they exchange some land. However, as Richard was not yet in possession of the land he had inherited from his uncle, he suggested using some of Louisa's property as security. She was then two months pregnant with a child Richard was already referring to as 'my son', and was adamant that her fortune, over which she had no actual control, would be for the benefit of their younger children and thus prevented the exchange taking place.

According to Tom, they lived as 'if both were regardless of posterity'. He wrote: 'I fear that they are neither very steady nor very economical, nor will they think till distress comes upon them, as she seems to love pleasure as well as her husband – they now have lodgings in Pall Mall at four guineas a week and giving dinners and going to publick places, so that one may fairly say that they are going Pell Mall to ruin.' Tom had made a pun on the old expression 'Pell Mell', meaning 'reckless haste'. The sum of four guineas a week for their lodgings at No. 28 Pall Mall, was one they could ill afford.

Although Louisa and Richard appeared to be gallivanting around London they had, by the end of January, completed a claim which they presented before the 'Commissioners for enquiring into the Losses and Services of American Loyalists'. They were among many hundreds of loyalists that had looked to the Crown for compensation for their property and land destroyed, or confiscated in America. Louisa was anticipating a hefty payout for her losses at Fairlawn.

The claim was substantial, covering the house and buildings, furniture and personal property, ships chandlery, impressments of slaves and other losses. This amounted to £21,183.17, from which they deducted the sum of £4,331 for the remaining 'negroes left on the estate, value of plate and horses', which left a net claim of £16,852.17.

Louisa sat before the Commissioners in London on January 25th 1788, and gave a sworn statement claiming her right as heiress to her father's estates, and that he had been 'one of the King's Council for that state of South Carolina'. She produced a certificate from William Bull, 'late Governor of South Carolina,' confirming that he knew both Louisa's grandfather and father, and that they had considerable land and slaves in the province. Bull reckoned that Devil's Elbow was the more valuable of the two plantations. The Commission, however, refused to allow Louisa's claim for Devil's Elbow as her agent had previously refused their offer of £8,000.

The first witness to Louisa's claim was Captain McMahon who, having been at Fairlawn with the British Army, verified that the house at Fairlawn was 'esteemed one of the best in the country', and that the house 'appeared exceedingly well furnished'. He believed it had been burnt down by the rebels because it had become a hospital. The next witness was the last Attorney General of South Carolina to serve under the colonial government, James Simpson. He testified: 'Sir John Colleton was in England when the troubles commenced. He returned to America to Charleston after the rebellion broke out. He had no merit as a Loyalist nor does he know he took any part against America – he was a drunken sot.'

The Commission would continue to gather evidence throughout the remainder of the year, and while they did so, Richard and Louisa considered the fate of her eldest half-brother, William Colleton Mutter. Sir John's will stipulated that as soon as he was old enough, Louisa should 'bind him out to some trade'. She was apparently very fond of William, much more so than his younger brother, John Snell.

William had but a shilling to his name, and from the time Louisa rescued him had been entirely reliant on his half-sister for his welfare. While John Snell had benefitted from a formal education, Louisa had educated William at home, with her. It must have been to her distress, that Richard, most likely to rid himself of an unwanted expense, followed Sir John's instructions to the letter.

On May 25th 1788, he paid £30 for William, just sixteen, to become an apprentice to Thomas Lingham, 'breeches and waistcoat maker' of the Strand in London. As a result of Louisa's endeavours, he signed his name on the legally binding contract in elegant handwriting. The apprenticeship was to last seven years and each year Richard had to pay Lingham a further ten pounds. William was left at his master's bidding and in return would be provided with 'sufficient lodging Meat Drink Cloathing and Washing Medicines and other Matters in Sickness and healths'. It would not be until 1795 that William would be at liberty. While Lingham was perhaps one of the fairer employers, apprentices with no money of their own were too often dragged into the underworld and into a life of petty thieving.

With the continuous pressure to live more frugally, Richard decided they would move to France. Even though the arrival of their first child was imminent, he travelled there to find accommodation for the family. Landing in Boulogne on June 19th 1788, he was soon advised that St Omer, where several other impoverished English spendthrifts had settled, was now the 'cheapest place' to live in France. It was a town he knew well, for he had lived there for some months while learning French. On June 25th 1788, only six days after Richard left for France, Louisa was delivered of a son at Hembury Fort. He was later named Samuel Colleton Graves.

CHAPTER 12

Disallowed

*

RICHARD sent word to Tom of his plans, and of his arrival in France. Tom then wrote to his brother John the same day to say, 'I hope most sincerely that his wife will be able to follow him, that they meet with a situation & adopt a mode of living corresponding to their present income, which I fear is extremely small, as I do not find that her English property is equal to the payment of her Mothers pension and if not regularly paid there is a penalty of one thousand pounds.' Although Louisa's mother had married John Robert Lea, a naval officer and 'gentleman', the payment of the pension was still due as it fell under the terms of her parent's marriage settlement.

Ann and John Lea were due to have married two years earlier, almost to the day; the banns were read three times at Nicholas Hawksmoor's masterpiece, Christ Church, Spitalfields. But as the wedding did not take place, it can only be presumed that Lea, who was then twenty-five, was called to sea. When he returned, he applied for a Special Licence, on September 10th 1787, so he could marry Ann almost immediately, and lodged a bond of £200 which would be forfeited should any impediment to the marriage come to light. Lea stated that Ann was a spinster 'aged thirty years old', when she was in fact forty-four. While Ann may have misled John Lea about her age in the early stages of their romance, she would have been unable to sustain the pretence. Lea must have been so besotted with her that he thought it worth lying, under oath, perhaps to prevent the inevitable questions about their seventeen-year age gap. He married Ann the following day, September 11th in St Anne's Church, Soho.

Ann's pension was not the only pressing debt, according to Tom. Louisa's paternal aunt, Elizabeth, and her husband, Dr Cook, were demanding repayment of £3000 for the mortgage on land in South Carolina taken out by Sir John shortly before his death. There were also several other debts in America. Tom wrote in exasperation that, added to this, Richard 'has his wife's two brothers to support. Sir John Snell Colleton is going down to Admiral Graves' [Admiral Thomas Graves] ship in five days which will relieve our poor Brother of some of the expense – was there ever a man so unfortunate by being made an Uncle's Heir as I know nothing that can save him but the old widow's death who certainly has been instrumental in his marriage which put the finishing hand to his ruin, for without a wife on his half-pay he would be rich & could live like Gentleman in any part of the world.'

Tom again laid the blame for the couple's financial troubles squarely on Louisa. He wrote that Louisa had married Richard 'out of pretence of affection & generosity' and 'without settlements to prevent an investigation of her fortune'. It is unlikely that Louisa would have deceived Richard as to her 'fortune'. He himself reported, shortly before their marriage, that Louisa's American estates would do little more for several years than sustain themselves 'owing to the ruinous situation of that country'. It was also not in Louisa's favour that they married without a marriage settlement, and it can only be presumed that such matters were of little concern to either of them in their haste to be married.

Louisa clearly could not face travelling to France with a new baby or indeed live in such circumstances, so Richard came back to Hembury Fort. Mrs Admiral, meanwhile, piqued that her husband had wantonly spent her money during their marriage, mostly on land which he subsequently left to Richard in his will, decided to let Hembury Fort and sell the contents. Richard was ordered to hand back the keys. While Mrs Admiral had use of her late husband's possessions, they were not hers to sell. In August, the admiral's 'elegant household furniture, china, glass etc. his various valuable stock of Wines and other liqueurs, Beer etc. particularly a large quantity of excellent Madeira' were put up for auction. Not only were contents of the admiral's cellar to be sold, but also 'eleven horses, some of which are famous hunters'. All the livestock was to be auctioned, and a 'handsome Chaise, almost new', with two horses and their harnesses. Also for sale were mahogany bedsteads, clothed in 'India Damask, Cotton and other furniture' which included the curtains, 'the best Goose feather beds', wool mattresses, counterpanes, quilts, blankets, 'various kinds of mahogany and other chests of drawers, dressing tables, bureaus, chairs, sofas, clocks, Wilton carpets, a set of 'Nanquin china', sets of table linen, and the contents of the kitchen. The auction was set to begin at eleven in the morning and finish each day at six in the evening. Mrs Admiral even sold the admiral's plate, which he had specifically wished to be distributed among his nephews and nieces.

Louisa finally saw sense; they could not continue to spend money they did not have. At her insistence, they rented for £8 a year, a tiny, thatched cottage in the village of Gittisham to the south of Honiton and not far from Hembury Fort. The house was very modest; indeed, the living conditions there were more suited to farm labourers. To add to their woes, the lawsuits brought against her by the 'friends' of Sir John Snell, now fifteen, were producing evidence of misconduct and deceit by the lawyer William Field, whom, it was revealed, fraudulently sold properties belonging to Louisa's father as soon as Sir John had left for America in 1775.

What the lawsuit did not reveal, however, was the full extent of Field's thieving. He had concealed title deeds to property and funds that belonged to Louisa's great-grandfather, his extremely rich spinster sister, and the 3rd baronet's youngest son, Robert – which in consequence, had left his family destitute.

There are several possible explanations why Field had stolen from the Colletons. He may have believed his mother, Arabella, had not been left a fair share of the spoils by her father, the staggeringly rich Earl Rivers. And, this was true: Arabella, one of the Earl's many illegitimate children, was left the sum of £1500 but the bulk of Earls Rivers' fortune went to Elizabeth Colleton, the illegitimate daughter of Sir Peter Colleton, who had been Earl Rivers' constant and favoured mistress, and then to their illegitimate daughter, the ravishingly beautiful Bessey Savage. Bessey at the age of fifteen had married the 3rd Earl of Rochford. Arabella, her half-sister, had meanwhile married Field's father, steward to the Rochford family at their seat, St Oswyth, in Essex. She was considered to have married below her station, with a local historian writing of the union: 'One wonders how the village attorney's son aspired to the hand of an Earl's daughter.'

William Field was bought up at St Oswyth and must have felt some sense of social inferiority, given his father's position. He saw first-hand, the extraordinarily opulent lifestyle of his half-aunt, Bessey, and afterwards that of his first cousin, the 4th Earl of Rochford. Field had no means of clawing back some of his grandfather's fortune from the Rochford's, so instead preyed on the more vulnerable members of their extended family.

As Richard Savage-Lloyd and the Reverend Willian spuriously funded Sir John Snell in his efforts to overturn his father's will, Louisa would get the upper hand. Her half-brother was then entirely reliant on her for funds. If Sir John Snell's 'friends' failed to have the will overturned, he risked being left without a penny. Before he left for Plymouth to join Admiral Graves' ship, the young boy was no doubt coerced into writing a letter to the court, wherein he denied any complicity in the proceedings: he formally stated that he did not wish to overturn his father's will and that he had no claim on the properties in London and Suffolk. After this, Richard and Louisa sued Savage-Lloyd and the venerable vicar, Reverend Willian, for the return of the Colleton properties. The case dragged on and in order to pay his lawyers, Richard sent word to his brothers that he was withdrawing his allowance to his spinster sisters.

On June 23rd 1789, Richard, and Louisa who was close to the birth of her second child, again appeared before the American Loyalist Claims Commission. They sat as the evidence from their memorial of January 1788, and subsequent sworn statements from witnesses were read out to them, after which Louisa said she did not have 'anything material to add to the circumstances therein generally detailed'. Asked about her father, she replied that she knew 'little concerning her father's conduct, but through writing his letters, knows he refused to be concerned with the rebellion'.

Louisa was thoroughly examined by the board and once more had to tell them what she considered to be the value of her possessions that had been destroyed. She took the opportunity to add that her vessels had been used in Public Service, but 'from neglect or ignorance did not procure certificates of the same, and when in America she was inexperienced and unacquainted, with what might be required in proof of her losses, as not to obtain any other documents than those produced, which otherwise she might have done when at the Bahamas in 1785, where Colonel McArthur then was; the officer who with a body of troops under his command took post at Fairlawn'.

McArthur was still understood to be in the Bahamas, and Louisa told the Commissioners she would endeavour to obtain his evidence. At this point, Richard interjected to inform the board that he remembered 'one of the Schooners [the *Success*] in the service of Government, as he apprehended going from Charleston to St Augustine, about the time of the evacuation in which voyage she was wrecked. Richard had commanded the convoy, but as it was a casual service, he did not take a List of the Vessels put under his case, nor enquired to whom they belonged or how employed'. Louisa asked the Commissioners if it would 'not be equitable to make some allowance for their hire'.

The Commission once again asked Louisa about the slaves at Fairlawn. She stated that 'above one hundred men, women and children were lost to the estate by various means, some attached themselves to the troops, and acted under orders, some to Officers and Individuals of the Army and others run away without any account being had of them'. A certificate was then read to the board, written by Colonel N. Balfour, in which he said that on his orders Fairlawn had been converted into a hospital, and that he had 'no doubt of considerable supplies having been given to the troops from that plantation, and think it very probable that proper certificates were not granted'.

While the Commission sat trawling through evidence from loyalists, news came from Paris that on July 14th a mob had stormed the Bastille. It was thought in England that any revolution would be peaceful; William Pitt, the Prime Minister, refused to be overly alarmed by the events.

The Graveses left London and went back to Gittisham. There, it was very wet; crops were underwater, and fruit rotted on the trees. They were unable to entertain, not just for a lack of space in the cottage, but because they could hardly afford the most basic of provisions. When Tom wrote from his house, Woodbine Hill, declaring his intention to come and dine with his brother, Richard asked that they be given ample warning so they could try to bring in something decent to eat.

Finally, at the end of August, the Commission received a statement detailing the wartime events at Fairlawn from an ailing Brigadier General Archibald McArthur. He confirmed that he had ordered a fort to be built to cover the landing on the River Cooper: and that a considerable number of cedar trees were cut down to open up the land and to surround the house with a log barricade. He knew that the estate belonged to Louisa to the prejudice of a son by a second marriage and that when he took possession, Mr Giles 'who married the widow Colleton coming there most of the furniture was put into garrets for security'. McArthur wrote that he could not remember the Carriage House, but admitted that he had ordered two of the slaves' houses to be burnt 'and had threatened the whole in order to oblige the negroes to attend the Public Works'. He also stated that he had lived in the overseer's house and had ordered a redoubt to be built around it.

James Nassau Colleton had also petitioned the Commission with an extensive claim. He explained how he had inherited Wadboo, and detailed his journey to America with his wife in March 1783. He stated that his time spent in South Carolina had cost him above £600, which he could ill afford on his pay as a Junior Clerk in the Home Office. He wrote of his unsuccessful attempts to have the confiscation of Wadboo overturned, until finally the financial penalties on the plantation were removed in March 1786. He had then been sued by the American Commissioners, in charge of forfeited estates, for the bills arising from the sale of Wadboo. James Nassau ended his memorial with a dramatic rendering of his hardships, including being unable to support his spinster sister.

James Nassau put in a claim of £17,523 for Wadboo: for the loss of his land which amounted to 12,724 acres at a value of 20 shillings per acre, the sawmill, the storehouses, cattle, horses, hogs, plantation tools, household furniture, and sixty-two slaves valued at £60 each. He deducted £72.50, which he had already been paid for twenty-four cattle supplied to the army, leaving a total claim of £17,450.15.

On February 11th 1790, the American Loyalist Claims Commission announced their decision on Richard and Louisa's claim.

For the buildings at Fairlawn burnt by the Americans in consequence of their being fortified and used as a hospital for the British Army: £1500

Furniture burnt and destroyed at the same time: £500

Overseer's and Negro houses burnt by Order: £85

Timber used and trees cut down for the purpose of fortifying the Post, some part whereof was carried to Charlestown, for the Kings works: £400

Demand for Negroes, it not appearing in proof that any of them were taken for Public Service. For the Hire of Vessels, there being reason to conclude that they were only employed by Government occasionally and payment for such hire is acknowledged viz, From the Chief Engineer in May 1782, From the Commissary General in Nov 1782. And Charlestown was evacuated in December 1782. For stock, carriages, Horses, no proof being actually adduced that they were taken for, or applied to the Service of Government: Disallowed

Total amount allowed: £2485

Richard and Louisa were horrified, this sum was a far cry from the £16,852.17 claimed. The Commission's view was that there had been a failure to produce 'documentary or other satisfactory proof of the definite loss of their property by confiscation or other means'. James Nassau was awarded a little more, but Louisa's cousin, Thomas Boone, once governor of South Carolina, was given £22,000, the highest single amount given by the Commission for American losses. Boone's Barony of 7420 acres had been presented in 1782 to General Nathanael Greene, commander of the rebels when Fairlawn was burnt down.

On hearing of the amount awarded to them by the Commission, Richard immediately wrote to them, protesting that he and Louisa would be 'reduced to extream distress – and must ultimately be ruined without some relief from Government'. They were now parents to two children, after the arrival of a daughter they named Sophia Louisa, and the amount of the compensation would not even clear their debts. The family left London for their damp cottage in Guittisham and waited for a reply to their appeal from the Commission through an interminable winter. As late as April 21st 1790, thick snow fell on the ground and high winds blew down many trees.

It was not until the early autumn that it became apparent that the Commission would not alter its decision. The vivacious Louisa had to sit at home while 'a good many Bath people' clattered through the village in their carriages on their way to the now fashionable resort of Sidmouth to enjoy a week of balls and other amusements.

CHAPTER 13

'Artillery of tears'

*

SEVEN years after Louisa had received her mother's miniature, Ann unexpectedly wrote to her daughter again in early 1791. Ann was clearly in need of funds and wanted to sell Shewte Manor on Dartmoor to raise a capital sum. Under the terms of her marriage settlement, she could not do this, despite it originally being her house, without Louisa's agreement, hence the letter. Louisa was magnanimous and agreed in principle to her mother's request, but as she did not wish to sell the estate she asked Tom Graves for a loan so she could buy out her mother.

A date was set for the documents to be signed, and on a bitterly cold day at the end of January, Richard, and Louisa then large with her third child, faced her unfamiliar mother and step-father, John Robert Lea, in the lawyer's office. The meeting, which perhaps Louisa hoped would lead to some sort of reconciliation, was but a mere formality in Ann's eyes. There was no idle talk before or after they signed the deed, and then went their separate ways. This was one of those occasions, as Louisa would write, when she had 'shed many an unavailing tear' over her mother. A few years later Ann and her husband would live but a few streets away from Louisa in Exeter. They did so until Ann's death in the summer of 1809, and it is improbable that their paths did not cross during this time. It is understandable since her mother had never shown the slightest affection for her only surviving child or any interest in her grandchildren, that Louisa would claim in public and in print that she was orphaned in 1777 after the death of her father.

A few weeks after the meeting with Ann, Mrs Admiral handed back to Richard the keys for Hembury Fort. This may have been because she had failed to let the house or because she had been put under moral pressure by the family to allow them to return. There were now three children, after the arrival of another daughter, Carolina Victoria. While it was a relief for Louisa to leave the tiny cottage in Gittisham, there was no furniture at Hembury Fort, and the house was in a state of disrepair. It was during this time that Richard began to sell parcels of Louisa's land, behind her back, in order to keep his wife in the manner to which she was accustomed. He was also relying on an annuity from Mrs Admiral, who had agreed to give him a share of profits from his late uncle's estates.

The Graveses social life now revolved around their nearest neighbours who, apart from Tom Graves, had left them off their calling list whilst they had lived in reduced circumstances in the cottage. Tom, his wife and their rather fat eighteen-year-old daughter, Mary, lived across the valley at Woodbine Hill, a substantial house which he had built over an old farmhouse. It had been so badly constructed that water often ran down the walls, the cook struggled to get the fire going on her range and had walked out, after which Tom's wife had left for Bath. He did not seem to have been unduly concerned by her absence and was left at home with Mary, whom he adored.

John and Elizabeth Simcoe and their several children were close neighbours at the newly built Wolford Lodge which, filled with a few good portraits and a great collection of maps and military treatises, was the scene of many county gatherings. Guests staying in the house would, however, endure very long sessions of morning prayers with the whole household in attendance. Perhaps Richard Graves was now thankful that he hadn't married Elizabeth. Mrs Simcoe's best friend since childhood, the spinster Miss Mary Anne Burges, lived in the neighbouring village of Awliscombe and both these women were very close in age to Louisa. Mary Anne was a blue stocking: she was fluent in several European languages and was a dedicated botanist and geologist. Her great friend was Jean-Andre de Luc, the Swiss geologist and natural philosopher, and she had contributed to his work. She also later had published, anonymously, a sequel to *Pilgrim's Progress*, which sold as fast as it was printed. Mary Anne, who would later remark that Louisa was 'really a very clever woman', was no doubt delighted that there was someone in the valley who could match her intellect.

Other neighbours included the Drewes at the Grange in Payhembury, who had long been friends of the Colletons and the Grinfields. Everyone liked Mrs Grinfield, but her husband, Colonel Grinfield was considered 'imperious and colonellish'. He also made provocative jokes about the cruelties of the slave trade when anyone was eating food containing sugar. Richard's brother, John, lived only a few hours' ride away at Barley House in Exeter, which belonged to his disagreeable wife. And, only two years later, Richard's cousin, Admiral Thomas Graves, would move into Cadhay, a Tudor house of some standing in nearby Ottery St Mary.

Richard still lacked employment: his arrogant nature and lack of social skills ensured that he failed to attract the necessary patronage to progress his naval career. John Simcoe, however, landed the post of Lieutenant Governor of Upper Canada, in September 1791. He had sailed for Canada with Elizabeth and their youngest daughter, and infant son. They had left behind their four eldest daughters, the youngest of which was just three years old, at Wolford Lodge in the care of governesses under Mrs Admiral's supervision.

Mrs Admiral was so cross with Elizabeth for leaving, that Richard decided to try to ingratiate himself with his aunt, in the hope of extracting more money from her. However, as always, he lacked the finesse needed for such encounters and began their meeting by making an unwanted caustic comment about Mrs Simcoe.

Mary Anne Burges, who had promised Mrs Simcoe that she would write to her with all the news, reported that Richard put his aunt in a 'furious passion'. Towards the end of their meeting, Mrs Admiral was 'very near turning him out of the house for insulting her by saying any-thing against her relations'. The argument escalated when Mrs Admiral told Richard, that 'since he kept two carriages she did not know any obligation she was under to keep him & she is actually almost resolved to withdraw her annuity.'

Tom Graves wrote that the 'old fury' delayed sending Richard his usual annuity of £100 by eight days, 'rather meaning to alarm him, than resolved to recall it, on which he sent her a letter, to remind her that it was due, & to request her to pay it immediately'. Incensed by Richard's effrontery, Mrs Admiral 'enclosed him the customary allowance but acquainted him that, since he did not know how to distinguish between a matter of favour & of right it was the last he should ever receive from her'. She added that Richard's demand of it as a debt was not only highly improper but extremely impertinent. Richard's subsequent letter of apology did nothing to appease his cantankerous aunt. Indeed, despite both Richard and Louisa calling on her and lending her their piano, in the words of Mary Anne: 'She is very civil & means to invite them to dinner, but is resolved never to give them another sixpence.'

The constant squabbles with Mrs Admiral began to affect Louisa's health. She was also bored with her repetitive social life. Mrs Simcoe was in the depths of northern Canada, living under canvas when she read Mary Anne's account of the latest gossip from the valley: 'Mrs Rd G. has avowed her wish to go to live at Bath & says that if she is forced to remain much longer at Strawberry Fort, [Louisa's nickname for the Hembury Fort] she shall nail up the window shutters & live by candlelight that she may not be longer tormented with the sight of the green fields.'

However, Louisa continued to attend the regular Assemblies in Honiton, at which the county aristocracy and gentry collected in a grand building on the high street boasting a ballroom. One evening in attendance, she was not well and had not bothered to dress her hair for the occasion. Mary Anne reported: 'Mrs Richard Graves was there, so extraordinary a figure that Mrs Bacon fell far short of her. Mrs Grinfield thought she looked most like a Squaw.' During supper, Louisa had a 'fit', and while this unfortunate episode improved the 'county' ladies' dull evening, it was to be the first of many.

Richard was also attracting public comment. The storming of the Bastille a year earlier and the subsequent revolutionary events in France had divided social and political opinion in England. The country, having recently suffered the American Revolution, split roughly into two main camps, with loyalists defending tradition and radicals calling for change. Richard and his brothers, John and Tom, openly, vehemently and unwisely supported the radicals.

Sympathy in England for the French Revolution was not uncommon. Poet William Wordsworth wrote of the storming of the Bastille: 'Bliss was it in that dawn to be alive.' Many liberal-minded Whigs hoped that the revolution would usher in a constitutional monarchy modelled on that in England. Some went further and took inspiration from Thomas Paine's The *Rights of Man*. Paine, whose writings were central to the fomenting of both the American War of Independence and the French Revolution, spoke to those who looked forward to a time when aristocratic privilege would be a thing of the past and merit itself would be the only measure used in government appointments.

It was hardly surprising that such views attracted the talented but relatively impoverished Graves brothers. Although the Royal Navy was meritocratic up to a point, no one was promoted to the rank of lieutenant unless they had spent time at sea, passed a tough exam and were at least twenty-one years old. After that, promotion to commander and then Post Captain was often a result of influence rather than merit.

The Graves brothers must have seen many such promotions of officers whom they considered inferior in ability to them, and naturally, this had rankled. Their Uncle, Admiral Samuel Graves, whom the brothers believed had been monstrously treated after he was recalled from America, clearly held similar views about merit. Inscribed on his monument were the words. 'His own merit raised him to the Head of His Profession without the support of Parliamentary interest and unassisted by splendid Connections. He served and loved his country with a Zeal seldom equalled, never excelled.' The inscription ends with the sentiment that his family and acquaintances 'emphatically styled him "The poor Man's friend". Although all three brothers harboured similar views, it was Richard who would later declaim them with the most vehemence, and with the reputation as a 'dangerous radical', he ensured the destruction of his naval career.

In October 1791, Louisa learnt that her aunt, Elizabeth Fulford, had died. The obituaries that followed only reminded Louisa of the obvious charm and generosity of someone she had considered her surrogate mother. They had never been reconciled and Louisa wrote sadly: 'I never saw Mrs Fulford after I left England.' Louisa's distress was later compounded by the contents of Elizabeth's will. Although Louisa was not directly related to Elizabeth, she must have hoped that her aunt would have left her some small memento or keepsake as a reminder of happier times; a small gesture to signify that she had once loved Louisa. But none was forthcoming. Elizabeth left her sister, Frances, many of her possessions, including her carriage, and she had not forgotten her other Fulford nieces, all spinsters, who inherited money, her expensive and coveted clothes, and other personal items.

Some four years after her marriage, Louisa's resilience was beginning to crack. Beleaguering tradesmen arrived at Hembury Fort demanding payment, and Mrs Admiral refused to give in to family pressure and reinstate her annuity to Richard. Over Christmas that year, Tom Graves' wife had interceded on Richard's behalf but her pleas were in vain. By the beginning of 1792, Louisa and Richard were in such a precarious financial position that on a miserable cold day in early January they drove in their carriage to see Mrs Admiral at Wolford Lodge. Mary Anne wrote to Mrs Simcoe: 'Capt & Mrs R. G. have been in person to beg for their pension. The latter tried her whole artillery of Tears & Spasms, but all to no effect.'

Louisa began having frequent and uncontrollable spasms in public and these became a hot topic of gossip in the county, as they were, according to Mary Anne, 'more extraordinary than ever'. Some of the county ladies spread malicious rumours that Louisa was perhaps possessed, but in the end all agreed that it was more likely she was suffering from St Vitus' Dance, as 'Sydenham's chorea' was then sometimes called. The condition manifests itself some months after an acute attack of rheumatic fever caused by a streptococcal infection. It was not life-threatening but rendered the victim at times unable to control their limbs or facial expressions. Mary Anne noted that Louisa's 'latest invention is rattling her fingers one against the other, to resemble the noise of a pair of Castanets'. On February 7th, when Louisa again attended the Honiton Assembly, she suffered, according to Mary Anne, another 'spasm in the middle of the room to the great edification of the whole company'.

Humiliated by the effects of her illness which, instead of garnering sympathy from her friends and acquaintances, served only to amuse them, Louisa remained at home. She was not thirty years old and there was no cure for the illness. It was believed the symptoms could be alleviated by 'repeated purgings and bleedings' and with doses of 'peruvian bark and snake root'. One physician wrote: 'A cold bath is likewise of singular service and ought never to be neglected if the patient can bear it.' Patients were also given doses of arsenic and laudanum to calm the spasms.

Because of the drugs administered to Louisa, she became increasingly emotional, unstable and irrational. She was also expecting another child. Mary Anne 'did penance' and went to dine at Hembury Fort on March 10th, where she found Louisa unable to prevent herself from verbally attacking Richard in public: 'She scolded him, & almost swore at him, for everything he said or did.' Louisa looked to Mary Anne for support, and three times Mary Anne actually lost her temper and told her it was not the custom of guests to 'beat people' when they went to visit them. 'And yet,' Mary Anne wrote of Louisa, 'she is so thoroughly unhappy that she excited my compassion.'

More worrying, Mary Anne wrote that Louisa's daughter, Carolina Victoria, then a year old, suffered from fits that were similar to Louisa's. She wrote of four-year-old Samuel and Sophia Louisa, who was nearly three: 'The other two are more tiring than ever. She adheres to her system of giving them whatever they cry for, but it happened two or three times while I was there that they both cried for the same thing. And then the point became extremely intricate.'

Louisa, as with so many other women of her class, had taken to heart the child-rearing theories of the philosopher, Jean-Jacques Rousseau. He advocated that a mother should breastfeed her children and that no child should be taught anything until the age of twelve. Until then, he recommended that children should be allowed to wander around the countryside unhindered and enjoy the fresh air. The manner in which she was bringing up her children was taking Rousseau's philosophy perhaps too far. Mrs Simcoe, by contrast, would not even allow her children to sit in her presence until they were given permission to do so. Louisa herself wrote that she 'sought to persuade rather than compel', which must have been exhausting for her and allowed her children to behave as they felt so inclined.

The Admiralty again rejected both Richard and Tom's request for a posting which served to inflame their radical ideals. They spent the hot August of 1792 setting up a 'Constitutional Club', but there was little appetite for such a political movement and it attracted a paltry twelve members. Tom, in his campaign for change in England, was to be seen in the streets of Exeter swearing at booksellers for failing to stock any republican pamphlets or copies of the Republican 'bible', Paine's *Rights of Man*. A warrant for Thomas Paine's arrest had been issued at the beginning of the year, and having fled the country, he was convicted in absentia for seditious libel. The government, under the Prime Minister, William Pitt, had no wish for republican ideas to gain traction on home turf. When Tom eventually found a copy of Paine's book, he 'walked the streets & coffee houses to make a parade of his acquisition'. Richard was called, not for the first time, as a second in a duel for 'one of his republican cronies', Mary Anne wrote, although he managed to persuade the parties to abandon their potentially fatal meeting. The behaviour of Tom, John and Richard Graves was unseemly and downright improper as they were now Justices of the Peace. Mary Anne referred to them and their cronies as loathsome 'Jacobins' and 'democrats'.

At Hembury Fort, Louisa was delivered of a third daughter, named Louisa Catherina. Meanwhile, at Wolford Lodge, the governess, Mrs Hunt, who disliked Richard, begged Mrs Admiral to write a new will. She had destroyed one that left everything to Elizabeth Simcoe in her fury at her niece's departure to Canada. The governess convinced Mrs Admiral that should she die intestate, Richard could make a claim against her personal fortune. Mrs Admiral called for her lawyer at once and signed a will leaving everything to Elizabeth Simcoe and her daughters.

Mrs Admiral, like Louisa, longed to escape from the country and on the pretext of her ill-health, she purchased a house that was part of a grand crescent being built by speculators in Bath. When No. 15 Lansdown Crescent was completed in November 1792, Mrs Admiral left her great-nieces and their governesses at Wolford Lodge. She took with her all her furniture, pictures, plate, and carpets – one of these a valuable Wilton, which the family later saw to their amazement, had been cut down to fit a back room. Her departure must have been a relief for the four Simcoe girls who, although reasonably fond of their great-aunt, must have tired of her capriciousness. Mrs Admiral often favoured one of her great nieces above the other – mostly the eldest Eliza, who was such a kind-hearted girl, that she would refuse any favours or presents from her great-aunt unless her siblings were also included.

The new year of 1793 began under the threat of a French invasion. From her desk in Bath, Mrs Admiral wrote to Eliza and scathingly asked whether Richard, whom she called 'Mr Dick', was still in Devonshire, or had gone to France 'to teach the National Assembly to dance'. News of Richard and his brothers' embarrassing political affiliations had clearly reached Bath, as it would the Admiralty.

After the execution of King Louis XVI on January 21st 1793, French Revolutionaries had declared war on all the monarchies of Europe, so Britain was now on a war footing. Richard was desperate for a ship and implored his elder brother Sam to arrange a captaincy, but Sam refused: Richard's republican views were all too well known. Neither was Tom successful, Mary Anne later reported that he was 'breaking his heart at not being able to get a ship. I fancy he has certainly only himself to blame for it, for Government would be mad to employ a man who talked as he did all last year. He is very silent now, but it is too late'. It was also too late for Richard, who nevertheless thought himself 'ill used'. Such was his chagrin and resentment at being rejected by the Admiralty that he wanted to give up Hembury Fort and take the family to South Carolina. However, his plans to leave England were thwarted by the Admiralty: whilst they did not wish to employ him, neither would they grant him permission to be unavailable to the Navy.

Mrs Admiral was still withholding Richard's annuity, and in desperation he grovelled to her, asking her to pay Samuel's school fees. She refused to do so, and as Mary Anne told Mrs Simcoe: 'Is it not an ingenious scheme of Capt Richard to have written to Mrs Graves to desire that she will undertake the education of his son? I suppose he could have devised no possible demand, of the rejection of which might have been more certain.'

CHAPTER 14

Cargo of Rice

*

THE early summer of 1793 had been wet and miserable, but in early June the weather changed. Mary Anne Burges wrote that it was so hot that she could little more than sit sweltering under a great walnut tree in her garden. Louisa was unable to resist the charms of Sidmouth. Regardless of the sore matter of Samuel's school fees and lack of funds, the family packed their bags and left for the 'gayest place of resort on the Devon coast'.

The *beau monde* was to be seen making their way down the charming valley to the town. On the seafront toys and trinkets were sold: there were bathing machines on the beach and a large thatched building where visitors could take shelter if it rained. In bright sunshine the sea was 'reddened by reflecting the colour of the cliffs', and pleasure boats and fishing smacks dallied on the water. It was a place where, as was noted by one contemporary visitor, 'every elegancy, every luxury, every amusement is here to be met with: iced creams, milliner's shops, cards, billiards, plays, circulation libraries, attract notice in every part'. Not everyone saw it in that way: a more jaundiced observer, a friend of the poet Samuel Taylor Coleridge, thought Sidmouth, 'a nasty watering place, infested by lounging ladies, and full of footmen'. Here, it cost visitors almost as much for them to stable their horses as it did for them to take lodgings for themselves. The Graveses rented their own hut on the shore from where Louisa could keep an eye on her children as they played on the beach. In the evenings they went to the Assembly Rooms, where there were frequent balls and rooms set aside for card tables.

Early in the morning on July 8th, Mary Anne saddled her aptly named mare, Placid, and rode to Sidmouth. It was, she recalled in a letter to Mrs Simcoe, 'the hottest day I ever was out in'. As the day progressed, the temperature in the sun was recorded as being over a hundred degrees. Mary Anne was surprised to discover that the Graves' children, five-year-old Samuel, four-year-old Sophia, and Carolina who was two, were being sent to school 'in an alley'. She said of the manner Richard and Louisa disciplined their children: 'I could not help being diverted with the progress of the system of unlimited indulgence; I met Capt. G & his son, & I heard him threatening to horse whip him & reminding him that he had done it twice the day before.' And she told Mrs Simcoe: 'I do not recollect that to have been your usual mode of proceeding with your children, notwithstanding your astonishing severity.' If anyone spoke to Samuel on the beach Mary Anne reported: 'He creeps behind them, & kicks them with all his might; & if they presume to remonstrate, he throws large stones at them. Miss Drewe assured me he had hurt her very much.'

The Graveses were still living in Sidmouth in late October 1793, when, to Tom's bemusement, he heard that Richard had been in Honiton purchasing land. He was told that Richard and Louisa planned to take the children back to Hembury Fort, and then go on to London. Tom wrote to John: 'I suppose he must have discovered a mine or some hidden treasure, but I fear he is *a la mode generale*, increasing his expenses without the means of raising the taxes.' Tom feared that this would be yet another reckless speculative investment plunging Richard even further into debt. But, in fact, his brother had discovered a mine of sorts – rice was now being shipped out of Fairlawn, just as the commodity was enjoying a boom.

Louisa's previous efforts in South Carolina were now beginning to pay a dividend. She was fortunate, many other plantation owners who had left their plantations in the hands of agents were unlikely to see any profits. Those who ran their own plantations, such as George Washington at Mount Vernon, worked hard to ensure they made money. Washington would be up at dawn ensuring his slaves were not feigning illness, stealing, using the horses for their own pleasure, or drinking. He also paid meticulous attention to his accounts. In a letter to one of his agents, he wrote: 'I cannot conceive how it is possible that six thousand 12 penny nails could be used in Corn house at River Plantation.' Perhaps Louisa from afar was making just such comments to her agents.

Only a few weeks later, Tom told John: 'Richard talks of going to London shortly and Madame accompanies him, so that you may think they are determined to spend the cargo of rice as soon as possible – you know they have ordered a new carriage at Exeter £100 cost.'

After a great spending spree, the Graveses returned to Devon at the beginning of 1794. In March, Mary Anne told Mrs Simcoe the news that Louisa 'has another daughter, which is a great disappointment; I am told it is to be called Seraphima'.

By early May, Richard was somewhere in London but would not divulge his location to avoid the expense of receiving a letter, so bad was the state of his finances. The onus of paying for postage, which was expensive, then fell on the recipient. He made daily overtures to the Admiralty hierarchy for a ship, but to no avail. Tom had hoped Richard would be employed by then, but he feared that a historic misdemeanour 'would stick by him – you know it was much talked of at Plymouth at the Duke of Clarence's table & the Admiral's – a trifle may ruin all the professional's merit & long service he has to plead'.

The Duke of Clarence, later King William IV, who had joined the navy aged thirteen in 1779, declared at the time that he would ensure Richard would never again be employed by the navy. The 'trifle' thirteen years earlier had occurred in Halifax on the east coast of Canada. Richard had raided a privateer's ship and struck the captain so hard across the face that had he not grabbed a sail, he would have fallen onto the deck below. Richard was ordered to appear at a makeshift Admiralty court, but when no one turned up to testify, the case was not pursued.

Now, an unwanted Richard Graves continued to haunt the Admiralty corridors. Around this time, rumours spread that Rear Admiral Thomas Graves had lost an arm in the battle of the Glorious First of June against the French. On June 17th, the family was relieved to hear that his wound was 'slight' even though the man standing beside him had been killed. Mary Anne recounted that the victory was much celebrated in Honiton and most of the laurel in her garden was cut to decorate the town. In November 1794, Thomas Graves was elevated to the Irish peerage, while his cousins, Richard, John and Tom, remained unemployed.

Louisa, who was so often treated with such derision by her neighbours, was of course now a most desirable guest because of Admiral Thomas Graves' glory, and no party was complete without her in attendance. In December, whilst at the Assembly in Honiton, Mary Anne told Mrs Simcoe that Louisa received a rude push from Mrs Drewe when going in for supper. Proceedings came to a halt as everyone watched to see how Louisa would respond, but instead of challenging her neighbour, Louisa succumbed to a spasm.

Many were highly amused by the petty slights that evening, but Louisa, who was seven months pregnant, refused to stay in Devon any longer. The family left for London only to return to Bath at the beginning of January 1795, where Louisa suffered the traumatic birth of a daughter.

They named her Ann Felicia, but she did not live for long. It was not until May that the family learnt Louisa had 'quite recovered', and would be returning to Hembury Fort. Only months later, in early July, Richard and Louisa were at the graveside of their 'heavenly angel', Seraphima, who had been only eighteen months old. Eight days after her funeral, Richard and Louisa called on Mary Anne who wrote that Louisa was looking 'so ill, I think she really must be in a very bad way'.

During August, it seemed that Louisa was well enough to attend a scientific lecture in Honiton, and joined in discussions on green tea and salamanders. But when Mary Anne called in to see her in the middle of the month, she found her terribly distressed. Louisa 'was crying all the time I staid, & has literally cried her eyes out; they scarsily contain any colour, & altogether she looks so ill that she might move any person to compassion'. Mary Ann told Mrs Simcoe: 'They are to go to America next month; and as all the children are to be left, the only objects which engaged any part of her affection, she has all to suffer that you had, without the support of your fortitude & just principles, & without any one of the circumstances which contributed to your comfort; for she has no eligible place to leave her daughters; Miss Lewis, after having consented to receive them has written to decline it, assigning reasons foolish enough; but I suppose she must have heard what troublesome children they are, & does not chuse to have the charge of them; & as for friends I do not believe Mrs Rd. Graves possesses one, so that if she does find any school that will take receive them, should that break up during her absence, they will be equally thrown upon the world. I know not why so situated, she leaves them at all; but I rather think it is Captain Graves's doing; for many people think that he has of late taken more upon himself than he used to do; & he told me nothing should induce him to have the plague of children on a voyage'.

Richard had had to take more notice of his children while Louisa was ill, and found them hard to tolerate. The children's reputation was such that no one wanted the onerous task of looking after them while the Graveses were away. Samuel, in particular, although he had benefitted from being educated, had been allowed to run wild. He was in his Uncle Tom's opinion, 'a sharp little boy & in proper hands would do very well', but Louisa spoilt him so much that Tom thought 'the poor little fellow will made unfit for anything but a man milliner, a confectioner, a maitre d' Hotel or a country squire'.

In late August, Mrs Admiral again added to Louisa's woes when she 'ordered Capt'n Richard to give up the keys of Hembury Fort', for the second time. Mrs Admiral had decided that her 'chief friends and favourites' were Richard's eldest brother, the recently promoted Admiral Sam. She offered the house to Sam and his wife, but Sam had no desire to take it over, particularly as it would eventually belong to Richard. Mary Anne believed Hembury Fort would be 'left to go to ruin; since in so bad state as its present there is less chance than ever that anybody will take it without furniture'. She was asked to dine there, but 'chose to be engaged'. Tom could not understand why Richard would want to live at Hembury Fort. In a letter to John, he wrote: 'I should have thought Bath would have been a more eligible place for our Brother than the country where the time will hang heavy on his hands as he is neither fond of any rural sports or pursuits or of reading – where as at Bath he is constantly meeting with one of his acquaintances with whom he can saunter the mornings & make little parties in the evening.'

Mrs Admiral subsequently became very ill: Tom reported to John, 'she is now supposed to be a lost cause an abscess in her side, & there is no hopes of her'. Richard told everyone he met that he could not find a ship to go to America, but many suspected that he was delaying the journey until Mrs Admiral died. After the Graveses had been forced out of Hembury Fort, they went to spend the winter at the Golden Lion in Honiton, much to the annoyance of some in the town. Relations between Richard and Louisa were then at a low ebb, and they were heard openly rowing at the Honiton assembly.

In December 1795, Tom, John and Richard, having ordered expensive new uniforms for the occasion, tried to make amends to their brother Sam for the harm their political views had caused their brother's naval career. In March that year, to his disgrace, he felt, he had been superannuated as Rear Admiral, which retired him from service. The demotion, as it was considered, also affected his pension. The brothers travelled to Weymouth to present a petition to the king, where they were publicly humiliated. Mary Anne heard a 'ridiculous account of the procession of Captain Graves's'. The king had 'looked at them all round & said 'Three post Captains!' & then walked on without returning them any answer.'

Surprisingly, Mrs Admiral had recovered from her illness and resentfully handed the keys to Hembury Fort back to Richard. It was from here that Richard wrote to his sister Catherine in Ireland at the beginning of 1796.

'My son is grown a very stout boy for his age, just seven years and a half, he goes to school at Honiton, which is only from us three miles, comes home on Saturday evening and returns on Monday morning to his school. He can ride his pony everywhere with me and has even been out hunting with me. He is mother's pet, no unusual thing with sons, and will soon lead or direct the House when I am out of it.' Richard told his sister: 'I hope to leave this country in the Spring for America, indeed I flattered myself last fall of being there now, but circumstances turned out to prevent me, and as fates will have it my Wife is breeding again, which is a disagreeable thing for her to embark with a big belly and I fear I shall not be able to prevail upon her to stay behind me.'

A few days later, Mary Anne reported: 'Mrs Richd. Graves will not allow any of her children to be taught to read, excepting the eldest, because she thinks it is cruel; & has put them to school with that express stipulation; but they all learn to dance.' It is bewildering that Louisa did not allow her girls to be taught to read, having placed such emphasis on the fine education she herself had received as a child. Samuel did not like going to school because all the boys called him 'Miss Molly'. He must have been disliked, and effeminate, as a 'Molly' was a Georgian word used to describe homosexuals. Richard and Louisa had threatened to remove him from school unless the headmaster, Mr Hayne, made the other boys act more kindly towards him. 'Yet', Mary Anne wrote, Mr Hayne had told her: 'the child would really be an exceeding fine boy, if he were not spoiled in so terrible indulgent home'.

Mary Anne called at Hembury Fort after church on a fine March morning. Richard, she discovered, was dangerously ill with rheumatic fever, but Louisa had been safely delivered of another daughter. They named her Septima Sexta, indicating in Latin, that she was the Graves' seventh child, and sixth daughter. Septima was, poignantly, christened on April 6th 1796, the same day as her late sister, Seraphima, had been two years earlier.

As Richard had failed to find employment in the navy, he and Tom became determined to capitalize on the 'industrial revolution', although neither of them had any expertise or knowledge in such matters. They had brought a mill and set out to purchase 'machinery for the woolen business'. Their brother, John, although not a partner in the business was, it seems, left to do the donkey work. Tom wrote to him at Exeter, where the machines were being manufactured: 'There is a man in North Gate

Street who makes Billies and Jennies, the Billy is sometimes called Hubbing or Scribbling engines & the Jenny is sometimes called Spinning Engines, I mention this to you that the man, I believe, may not understand you – you will be so good as to call upon him as soon as possible to know his prices for each sort of engine & to be particular in the number of spindles each sort of engine should have to make the greatest dispatch & best yarn & also what room each engine will be required to be worked in, that we may know how many our present building will contain.' John Graves, who had married an heiress, and had no financial incentive to join forces with his brothers in their new business, must have been annoyed after his brother's demands, to read at the end of the letter: 'You Gentlemen can command your time but we Tradesmen must look after our business.'

Towards the end of April 1796, Louisa and Richard went through Bath on their way to London, with the intention of visiting Mrs Admiral. However, she declined to see them. Although she knew it would be a short carriage ride from the White Hart, a coaching inn near the Pump Room, to her house in Lansdown Crescent, she was not 'willing to give them the trouble of coming so much out of their way'. While in London, Richard badgered the Admiralty to extend his leave of absence in case he and Louisa wanted to make the journey to America. Louisa, meanwhile, sent word to Mr and Mrs Hayne that she wanted a lock of Samuel's hair and 'a whole page was filled with injunctions to cut it from such a part of his head as he might not take cold.' This caused much mirth in the neighbourhood and, eventually, Doctor Teed was called to perform the operation.

The Graveses returned to Hembury Fort, and on July 9th dined with Mary Anne. She told Mrs Simcoe: 'Mrs Ed Drewe seemed to come with a set purpose to be agreeable; & I was promising myself a very pleasant day, when Mrs Rd G arrived with a set purpose to be disagreeable; in which she succeeded so completely, that I believe no party was ever more glad when the hour of breaking up arrived.' Mary Anne added of Louisa: 'I knew not what I should do to get her out of the house.'

The Admiralty eventually agreed to extend Richard's leave, but it would take more than a year before he and Louisa would sail for South Carolina. It seems that Richard had not fully recovered from his bout of rheumatic fever. Mary Ann wrote: 'Capt RG is so much altered by his long fit of illness that I should suppose he is twenty years older.'

In 1797, the journey to America was further delayed by the discovery that Louisa's half-brother, Sir John Snell Colleton, in collusion with Richard Savage-Lloyd, had mortgaged property in Suffolk which belonged to her, and with the money had purchased other property in his own name. The Graveses were incensed by Sir John Snell's behaviour and employed an expensive Lincoln's Inn lawyer to embark upon another lengthy lawsuit to retrieve their property. Savage-Lloyd, (the Reverend Willian was by then dead), refused to hand over the Colleton papers and claimed that the cost of the repairs to the properties far outweighed the loan given to Louisa's father in 1775, some twenty years earlier. The court later ruled in favour of those in possession.

It was during 1797 that Mrs Admiral was threatening, again, to take back the keys to Hembury Fort and Louisa, unwilling to suffer this uncertainty any longer, made plans to move the family to Exeter.

CHAPTER 15

Captured

*

LOUISA had not been in South Carolina since 1787 and was desperate to see for herself the state of her plantations after a decade's absence. Such a journey though was now considerably riskier due to the continuing war with France and the proliferation of French privateers operating in the Atlantic on the lookout for British merchant ships. The Simcoes had returned from Canada in October 1796, bearing a harrowing tale of the near-capture of their ship by two French frigates. This did nothing to deter Louisa, but Richard decided they would be safer if they sailed under a neutral flag. In January 1798, they boarded an armed American brigantine, the *Eliza*, bound for Charleston. Their five young children would remain in England at Richard's insistence.

A month later, the *Eliza*, under the captaincy of Neil McNeil, was still sheltering in The Downs, off the Kent coast, waiting for the weather to turn so they could set sail for South Carolina. Once underway, the voyage proved uneventful and they arrived in Charleston at the end of March. But, within six weeks Richard was overcome with a 'severe illness': he had caught malaria, compounded by a respiratory infection. They decided to leave for England as soon as possible. The Graveses were fortunate that they had, by then, employed the dependable William Robertson to manage their affairs in South Carolina.

By chance, the *Eliza* was being turned around to make a return voyage to England. Captain McNeil advertised in the *Charleston Gazette* on May 28th, that the copper-bottomed ship of 380 tons, which 'sails remarkably fast', was mounted with ten 24-pounders and two 9-pounders with a crew capable of manning of the guns. She would, he boasted, be ready for sea before the 31st 'For Freight or Passage, having elegant accommodations for passengers'.

With some haste, the Graveses booked a berth and had loaded onto her a large consignment of rice and indigo from Devil's Elbow and Fairlawn. As the *Eliza* eventually set out across the Charleston bar, on June 12th, it was carrying a great quantity of white sugar and brown sugar in chests, 400 bags of coffee, 260 bales of cotton, 65 hogsheads of tobacco,

317 barrels of rice (approximately 50,000 pounds), 12 barrels of indigo and 18,000 wood staves.

Louisa later wrote of her feelings on leaving Charleston, believing then that it was unlikely she would ever return to America: 'Adieu, adieu my native land, the light breeze wafts us from thy strand,' she wrote, as the shore drifted out of view. 'I sigh my last adieu to thee.' She regretted not only leaving her native land but her 'friends most dear'.

Amongst her fellow passengers was her neighbour on the River Cooper, Sir John Nisbett. He had much in common with Louisa: he, too, had been a minor, living in Scotland, when his plantation, Dean Hall, was put on the 'Number One' List for confiscation. His American uncles managed to retain it, and as a young man, not yet twenty-one, he went to live on his plantation.

Nisbett was a noted lothario, who had now left his young wife at Dean Hall,* to attend to family business in Scotland. His uncle had advised his 'imperious, haughty and stubborn' nephew to sail for Glasgow to avoid the enemy as the French privateers tended to hunt in the seas within easier reach of their ports. It was advice the baronet ignored. Perhaps another reason that Louisa mentioned Sir John Nisbett in her memoirs was because women were known to swoon in his presence. The baronet's uncle wrote Sir John was 'an Adonis, particularly beautiful'.

Some three weeks after the *Eliza* had sailed from Charleston she was nearing Europe. Louisa wrote that they enjoyed a late evening on July 4th 1798, in the 'highest degree of hilarity', but were woken at daybreak by the frantic cry of 'all hands to quarters'. She now, in some terror, remembered a vivid dream she had had five years before when she was ill, 'Being subject to faintings, in which I have frequently lain for five hours to all appearance dead,' which she wrote, foretold of her capture at sea.

A 'strange sail' was spotted by the lookout and appeared to be giving chase. Louisa could hear the gunners open the magazine below to fetch gunpowder, but it was not until 7 a.m. that she went up on deck: 'Never can I forget the awful silence which reigned universally, all, not actually engaged in working the ship, were busily employed in making cartridges, or preparing the small arms; the captain's voice alone was heard, and was obeyed with promptitude.'

The pursuing ship was identified as an armed French Privateer, and

* Dean Hall is now the site of the renowned Cypress Gardens.

the captain of the *Eliza* feared that although the *Eliza* flew the American flag and should have been safe from attack, the Frenchmen would not ignore the chance to take such a potentially rich prize. And so it proved. Louisa retreated to her cabin only to be immediately hustled out by Richard and rushed into the magazine along with her maid, Bath, and another passenger, 'Mrs C'. The women were in a state of shock, listening to the sound of waves walloping against the stern of the ship and unable to see what was going on outside.

Louisa and Bath sat on two empty casks of gunpowder, and beside them were two more covered with a mattress. Both of these had the lids prised off should the crew need to refill their cartridges. Richard then fueled their fright by calling for 'buckets of water and wet swabs, in readiness, lest we should take fire'. Louisa shouted to him, asking how the ship would catch fire, and he 'cooly replied, by a shot or wadding falling through the skylight' immediately over their heads. Louisa screamed to be allowed out, but Richard cut her short, mercilessly telling her that should the powder catch fire it would be an advantage 'as you will not only be the first victim, but without the possibility of lingering, be killed in the instant of the shock'.

With this 'horrible consolation', Louisa 'sat in dire suspense, till the tremendous sound of a broadside burst in my ear! My whole frame vibrated to the shock!' The French had fired a 9-pound shot at the *Eliza* and continued to attack with a 'volley of musketry'. A battle then ensued 'within pistol shot'. For nearly two hours, with her head enveloped in a pillow to deaden the cacophony, Louisa clasped Bath close to her. Then, an ominous silence descended until Louisa heard the shout: 'We are taken.' The *Eliza*, and her crew of thirty were no match for the French ship, *L'Heureux Décidé*, boasting sixteen guns and a crew of just more than a hundred. The 'sails, rigging and braces were shot away' on the *Eliza*, the mainmast damaged and Captain McNeil was later quoted as saying that 'the brig could not be steered'. Two of his crew were dead and several wounded. It was later reported in American newspapers that Captain McNeil had struck his flag 'in tenderness to some of the female passengers he had on board'. Sentiment aside, given the strength of the *Eliza* compared to the *L'Heureux Décidé*, anything short of surrender would have been suicide.

In aftermath of the fighting, Louisa became 'inert' and let go of her hysterical maid. Her fear now was for Richard, 'he being in the British Navy.' Motionless and incapable of uttering a syllable, the shrill voice of

Mrs C aroused her from her stupor. The steward then called down and told Louisa that the bloody flag had been hoisted by the enemy, signalling that no prisoners would be taken. Louisa shuddered and now believed that their attackers would find her in the magazine and murder her. Determined to get out, she had climbed onto the top of a barrel when Richard arrived to rescue them from the magazine.

He took them to the captain's cabin to await their fate. The French boarded the ship, and the first to enter the cabin was a man they later learned had spent six years in an English jail. Louisa recalled: 'His countenance was as gloomy as his form was uncouth, with a lowering brow, he stalked around the cabin, without deigning to bow to the hapless victims of war. "You are English," at length said he, in the English language; his reiterating this expression induced me, being a native of South Carolina, to reply, "pardon me Sir, we are Americans." "You are English" repeated he, casting his eyes towards me as he spoke, "all English". Mrs 'E', on this burst into a violent fit of tears, her daughter, a beautiful child of five years old, hung on her mother's neck and wept most bitterly.' Richard tried to comfort them by saying that although they were prisoners, he was sure their captors were gentlemen and the ladies would remain unmolested. The sailor turned on his heels and left, stating again, 'you are English, you are all English.' However, he soon returned and began to plunder the captain's bureau, but, thinking better of it, instead went to the sideboard and picked up small items of value, which he then concealed in his pockets. All the while, he kept an eye on the door for fear he might be caught by an officer.

Then, 'a tall stout elderly man' entered at which the 'savage plunderer', as Louisa referred to him, left. The elderly man, in charge of weapons, addressed them in French and Louisa translated for her companions, Richard having by then left the cabin. The Frenchman comforted the prisoners by telling them: 'You have fallen into good hands, our captain is honourable and humane.' After offering Louisa some snuff, which she declined, he asked her what ammunition there was in the magazine. Louisa showed him the 'seats' she and her maid had sat upon and the two barrels of gunpowder. After that, 'a tall slim elegant and lively young Frenchman now skipped into the cabin' and said 'be soothed ladies' before he began to search the room. 'On looking round the cabin he discovered English Colours rolled up and quite new' and unfurling the flags he exclaimed with joy: 'You are English, you are all English.'

Louisa bravely retaliated to the assertion, saying: 'belligerent and neutral powers carry not only their own colours but those also of other belligerent and neutral nations, to hoist as occasions require.' She then challenged him to admit, that he, too, no doubt had colours of other nations aboard his ship, to which the Frenchman replied that it was not the point, and continued his search. He then found the steward's pantry, where, to his delight, he spotted a 'cold roast fowl', and tore it to pieces in his fingers. Louisa wrote: 'never before having seen the French mode of eating it shocked me; it appeared quite savage.' The Frenchman then asked for bread, two or three times in French, and believing that the assembled company did not understand, repeated 'bread' several times in English.

'Good God,' Louisa exclaimed, her sovereign arrogance overpowering any sense of fear, 'surely if they do not murder us, they will make us wait on them as servants.' But, on reflection, she asked Bath to go and fetch the man some bread, which she did and offered it to him with a curtsey. The Frenchman bowed most politely and then calmly explained in English to Louisa that they had been chased by an English frigate the previous day. They had just escaped when they sighted and decided to attack the *Eliza*, so he had not eaten for some time. Louisa could not resist remarking to him: 'I exceedingly regretted that his time having been so taken up.'

This Frenchman, to whom Louisa referred to as Monsieur La R— , smiled at her last aside which encouraged her further, 'Are you to remain with us Sir?' to which he replied, 'I shall have that honour, Madam.' To Louisa's disappointment, he told her that he was not the captain, merely a lieutenant. He asked Louisa to withdraw to her staterooms and to take anything of value with her as although his men were ordered not to plunder, he could not assure Louisa that they would not do so in his absence. While Louisa was collecting her books from around the cabin, Captain McNeil was brought in by his impatient captors.

That Lieutenant La R— spoke English, prevented any open discussions, but, 'While Captain McNeil was at his writing desk, taking out some papers he raised his eyes more than usual, looking at me steadfastly; it instantly struck me that he wanted me to receive some papers in his hand unobserved…'. Louisa distracted Lieutenant La R— and the captain was able to walk behind her and surreptitiously slip the documents into her right hand behind her back. They were then disturbed by the entrance of another lieutenant, who had come to take Captain McNeil away to the *L'Heureux Décidé*.

As they were saying their 'mournful goodbyes' to their brave captain, whom they had sailed with on two voyages, Louisa managed to whisper to him and ask him what the contents of the papers were. He told her they were bills drawn in England 'to the amount of 2200 pounds in gold and jewels', and as he left, he said, 'keep them if possible till we meet again.' Louisa and Richard watched as the captain and most of his crew were hurried off the *Eliza*. The passengers returned to their staterooms where one of the officers asked Louisa who Richard was, and when she told the officer that he was her husband, the officer bowed to her and said: 'He shall not be separated from you, Madam.'

The entrance of a 'tall, sallow looking Frenchman' made Louisa 'shudder' for 'his complexion made me believe he was one of the St Domingo Savages, called in Europe men of colour'.* Louisa was duly very surprised when Lieutenant La R— 'gayly stepped up to the table around which we were standing, and introduced him to us, as Monsieur S— capitaine du Prize'. The captain told them, in French, that they were as free that day as they had been the day before, except they were now in France. He asked Louisa 'to order everything to be conducted as we had been accustomed to have it'.

Louisa took charge and at once sent for the steward and told him 'to regulate everything as usual'. The steward, along with the second cook and the cabin boy, had been allowed to remain on board to look after the passengers. The first cook had been injured and taken over to the corsair and Louisa discovered that the second cook had refused to work for his captors. Only after a second flogging by the French did he 'dress the dinner'.

After dinner, the passengers were sent to their staterooms and the passages adjoining them were filled with armed men. One appeared to try to enter Bath's room and Louisa complained to the captain who put a guard outside to ensure that no passengers were so threatened.

The passengers could leave their staterooms at meal times but had to be back by 8 p.m., and the lights extinguished. For three days after the capture of the *Eliza*, Louisa did not leave her room except to eat dinner. She was, therefore, surprised when the captain knocked at her door and

---

* Louisa was presumably talking of mulattos from what is now the Dominican Republic or Haiti, both having an unfavourable reputation at the time.

told her that he was apprehensive that her confinement would make her ill. He had ordered the deck to be cleaned so that Louisa might take the air. The captain offered his arm, which Louisa took hold of out of politeness, and accompanied him up to the deck.

While walking on deck she pointed out that the sails, which were flapping, were set incorrectly, and the captain had them altered to her approval. Louisa also saw someone that she thought was English, and who proved to be the carpenter's mate. She asked him why he was still on board when he should have gone with the rest of the crew over to the corsair: he replied that he had hidden himself in the hold until his fellow crew members had left. Louisa asked him, 'Did I not see you pull a rope just now? Are you gone over to the enemy?' He told Louisa that he had not gone over to the enemy but since the French were civil to him, he was, 'willing to be civil to them'.

A thoroughly alarmed Louisa returned below deck to Richard. He had maintained that he, too, was an American because of the danger should it be discovered that he was a captain of the British navy. As Richard had been at the forefront of the action while defending the *Eliza*, the carpenter's mate would surely have recognised him as a naval officer. Louisa, fearing for him, begged that he immediately 'throw himself on the honour of the Captain of the Prize'. Richard did so, and Monsieur S— told him that as a fellow naval officer, he was incapable of 'betraying him' and advised Richard to continue to claim that he was an American, or he would undoubtedly be taken as a prisoner of war.

On their way to port, Monsieur S— encouraged the passengers to come on *Eliza*'s deck to listen to the band of the escorting *L'Heureux Décidé*. At one point, unable to hear what was being played, Monsieur S— allowed his own crew to entertain them. They had begun to sing a rousing version of the 'Marseillaise' when Monsieur S— 'turned his large black eyes, which could well express either rage or gentleness, fiercely on them, exclaiming, 'If you mean to entertain the company, respect their feelings.' The crew subdued their exuberance but Louisa was so fearful of what they might do that she made a hasty retreat to the cabin. This was understandable as Monsieur S— had previously told Louisa that if the crew on board the *Eliza* had retaliated once the corsair's 'bloody flag' had been raised, they were obliged under orders, as officers, to treat their captives as pirates and 'to give no quarter, and to save no prisoners', and he added, 'you would all have been obliged to walk the gauntlet.'

Lieutenant La R—, however, appeared in the cabin and told Louisa that all was calm and entreated her to return to the deck. Louisa was then formally seated between Lieutenant La R— and the captain and both men offered assurances that they would protect her from their crew. She then rather enjoyed the crew's impromptu song about the battle, the glorious prize they had captured, and one in which the chorus paid compliments to the women on board. A sudden change in the wind then sent the passengers to the cabin as the sails were altered.

Having observed both the captain and Lieutenant La R— for a few days, Louisa and Richard suspected that they were not fanatical revolutionaries. In public, they referred to each other as citizen but when none of their party was present they called each other Monsieur. The captain told Louisa that his once noble family had been in great danger during the revolution. He had placed his wife and children in safekeeping, but she had then written him a letter under 'circumstances of peculiar distress', and it had, he implied, been intercepted by their enemies. They had survived the purge but he, too, was separated from his children. This intimate brief encounter, where both revealed to each other their heartache, sealed an unlikely friendship. Louisa had brought 'beautiful and curious' plants from South Carolina, which she now begged Monsieur S— , when the opportunity arose, to present to his wife.

On the evening of July 11th 1798, eight days after the *Eliza*'s capture, she came into the harbour of Passage on the west coast of France near the Spanish border. From the deck, the passengers marvelled at the romantic scenery, but as they did so the American flag was thrown into the sea. French colours then flew triumphantly above the English colours found on board the *Eliza*. This was as much as Louisa could bear, 'none but those who experienced it, can tell what a pang it gives the heart thus to behold the colours of their nation drooping beneath those of the enemy'.

After they docked, the ship was swamped by the French who had come to congratulate the captors on their prize, Richard told Louisa that he had heard they were to be given up to a civil power. Their situation, Louisa wrote, 'was now highly distressing, fear magnified danger'. They soon heard that officers of the *L'Heureux Décidé* were claiming that because the American *Eliza* had fought back, all on board her were to be considered pirates. Although war had not been declared between America and France, Louisa pointed out that, 'France under pretexts the most trivial and unjustifiable either stopped or captured every American vessel they fell in with.'* Captain McNeil stood his ground against what he claimed was an unwarranted attack. But even so, Louisa feared 'that either a long captivity or perhaps death awaited us'.

Amidst the mêlée, Monsieur S— as captain of the *L'Heureux Décidé*, pointed out a man to Louisa and told her to attend to what he was going to tell her. He told her she was free to go and Louisa believed this was because she was an American by birth, and could potentially become an embarrassment to her captors. She beckoned to Richard and to Bath and said to the stranger, 'this is my husband and this young woman is my attendant: they must share my freedom or I will share their captivity.' He replied that they were all free to go, but Louisa suspected he had 'exceeded his powers' as they were later told that they would remain with the other passengers.

That evening, the ship filled with yet more noisy visitors who had come to gawk at and harangue the captives. Hemmed in by the crowd and unable to retreat to their staterooms, the heat being intolerable, they sat in silence as the visitors slandered the English for their insolence and haughtiness. The mood turned, momentarily, when one of the visitors expressing sympathy to the prisoners exclaimed: 'The people are not to blame on either side; the government plays the game the people are only the counters.' This led to more heated discussions until two men decided to wager on the argument and chose Louisa to hold their stakes.

It was at this point that a terrified Louisa began to wobble on Richard's arm and Monsieur S— stepped in, and taking the money returned it to the men and added, 'It is time to break up; the ladies cannot retire to rest, while this noise continues; and that Lady,' pointing to Louisa, 'you see is very ill'. Richard was holding Louisa up as 'convulsive spasms' twitched in her arms, whereupon the assembled company gave opinions as to the best cure but they eventually withdrew. She was taken to her stateroom, which enabled her to take the 'rest so essentially necessary for my recovery'. The next morning, Louisa heard angry voices in the cabin through her stateroom walls. Richard came in and said a government official, the 'Commissary' had ordered that she go to the cabin at once.

---

* None present would have known that America had rescinded its treaties with France only a few days before on July 7th. This would lead to what became known as the Quaisi-War, fought mainly in the Caribbean and off the Atlantic coastline of the US from 1798-1800.

She protested that she was not dressed, to which he replied, 'Never mind being in your dressing gown, gather up your hair and wind it around your arm, for you must come immediately.'

With all the dignity the vain Louisa could muster, she did as her husband had ordered. As she entered the cabin, she found the commissary and several soldiers, two of which were 'holding their drawn swords over the head of our brave Captain McNeil' in an effort to force him to sign a paper. Initially, he refused and calmly made the observation, 'I am your prisoner, gentleman, respect me as such: remember I am unarmed; the statement contained in that paper, that we first fired on you, I utterly deny being true: should you compel me to sign it, I shall declare that I signed from compulsion, as you undoubtedly fired on us first, and thereby obliged me to stand on my defence.' With a sword resting on his neck, Captain McNeil was obliged to sign the paper and the other passengers were told to sign their names, ages and countries. Louisa asked the captain if it would be wise if she signed the paper, and he replied she should, 'it is but a form,' and gave her pen to ward off the 'ferocious band tumultuously assembled in the cabin' who were coming closer to her.

With the signed paper in their hands, the privateers could now claim the *Eliza* as a lawful prize. The commissary then examined the prisoners' passports, after which he announced, 'Ladies, you are at liberty to land in Spain; gentlemen you will be conducted to the other prisoners.' Louisa, clinging to Richard's arm, at once objected: 'You will not surely heighten our calamities, by separating us, grant us at least the consolation of sharing the same fate, be that fate what it may.' The captain of *L'Heureux Décidé* also appealed to the commissary, to allow them to stay together. 'I must know', replied the commissary, 'where to lay my hands upon them at a moment: will you take on that responsibility?' The captain remained silent, which prompted Louisa to exclaim, 'I pledge my word to be forthcoming, though it be to lay my head on the guillotine.'

Louisa later wrote: 'Uncouth though the commissary was, he seemed affected, and involuntarily paused, struck with the fortitude of a feeble woman, thus braving all danger, even though surrounded by armed men, whose ferocious manners and appearance might appall. There are moments in which even the most rugged feel: this was one of those moments; he surveyed me in silent astonishment, as if to feel assured that he had heard aright, that on the honor of the party I pledged my life, rather than be separated from my husband.'

The commissary agreed to allow the passengers to stay together. Louisa added that this had taken place during the Reign of Terror. It was not true, as Robespierre had been executed five years earlier, but she still believed there was the possibility they could be put to death. It was, Louisa wrote, a time when 'neither age nor sex was spared'. The commissary departed and the ship was once again under the command of the privateers, who were no doubt also relieved to see him go.

The prisoners now were surprised when Monsieur S— asked Captain McNeal to arrange a large dinner for the multitude who would board later to see the prize: 'A superb dinner was served to the numerous party who came to congratulate the captors on the richness of the prize', which was estimated to be £50,000. Richard and Louisa could only watch as the assembled company gloated over their losses, which were to them considerable. It was only when the party ended, that the prisoners were disembarked.

CHAPTER 16

Joy to Agony

*

THE prisoners were to be escorted, by officers only, from the *Eliza* to the Spanish town of St. Sebastian. The privateers came ashore as well, being wary of the French authorities. Louisa waited for her turn to leave the ship and called for the 'accommodation chair', only to be told by Captain McNeil: 'Oh for heaven's sake, make no difficulty lest it should mar our landing, but put your foot on the ledges on the side of the ship, and hold fast by the ropes, and you will reach the boat very safely, as Monsieur S is waiting to guard you down the side of the ship.' Without any more fuss, Louisa duly did as she was ordered. Two beautiful women, dressed in 'highly picturesque' national costumes, waited to row the captives to shore.

The party was kept at sea until other boats carrying the wounded from the *L'Heureux Décidé* were taken ashore, 'a mournful sight', Louisa wrote. She, however, never mentioned that Richard was amongst those wounded. During the battle, he had either been hit or his exertions had caused the old wound to his thigh to re-open, and his leg was now tightly bound.

St. Sebastian lay some three miles along the coast from where they were landed, and the gentlemen of the party were required to walk, while two horses, each with an armchair slung over either side, were brought for the ladies. Louisa and her maid, Bath, clambered onto the wobbling seats. 'The woman who led my horse, in despite of the roughness and steepness of the road, which lies at the base of the Pyrenean Mountains although barefooted, walked so fast that I lost sight of the gentlemen, who wisely kept pace with the baggage; added to which the motion shook me so severely, and I feared at times lest I should fall out of the chair on which I was seated, the declivities in some places were so abrupt; it was in vain that I either entreated or remonstrated; the woman either did not understand me, or would not attend my request to moderate her pace.' To Louisa's further alarm, a Spanish peasant suddenly sprang forward, grasped the reins and began an argument with the woman leading Louisa's horse.

The peasant then approached Louisa, gently taking her arms and placing them on the side of the chair so that she might steady herself, and brought the footrest up. The delay meant the rest of the party appeared and one of the French officers took the lead of her horse for the rest of the journey. The officer, while walking beside her, talked gaily of the 'pleasure' Louisa would have in St. Sebastian. Louisa asked if she was as free as the bird that flew above them, to which he had to admit that she was not. The motion of the horse eventually proved too much for Louisa and choosing to walk, she reached St. Sebastian 'with great difficulty, being then in a very feeble state of health'.

The party was lodged at the Hotel St Juan and that evening endured dinner with the captain of the *L'Heureux Décidé*, and the officers guarding them. Sir John Nisbett must have played some role in defending the *Eliza*, as the captain remarked that when the ships were in close contact during the action he particularly remembered seeing the baronet. The baronet was clearly on the point of discussing the engagement further when, Louisa wrote, he remembered 'in the instant how perilous a situation this put him in', as those on the *Eliza* had no justification for fighting, 'neither being a letter of marque, nor being at open war with France.'

Louisa retired to bed exhausted. She woke in the morning to see 'the windows were grated with iron bars, and the hardness of the bed caused me to observe that I had slept on straw, the heat was intolerable: I fancied myself suffocating'. In her panic, she roused Richard who was sleeping beside her and said: 'Oh Graves, they have put us in a dungeon while we slept.' Richard soothed her and told her that had they wanted to put them in a dungeon, they would have done so already.

The next day, Louisa arranged to move into a larger room that led onto a sitting room with a balcony overlooking the sea. She and the others were objects of curiosity: 'A very pretty lady with a small dog under her arm walked into the sitting room, which was allotted for our use, without the least ceremony; after surveying us for some moments, she exclaimed, as if to account for her intrusion: 'What a beautiful view of the sea you have ladies.' Louisa replied, knowing her wit would not be lost on someone who spoke such good English, 'the view has few charms for those whose stay is par force.' However, they had been fortunate that the Swedish consul, who happened to be visiting St. Sebastian, came to see them and was given the role of interpreter.

It was not only being the object of curiosity amongst the citizens of St. Sebastian that annoyed Louisa, but also the way in which her food was served to her. Her first complaint began with breakfast: 'Foreigners have no idea of the comforts of the matin meal, this struck me forcibly; for at 8 o'clock without enquiring whether I was ready or not the chica who attended us, brought in a cup of chocolate and a slice of dry toast; the gentlemen had eggs and a jug of wine in addition but no cloth laid on the table. It does not appear to be a meal that gathers the domestic circle: the chocolate for the Ladies being served them in their bed rooms; I asked for another cup; but the chica shaking her head told me that no person ever took more than one; I was therefore obliged to rest content until dinner, to which we were summoned at one o'clock.' Louisa was hungry by one o'clock and one can imagine her dismay when she saw on the table a tureen of soup. To her further dismay after this was removed a 'large dish of white cabbage, chopped up with pepper, vinegar, oil, and salt, and another dish with a very small bit of coarse beef, without an atom of fat, to supply which there was a very small piece of bacon without an atom of lean to it'. Louisa complained to the maid that she had not 'half dined'. The maid ignored her protestations but soon returned with 'roast meats, poultry and made dishes of great variety exquisitely relished'. More was to follow, 'the fourth course consisted of a variety of pastry, and creams and the fifth of dried fruits, nuts and cakes, and sweetmeats wet and dry; with the two first courses they gave us small wine of the country, with the third claret, with the fourth malaga and with the fifth liqueurs'. Supper, served at 10 o'clock in the evening, was a similar feast of three courses.

Louisa's fellow captives now wanted to escape, but Louisa protested that the only reason some of them had been allowed off the *Eliza* was her pledge to the commissary and the captain of the *L'Heureux Décidé*, 'and they could not therefore in honor endanger me by making the attempt.'

The captive's uncertain fate darkened when, on Sunday morning, a French soldier arrived and summoned them to appear before the commissary in the offices of the viceroy. Louisa kept everybody waiting; her long hair had to be brushed, coiled and pinned. The soldier began to lose his patience and told her she must follow them when dressed. Again, Louisa pleaded: 'I will not be parted from my husband, we will go together, do not leave me Graves, we shall never meet again if you do.' She refused to let go of Richard's arm, even though the others urged them to hurry. But Louisa was adamant, and the group left without them.

Captain McNeil, who had left with the group, then bribed one of the guards to be allowed to return to the hotel to collect some shirts. The

French soldier guarding the hotel believed that by remaining at the head of the staircase, McNeil would be secured. But McNeil had opened the door of the first room he came to and slipped inside. The soldier, soon bored of waiting, walked along the passage and entered the Graves' sitting room. McNeil then ran down the staircase and out of the hotel. The soldier asked Richard where the captain was, to which he replied: 'How should I know, he is not in my charge.' After searching the hotel, the soldier returned, 'his fury unbounded, he rushed in to the room where we were sitting with his sword drawn and stamping his foot, shook his sword over the head of the mate of the *Eliza*, addressing him thus: "I order you in the name of the Revolutionary Tribunal of France to follow me.".'

Captain McNeil later returned and took refuge in Louisa and Richard's rooms. After the rest of the party had returned from the interview with the commissary, Lieutenant La R—, whom they had not seen since they arrived in St. Sebastian, came to give them an urgent message from the captain of *L'Heureux Décidé*, Monsieur S—. The captain strongly advised the captives to escape. The commissary, he said, had written to Paris to obtain the necessary powers to take the party to French Bayonne, where they would likely be imprisoned until the end of the war. Although they were the captain's prisoners, the *Eliza* had legally been handed over to him as his prize, and he had no further wish to detain them. Louisa wrote that she now 'no longer objected to make the attempt, which our party had so often urged in vain; now I felt myself exonerated from my promise by the Captain of the Corsair'.

On the advice of the Swedish consul, Louisa pretended to the officers that her ill-health would currently prevent any of the party from escaping. The next day, the gentlemen all left the hotel in different directions on the pretext of visiting the local sights but later met to make arrangements to escape. Louisa, hiding Captain McNeil in her rooms, was left to fend off any inquiries as to where the men were. She soon heard two French officers asking the maid where the gentlemen were and, with her long hair unbound and a comb in her hand, she opened her bedroom door to them. She told them that the men were probably visiting the churches, to which the officer replied he could not think of a better occupation than praying for the 'welfare of the Republique Francaise'. To avoid further conversation, Louisa gathered up her hair and appeared occupied in arranging it so the officers eventually left to allow her to 'finish her toilette'.

The following morning before daybreak, Captain McNeil along with Sir John Nisbett left St. Sebastian for Madrid. The rest of the party were not to leave until the next day and had to attend a long supper with the French officers. Louisa eventually complained 'of indisposition' and withdrew to her rooms, where she hastily packed her bags. All the officers left, except one who remained in the hotel to sleep on a camp bed in the passage outside Louisa and Richard's rooms. That night with 'a light step and palpitating heart', they crept past the officer and out of the hotel. The Swedish consul was waiting to bid them farewell as they climbed into their coaches. The party did not stop until they were 'far beyond the dreaded pass, about six miles from St. Sebastian'.

After clearing the pass, they travelled on for another ten miles to Toloso, where Louisa wrote, 'Our felicity may be better imagined than described when we found ourselves safely arrived at a miserable Posada.' There, they met with two other equally delighted travellers, an Englishman and a French priest, who had escaped from France across the Pyrenees. They suggested they dine together, as they were 'all rejoicing the same cause'. The maid had not put out a spoon and fork for Louisa, and as her soup was served Louisa asked for a spoon, at which the Priest looked astonished, 'which was again evident when I called for a fork, and also when I spoke.' Louisa thought his conduct very strange, 'but forbore noticing it.' Immediately after they had eaten, Richard, still unwell, retired for a siesta. After he left, the priest took Richard's chair and sitting by Louisa exclaimed in French, 'you are an American', to which Louisa replied she was; he continued, 'but you talk like us, you eat like us'. 'Mon Dieu', Louisa exclaimed, asking if he thought all Americans were savages. He replied that he had, but that now he had seen otherwise. Louisa wrote, 'I at once saw the error into which the Priest had fallen; but time was then too precious to permit me to set him right; I therefore rose to take a siesta, leaving the Priest at more leisure to learn the distinction between the Indians and the European settlers in America.'

The party, now joined by a fleeing Irish priest, Father Gough, headed for Madrid, and the journey took them through Vitoria. Despite the danger,` Louisa was much taken with what she saw and wrote: 'The roads are, in some places, over mountains, which rise above the clouds, never having before been in so elevated a region, I was forcibly struck with the wilderness of the mountain scenery, the stupendous works of nature awfully sublime; the sun arose in a clear blue sky over our heads, and the clouds rolled like a thick mist beneath our feet, veiling the base of the mountain from our view; as we descended to the region where the clouds floated, we found our breathing affected, till we had passed through it, when again we were cheered by the brilliant beams of the sun which had been obscured by the dense atmosphere of the clouds.' At Pont du Corbeau, they crossed a natural bridge of stone, which ran from mountain to mountain, across a deep narrow valley, which Louisa wrote 'was truly terrific'. They were so appalled at the danger of crossing in their carriage that they climbed out and walked over the bridge; 'on looking down the head turned giddy'. Ahead, lay the city of Vittoria, where they saw the 'remains of a magnificent aquaduct in ruins.'

From Vittoria they travelled to Madrid along the royal roads, where there were 'stone seats by fountains of clear water, gushing into stone troughs, for the refreshment of both man and beast'. During the journey, Richard had lamented greatly the loss of their valuable cargo, and that the journey home would involve him in much expense. On hearing this, the *Eliza*'s surgeon said, 'but to you, it will only be an expense, to me it will be ruin, for the sum the journey will cost me would have enabled me to have established myself in America with my family, where I had good prospects, which I must now relinquish.' He added that he would have to leave Madrid for England on foot after selling all his clothes, 'except what I can carry on my shoulders in a bundle'. Louisa begged Richard to help the surgeon, to which Richard, who was ever charitable, readily agreed even though he could ill afford another expense.

On their arrival in Madrid, they found themselves in the midst of the funeral procession of the Infanta Maria Amalia of Spain. To their alarm an embargo was placed on their coaches and mules but they later learnt this was because the Spanish court were leaving Madrid for their palace in Aranjuez, and the roads had be kept clear until the Royal party had left the city.

Captain McNeil had also arrived safely in Madrid, two days before Richard and Louisa's party. He had been to see the American Consul, Moses Young, to protest about the taking of his ship and subsequent imprisonment. McNeil then sought refuge in the palace of the viceroy, the Duke of Santa Fe, in charge of Spain's colonies in America. The 'Vice-Queen', Louisa learnt from McNeil, had exerted all her influence on the viceroy to obtain his protection for them which, although of little use against the French, would shield them from the Spanish. Louisa referred to the 'Vice-Queen' rather condescendingly as an 'amiable lady', and her story was one that Louisa could not omit relating. 'This lady', she wrote 'was a native of France and of very high rank, who had bitterly experienced the horrors of the Revolution and had escaped almost miraculously once from off the guillotine, where she had been conducted with many others for execution. The dreadful scene before her, as her fate approached gave energy to despair, she leapt from the platform amidst the populace, who gave way either from compassion or surprise, and she escaped to a vineyard, where she lay concealed by the foliage [for] three days, sustaining herself on the grapes, when she was discovered.' The Vice-Queen was once again taken back to prison and condemned to death. But a friend managed to smuggle two pistols to her and, later that evening, she threatened her two guards and made her escape. Concealing herself by day, and travelling by night over the Pyrenean Mountains to St Sebastian, the 'beautiful young woman of eighteen' then threw herself on the mercy of the viceroy, who, according to Louisa, subsequently married her.

Louisa and Richard took lodgings in the Hotel de Santa Crux where they posed as Americans. There was now no sign of Louisa's character traits that had so antagonised her Devon neighbours. She sparkled in the new company, her ailments forgotten, and people all but queued for the opportunity of meeting her. Their hotel was near the residence of the American Consul, 'Whose lady,' Louisa wrote, 'paid me every attention, always calling on me after the siesta to take me to the Prado in her carriage,' which she noted was 'celebrated as the finest thing of the kind in Europe', and at which there were often a thousand carriages. One traveller wrote of the spectacle: 'What vivacity! what art! what a struggle to attract attention, to bow to one another, to be observed, and to make mutual signs! Young girls with their duennas, belles with their *cortejos*, old dukes with their *conssesors*, nurses with children, priests with pampered faces, officers full of impudence, old mummies of duchesses, and young children playing. A moving picture... dragoons on their horses.' This took place from the botanic garden to the other end of the Prado and it was only at twilight, when the Angelus was rung, that 'the whole company become as fixed as statues, and every carriage stops.' Only at dark did the people retire.

Richard and Louisa would always spend the evening with the American Consul and his wife, where Louisa became an attraction for many visitors 'as they had heard of the extraordinary length of my hair'. Guests at the Consulate, having paid their compliments to the Consul's wife, approached Louisa and addressing her 'in French, Spanish or Italian and when they found they were not understood bowed and with the utmost politeness, took the comb out of my hair which they shook around me in order to gratify their curiosity'. One can understand their curiosity when Louisa describes the appearance of her hair, 'it was above seven feet long English measure, and so thick that when shook round me, I was completely concealed as if wrapped in a mantle: the colour of my hair was black auburn and very fine, with a slight wave in it.' It was then left to Richard, or the Consul's wife, to sweep her hair into a Grecian coil and pin it up again.

The next day, the Consul's wife took Louisa to one side and begged her to warn Richard 'to be more guarded in his expressions' as one of the gentlemen at a gathering had remarked after Richard and Louisa had gone back to their hotel: 'They must be English.' On seeing some children pass by, Richard had been overheard to say how differently they dressed to children in England, and he had also been heard addressing someone by their title, a practice obsolete in America since the Revolution. The Consul's wife had covered for Richard but warned him that should anyone believe him to be English, the French ambassador might demand him as a prisoner. The Spanish would then be unable to prevent handing him over.

Richard and Louisa could not yet leave Madrid because their coaches and mules were still being held by the Spanish authorities. However, the surgeon had told Father Gough of the Graves' generosity towards him, who, as Louisa wrote, 'Determined to exert all his influence to reward my benevolence.' Father Gough made a plea to the mayor of Madrid that their property be released, but this was refused. The priest asked him, 'Would not your conscience reproach you, if this lady who is so ill as to have her physician travel in her coach with her, should die without seeing the five children she left in England?' As a result of his efforts, the coaches and mules were duly released and Louisa and Richard 'lost no time, as we feared the French ambassador might demand us as prisoners of France, should an account of our escape from St Sebastian reach Madrid before we left; we therefore resumed our journey by the dawn of day'. The Portuguese ambassador had given them passports allowing them to travel to Lisbon, where they arrived after a journey of more than 350 miles 'without incurring any discomfiture, but what was incident to travelling in such a country'.

At the beginning of August 1798, Tom Graves was worried about Richard and Louisa, as ships leaving Charleston after the *Eliza* had reached England. He was relieved when Richard managed to send word from Lisbon that they were endeavouring to find a ship to bring them home. The children were told of their parents' dramatic adventures, and Tom hoped 'Sam and his sisters bear the news of their Father & Mother's capture without much disappointment'. In fact, they were delighted, as their parents would be home much sooner than expected.

From Lisbon, the Graveses were able to take a packet to Falmouth. The passage, Louisa wrote was 'long and stormy, having contrary winds. The captain remarked that he feared we would be driven into Cork, which greatly alarmed us'. News of a rebellion and violence in Ireland had reached them and the coast abounded with French vessels. Louisa and Richard were so nervous that when they saw a small vessel, which they discovered hailed from Ilfracombe on the North Devon Coast, they transferred from the packet. 'We narrowly escaped terminating our voyage by being wrecked on that rugged coast: our little bark at one time mounted on a billow, at another sunk in a hollow between the waves; at length we weathered the storm and safely landed at the port of Ilfracombe, about sunrise, and joyfully made our way to the George Inn.'

They had been away from home for nearly eight months. To Louisa's delight, she was at last able to enjoy an English breakfast, and as it would be some time before a coach arrived to take them home, they ordered the finest dinner the George Inn could serve that evening. 'On the following day, being Sunday, 22nd August, I arrived in Exeter, when I folded you, my dear children, to my heart, when the feelings of a mother were overwhelmed by joy even to agony.'

CHAPTER 17

Dark Scene

*

ON arrival at Hembury Fort, Richard at once sent what he considered to be valuable intelligence to Lord Spencer, the First Lord of the Admiralty. The Anglo-Spanish War had entered its second year, and whilst in Madrid, he had learnt that a Spanish convoy of nineteen ships, escorted by three frigates, was shortly due in Europe. One of these frigates, 'a very fast sailor', had on board treasure for the Crown. Moreover, additional Spanish frigates and an eighty-gun ship, carrying 34 million dollars between them, had recently arrived at Vigo on the north-west coast of Spain. Richard must have hoped that this intelligence would help mend bridges with the Admiralty. Instead, to his consternation, he received only a very brief reply of thanks from the First Lord.

Louisa was, meanwhile, excitedly packing for their move to Exeter; she would, aged thirty-five, at last be mistress of her own house. Within two weeks of landing, she had opened the door to the family's newly built terraced house in Southernhay, designed by the speculative builder and architect, Matthew Nosworthy. The four-storey red-brick building, with all the latest conveniences, had views over gardens planted with elm trees, and to meadows beyond; yet it was but a short walk to the Cathedral.

Richard's old wound, which had broken open again some four months earlier during the battle with the privateer, had still not healed. Indeed, it was showing every sign of worsening and was now giving him such pain that he agreed, finally, for it to be operated on. Fortunately, there was an extremely capable surgeon at the newly opened Devon and Exeter Hospital in Southernhay, and his brother John held him down as the surgeon set to work.

The operation was successful and it was during his convalescence that Richard received an unexpected letter from Monsieur S——, captain of *L'Heureux Décidé*. To Richard's utter astonishment, the captain was languishing in a Portsmouth jail. The *L'Heureux Décidé* had been captured by one of the great heroes of the wars against the French, Captain Sir Edward Pellew, who had proudly informed the admiralty that she was a 'very handsome ship, coppered and perfectly new, and in every respect fit for His Majesty's service'. The crew had been sent to England and imprisoned.

Monsieur S— wrote that the day after Louisa and Richard escaped from St. Sebastian, the commissary received an order from Paris to take all the passengers and crew of the *Eliza* under armed guard to Bayonne. Louisa wrote: 'Such a journey with such guides, in a time of such ferocity would indeed have been dreadful.' Richard at once sent funds to Monsieur S— to alleviate the hardships of a long winter in jail. Louisa commented: 'We felt happy to shew we were not un-mindful of the attentions we had received when it was our fate to be his prisoners.' Richard made endless appeals to the authorities on Monsieur S—'s behalf, and managed to secure his freedom. The Frenchman returned to the South of France, where Louisa hoped her present of the parcel of plants, which she had given him on board the *Eliza*, would flourish in his garden.

Tom and Richard Graves again sought employment in the navy. Tom had been forcefully told in a previous interview with the Admiralty that he would not be given a command because of his republican principles. Nevertheless, in September 1799, he was given command of HMS *Cumberland*, a third-rate ship of the line forming part of the Channel fleet. On hearing of this, Richard wrote the Admiralty: 'I have repeatedly, as my letters to the board will testify, made tender my service, and I know no professional reasons why I should not have taken my chance for service with the officers that have been employed during this war. In justice to myself I must say that my conduct during the last war entitled me to some notice of this, and I hope their Lordships will excuse my saying that I feel myself a little hardly used.' The Admiralty never doubted the ability or bravery of the Graves brothers, but Richard's detractors triumphed, and ensured he remained on land.

Louisa, having settled her family in Southernhay, turned her attention back to the Bahamas. She wrote to the Duke of Portland, then Home Secretary and also responsible for the West Indies, 'for the purpose of obtaining from him some of the lands that had not then been appropriated since the occupation of her Property by the Crown.' This was not an unreasonable request; the government had parcelled out much of the land she owned in her own name, without compensation. The duke did not personally answer Louisa's letter, but she did receive a reply from his secretary who told her that the duke refused to see her 'lest he might have his feelings worked upon by the entreaties of an eloquent female'. Perhaps because she was expecting her eighth child, Louisa did not have the inclination or strength to pursue the matter at the time.

The Graveses' fortunes changed in February 1800, thirteen years after the death of Admiral Samuel, when Mrs Admiral relented and formally handed over to Richard part of her late husband's Devon estates, and the income that came with them. This included Hembury Fort, a thousand acres surrounding the house, and Hawkerland, an estate of a thousand acres some thirteen miles away, both of which it has to be said, Mrs Admiral was entitled to keep until her death. After the christening of the Graveses' seventh daughter, Olivia Septima, on March 30th, Louisa, who had always loathed Hembury Fort, decided to rebuild it.

At considerable expense, she would transform the dilapidated house into a 'Capital Mansion'. Under the direction, it is thought, of Matthew Nosworthy, walls were knocked down and the house extended to include a salon measuring forty by twenty-four feet. On the other side of the entrance hall, there were two drawing rooms, a library and a billiards room. Louisa employed skilled carpenters to make heavy mahogany doors, and ironmongers to fashion elaborate handles for them: great lumps of marble were carved into delicate over mantles. Artisans painted the ceilings with clouds and furnished the rooms with rococo plasterwork. At the back of the house were 'water closets', larders, and servants' quarters.

A handsome new circular staircase led to the first floor where there were eleven 'superior chambers', each with their own dressing room: a large nursery and a 'Lady's sitting room', from where Louisa could see the sea. She took advantage of the latest innovations and installed a bath supplied with hot and cold water from a boiler below, and added more 'water closets'. On the top floor were a further ten bedrooms with large built-in cupboards, most of which were needed for her ever-increasing family.

Outside, behind the house in an enclosed yard, was a new dairy, a cold store for cheese, hot houses for melons and grapes, a brewery, a larder, a bakehouse and oven, a wood house, a coal house, laundry and drying rooms. There was stabling for eight horses, and sufficient room to house four carriages. When the house was finally finished, Louisa would almost be able to outdo the Simcoes at Wolford Lodge, where on reception days 'the drawing room was filled with well-dressed men and women'.

While Hembury Fort was being transformed, Richard and Louisa remained in Exeter. On one of their summer evening strolls there, they passed the new jail, built on the plans of Mr Howard whose 'intention it was, that punishment should effect the reformation of the criminal'. Richard suggested that they have a look inside. The large building was, Louisa wrote, 'well adapted to the melancholy purposes to which its apartments are appropriated'. The jailer's wife had the 'honour' of showing visitors around and asked the Graveses if they would like to see the 'prisoner under sentence of death, in the condemned cell'. Louisa replied that she most certainly would not. The jailer's wife retorted that she showed him to everyone: he was an American officer who had killed an English officer in a duel. Louisa realised that she had been present during part of his trial, at which everyone had believed the American to be innocent.

Louisa asked the jailer's wife if the American would receive her, and was consequently shown to his cell, where there was a trapdoor in the floor. Louisa wrote that he 'rose on our entrance and walked towards the window, as if to avoid gaze of impertinent and unfeeling curiosity to which he had no doubt often been exposed. To relieve him of this idea, I hastily stept up to him and addressing him, told him I was his countrywoman'. Louisa politely said that she had only intruded upon him because she wanted to offer help and that she was by chance travelling to London the next day. She proposed to take his case to the American Minister, and this she subsequently did. The Minister told Louisa that he would 'request his life as a matter of favour'.

Two weeks later, Louisa was back in Exeter. 'One morning,' she wrote, 'the library door was suddenly thrown open, and an officer in uniform entered,' whom she recognised as the American whom she had met in the jail: 'Oh, Madam,' he exclaimed, 'I am come to thank you not only for life, but for more than life: for liberty; I shall immediately return to America, to relieve the anxiety of my wife and children, who will join me in thanking you and in praying for you.' He had good reason to be thankful. For eleven months he had languished under the sentence of death, expecting at any moment to be executed.

It was soon after this that Louisa received a letter from a man who, curiously, she did not name in her memoirs. It requested she visit him as a matter of urgency. This she did, travelling to London, where she found an elderly man on his deathbed. For years, he told her, he had felt guilty about an act of deception to which he had been a part. Now, with death approaching, he wanted to clear his conscience.

As Louisa sat by his bedside, the old man told her that he had been employed by Messrs Chamberlayne and White, the Treasury Solicitors. He had been asked to obtain a deed pertaining to the ownership of the Sovereign Rights to the Bahamas, which was believed to be in the possession of Mrs Fulford. Initially, he had written to Mrs Fulford to ask her for the document, but he said: 'Mrs Fulford refused to give it up, alleging, that she had been advised not to part with it, at length after a month's discussion, they requested her to bring it merely for them to look at it, "and then, said he, I got hold of it, and would not give it up again:" Oh! what a piece of work she made, and how she cried, exclaiming, what could she say to her niece? Oh! she could never again see Miss Colleton again without the deed'!'

Louisa listened, with profound attention, to the man's every word and asked him how the business had concluded. The deed, he replied, 'was sent to Mr Pitt who was glad enough to get it, for he said it was the only thing that could give them a title to the Islands'. The elderly man then faltered, and said he was bound not to give Louisa any information on the subject, 'but as I was not restricted respecting any other person, if I am called before the House of Commons I will give the whole particulars'. He was then overcome with fatigue, and Louisa waited patiently until he regained enough strength to continue. Sometime, he said, after the Prime Minister had taken the deed, he prevailed on Pitt's housekeeper to take a copy. Then, dramatically, he reached into a box by his bedside and fished out a copy of the very document, tied together by a pink ribbon, and handed it to Louisa.

Louisa untied the ribbon and began to read, and as she did so it dawned on her that what she held in her hand was a paper that documented the purchase by her great-grandfather, the 3rd Colleton baronet, of the Sovereign Rights over the Bahamas from his fellow Lords Proprietors in 1729. Louisa believed it to be a copy of the very document that her great-grandfather had deposited in the Bahamas, to 'prove his title to the whole' and which was then taken by the British Government when they took possession of the islands. She remembered that her distinguished neighbour, Judge Buller, had seen a paper in one of the public offices, which should not have been there as it belonged to her, and that he had told Louisa that he would send it to Mrs Fulford for safekeeping. This he had subsequently done.

If only, Louisa later wrote, her aunt had had the courage to tell her about the deed being snatched from her hands in 1787, she would have had a far better chance of reclaiming it while all the parties concerned were living. The old man rustled around on his bed for another paper, on which he had written for Louisa a memorandum which would explain her family's involvement in the Bahamas over the years. Once again, Louisa bent her head and began to read.

It appeared that the first attempt by the British Government to buy the islands had occurred when the 3rd baronet, Sir John, was still a minor and this was thwarted by his guardian, William Thornburgh. During Queen Anne's reign a similar attempt was again made. The 3rd baronet was then of age, 'and threats were used on the occasion, which giving the public much dissatisfaction, government abandoned the measure after having incurred great censure for the attempt.' Subsequently, in the reign of King George I, a third attempt was made to persuade the Proprietors to give up the islands. All the Proprietors agreed to do so with the exception of Sir John who told the King 'he wanted them for himself'. The memorandum continued, 'after much contention, parliament inter-fered, and the king gave up the point'. It was no wonder that Sir John wanted the islands for himself. Amongst other deals there, he had, before he bought the Sovereign Rights to the islands, sold to a group of mer-chants in Nassau a piece of ground 'for the company to build on', and three thousand acres around it. These merchants were acolytes of the South Sea Company which was to go spectacularly bust in 1720.

At the time of the old man's revelation, Louisa could only hope that there was another copy of the deed in the Bahamas. She employed an agent, Robert Wood, to search the records. On hearing of this, the British government sent word to the government in the Bahamas, to prevent such a search. When they discovered that the Collector of Customs had been helping Wood, the Collector was duly dismissed from his post. Wood then employed a Liverpool merchant, who travelled to and from the Bahamas, to try to gain access to government papers, but after 'an ex-pense of upwards of four thousand pounds', much of which had presum-ably been spent on bribes, Wood 'failed in his pursuit'.

Later, Louisa wrote: 'Mr Pitt took great pains to place these Islands in the hands of the Crown, in which he was successful; but the means used to obtain them do him no credit and are also illegal.' She believed, how-ever, that it was not only the case that the Crown needed land to settle loyalists, but that their great inducement was salvaging wrecks which, Louisa claimed, in the last twenty-five years had produced 'near one million of money, which is in justice the right of Mrs Graves, formerly Miss Colleton.' The value of the timber, Louisa added, 'is beyond calculation, and is in itself an object of the utmost *importance*.'

'I appeal to the world,' she wrote, 'whether an Orphan, young and friendless as I was then, could resist a powerful government resolved to wrest her property from her: could I at this time do otherwise than bow beneath the blast that blighted me...'

CHAPTER 18

Upon Velvet

*

LOUISA would later write of Richard, that he was 'in his house, ever hospitable, polite and attentive to all'. But the same could not be said of Louisa when her house in Southernhay became a refuge for Richard's 'worthless' nephews, the sons of his younger sister Jane. They had left Ireland to join the navy, and relied not only on the patronage of their uncles but also on their purses. The eldest of Jane's sons, Adam Averell, had been in jail for debt, and in 1794 had been in danger of losing his commission. His younger brother, Sam, had been imprisoned in the West Indies, spending a month sleeping on bare earth. Subsequently, he suffered more at the hands of his elder brother, Adam, than at those of the Royal Navy. The 'inhuman' Adam, had, according to John Graves in a letter to his sister Catherine, 'bound him to the Master of Transport, where he was kicked about at the crew's pleasure'. This suggests that Sam was sexually exploited by the crew whilst on board ship. John continued: 'After a voyage to Russia and suffering in a prison there on his return to England he ran from the ship.' Sam had fled to their cousin, George Graves, in London. George fed and clothed him, but to rid himself of the lad he paid for Sam to travel to Exeter, where he had found John Graves at Barley House in August 1800.

Wishing Richard to share the burden, John Graves took Sam to Richard and Louisa's house in Southernhay, where John wrote that Adam Averell was 'daily entertained at our Brother Richard's table'. Richard was not at home when John and Sam arrived, but they were shown into the drawing room, whereupon Adam was horrified to see his younger brother. Louisa, who heartily disliked Sam, was also not pleased to see him. Adam at once set to, with Louisa, according to John, encouraging Adam in his 'ill treatment' of his brother.

John Graves wrote that he then proceeded to have 'smart altercation' with Louisa, 'who behaved in the most insulting manner. Rated us all over at a fine rate. Said our father had sent us over from Ireland without any education; that her husband was pennyless when she married him, and that it was her house etc. I bid Sam follow me and told her it should be the last time I would ever set my foot in within her doors or any of mine, which resolution I shall firmly adhere to.' John Graves was so incensed at Louisa's behaviour that he could barely finish a sentence coherently. Louisa, it can be surmised, never again would set foot in one of his houses, nor would he ever again set foot in any of hers. On reflection, Louisa may secretly have been thankful. Although she was, in essence, fond of John Graves, the same could not be said of his notably unpleasant wife, Elizabeth. John had had to put his daughter, Mary, when very young, into a boarding school, 'fearing her health and disposition might be entirely ruined by her mother's inaccountable temper.'

Louisa may have spoken in anger, but it must have cut deep that the house in Southernhay was hers, not her husband's, and that he and his brothers had had little education. Richard's uncle, Admiral Samuel, had complained to his brother, the Reverend John Graves: 'One thing I have wondered at is that so sensible a man as you are in most things should give your sons so paltry an education. What have they not to struggle with by that means? You have much to answer for.' The Reverend Graves did not take much notice of the missive from his brother. He had sent his sons, Sam, John and Tom off to sea at the age of ten or thereabouts. Of the brothers, only Tom had attended an academy, and briefly at that. Admiral Samuel later berated his brother for allowing his remaining sons 'to hang about on their mother's lap until they were fourteen or fifteen, and treated as children.' Richard, indeed, did not leave his mother's lap until the age of fifteen, and whilst a lack of education appeared not to have hampered his naval career, Louisa had possibly come to tire of a man who never read a book.

She now had to suffer Richard's frustration and anger at repeatedly, and brusquely, being rejected for employment by the Admiralty. At the end of 1800, Lord Spencer advised the king that Richard was one of five Captains who should not be promoted to flag rank because they had not been employed 'either on shore or afloat' for a considerable amount of time. This would have been a major break with custom but the king seems to have taken Lord Spencer's advice because when the new list was published on January 4th 1801, Richard found to his fury that he had not been promoted to flag rank as he considered was his right.

That evening he wrote to Evan Nepean: 'Sir, Having seen in the Gazette last night the list of officers promoted to their flags, I have to request you will be pleased to represent to the Lords Commissioners of the Admiralty my very great concern & astonishment at not perceiving my own name among the number. – That this has happened from inattention I cannot persuade myself, - & I am equally at a loss to assign any reason for so marked a disgrace. – I have ever looked forward to my flag as the reward for long & faithful services, - as well as the satisfaction of every flag officer I have served with, - & I have been unremitted from the commencement of the present war to the hour of the promotion – & yet I have unfortunately never been able to procure employment.' Richard demanded of the Admiralty whether it was his character as a 'sea officer' that had caused him to be overlooked.

On the day Richard wrote this letter, the Cabinet, fearful that the Baltic powers would ally with France against them, ordered the fleet to seize all their ships, at sea or in harbour. In late February, and at Admiral Horatio Nelson's specific request that Tom should join the fleet, Tom left London and raised his flag on the *Defiance*, which he found in a 'deplorable' state but hoped the ship's company would sort her out. Richard, meanwhile, pressed the Prince Regent with a short, printed rendition of his virtues as a naval officer, and appealed for reinstatement as an active officer.

The situation was made more intolerable for Richard, when only a few months later, on April 1st, his brother Tom, alongside his good friend and the nation's hero, Admiral Nelson, covered themselves in glory at the Battle of Copenhagen. After reports of his brother's heroics reached England Richard again wrote to the Admiralty stating his case. Earl St Vincent had by then replaced Lord Spencer, or 'that blockhead' as Tom had once referred to him, as First Lord of the Admiralty. Tom was a 'great favourite' of Earl St Vincent, and on this occasion, the First Lord seemed to side with Richard. On April 23rd, he wrote to Earl Spencer saying that he thought Richard had 'exerted every possible endeavour, publicly and privately, to obtain employment, and therefore no blame can fairly be attributed to him for his not having been called into service'. It therefore only remained for Earl Spencer to discover if it was indeed Richard's character 'that appeared to render it improper to include him' in the promotion of flag officers.

John Graves had written to his sister, Catherine, with news of the Battle of Copenhagen and wrote that Tom was to be made a Knight of the Bath. He continued: 'The Dowager Mrs Graves is like old oak. Still lives in Bath and enjoys herself. Richard has made great alterations to Hembury Fort. I believe they are soon going there to reside.' He then wrote unflatteringly of Louisa, who was clearly in her element: 'His wife is a true votary of pleasure – at the play every night – gives balls and frequently Masquerades. She and her husband was lately at a Masquerade given by Earl St.Vincent and they represented the characters of [sadly, this is indecipherable]. She was superbly draped in white satin, ornamented with a number of diamonds, and a fine skin of some animal around her shoulders, which reached her middle. They say it cost ninety guineas.' John's animosity towards Louisa was still evident, as he added of his sister-in-law: 'How her delicate nerves can bear the hurry of such entertainments is astonishing for even loud talking in her own house makes her clap her fingers in her ears. This disgusting trick has given offence to many.'

Some six weeks after the Battle of Copenhagen, Tom knelt on a velvet cushion belonging to Nelson's mistress, Lady Hamilton, whilst Nelson, now a Viscount, acting on behalf of the king, knighted his old friend on the quarterdeck of the *St George*, with all the captains of the squadron in full-dress uniform and a guard of marines in attendance. The newly knighted Sir Thomas Graves had let St Vincent know that he wanted nothing more than for his brothers to be promoted, and not long after his masquerade, St Vincent wrote a letter to Richard on the subject of his promotion. It was perhaps with the image of Louisa dressed in clinging white satin and festooned in fur and diamonds uppermost in his mind: 'Now Graves, you are upon velvet, and you make yourself easy; for we passed your Memorial yesterday at the Council, and nothing remains but forms of office to give it effect, which forms shall be gone through as fast as possible.'

A few days later, Richard called into the Admiralty but instead of receiving a formal assurance of promotion, he was requested to make a list of every ship in which he had served. The Admiralty claimed that two months in his service as lieutenant could not be accounted for, hence he was not eligible for promotion. Tom, later discovered that it was 'some malignant fiend' who had informed the Admiralty of the discrepancy.

While the matter of Richard's promotion festered, both of Louisa's half-brothers had died. It had been fourteen years since Richard had indentured William Colleton Mutter for seven years to learn the art of making breeches. William, at his death that summer, was not yet thirty years old. He died intestate, suggesting that his death was sudden, or that he believed that he had nothing to leave in a will. However, the news of the death of this 'gentleman' had reached Charleston. On July 23rd 1801,

Othniel Giles's son successfully applied for administration over the goods and chattels of his stepbrother. William's estate amounted to $2,521, and this was perhaps money that his mother, Jane, had managed to leave him, but of which he appears to have been unaware. Presumably, Louisa was also unaware of these assets, otherwise, she or William's brother, Sir John Snell, would have been able to make a superior claim. In late July 1801, Sir John Snell, aged twenty-seven, was carried off his ship in Weymouth and died onshore. Often mentioned in dispatches, he had been captured by the French but released in July 1796 in an exchange of prisoners. At his death, perhaps of tuberculosis, to which the family were vulnerable, Sir John Snell had reached the rank of commander, only one below that of post captain.

Louisa's father had stated bluntly in his will that John Snell and William Mutter were not his sons, but Louisa must have doubted this as she had, ever since rescuing them in South Carolina, treated them as though they were her half-brothers by blood. She had ensured that Sir John received a suitable education, and Richard had used what influence he had to gain him employment as a midshipman. They also had happily entertained him at Hembury Fort whenever he was on leave. Was Louisa then surprised when he had repaid her by trying to overturn her father's will? Or, when he tried, with mixed success, to alienate property from her estate to his? They certainly became estranged as a result, but it is hard not to have some sympathy for Sir John Snell, who, assuming he was his father's son, was unjustly disinherited through no fault of his own.

Sir John Snell's will was to be a parting shot. In the first lines, he gave Louisa further reason not to mourn his death. He left her the sum of one shilling, and the same to James Nassau Colleton, heir to the baronetcy. Unlike his father, Sir John Snell did not pass comment on the reasons for his insultingly paltry bequests, but they ensured that neither Louisa nor Sir James Nassau could contest the will. Sir John left the remainder of his estate to his 'dear and beloved wife Martha', whom he had only very recently married. Little is known of Martha except that she excelled at needlework and the press would note a few years later that she had made exquisite gifts for the Royal family. She was not left as much as she might have been. Shortly after Sir John's death, Louisa took the opportunity to retrieve some of her property. This included taking back possession of 21, Threadneedle Street, which stood in the heart of the city of London, near the Bank of England.

The following year, on March 25th 1802, Joseph Bonaparte and Lord Cornwallis signed the Treaty of Amiens, which brokered a temporary peace between France and Britain. And, now that the building works at Hembury Fort were completed Louisa turned herself to a far more ambitious project. She and Matthew Nosworthy drew up plans for a grand crescent to be built on her land known as the Friars. The bluff overlooking the River Exe had been settled in the 13th century by the monastic order of the Grey Friars – hence its name. Alexander Jenkins, the Exeter historian, wrote: 'On this site they founded a sumptuous house and church, with large orchards and gardens.' He added the choice of this place confirms the old adage 'that wherever there was a good prospect or a pleasant spot of land, a Friar was sure to be found'. The Friars' house, church and orchards had long disappeared, but the situation had not altered.

Alexander Jenkins noted that on September 3rd 1802: 'The first stone of these buildings was laid by Mrs. Graves (wife of the present and daughter of the late proprietor.) When it is finished it will be an ornament to the city.' Jenkins was either not present when Louisa laid the foundation stone, or felt it unnecessary to describe the wonderfully theatrical scene that day. Louisa, however,did so:

'I laid the foundation stone of the centre house of Colleton Crescent on the 3rd September 1802. The ceremony,' she wrote, 'was 'carried out amidst a concourse of spectators: General Simcoe, who was then General of the Western District, handed me down the platform, where the architect with the plan, and the master mason with his attendants and implements for building, awaited me. The band of the Inniskillin Regiment of Horse, attended on the occasion, ready to strike up 'God Save the King' the moment I appeared, which they continued playing till I drew off my glove and laid my hand on the stone, the signal for the music to cease. While I addressed the architect, after having laid the foundation stone, under which was deposited a box, containing coins of gold, silver, and copper, I presented a purse of gold to be distributed amongst the workmen on this occasion; the purse was emblematical.'

Soon after she had buried gold coins before the good and worthy of Exeter, her brother-in-law Tom Graves admitted that he could barely afford the postage for a letter. His house was in a dreadful state and he needed £400 to make the necessary repairs. Never defeated, he told John: 'I must make a short campaign this winter at Bath, as fortune, like all females, must be courted & in peace I can only try my fortune in the field of Venus & I believe Bath is the best cruising ground for rich widows & antiquated maids.'

Before Tom reached Bath, his eldest brother, Sam, had died at the age of 61, on November 29th 1802. The retired admiral had been so ill that John wrote: 'He can scarcely articulate and is obliged to be fed like a child with a spoon.' His death left his wife and children with little money. Tom at once rallied in support of his sister-in-law and implored the Admiralty to give her a decent pension. It was not the only letter the Admiralty received from the Graves family, as Richard had sent an impertinent missive on the subject of his promotion. He received a sharp letter back from Evan Nepean, in which he said he was commanded by their Lordships to acquaint Richard that: 'The language you have thought fit to use, is not such as they have been accustomed to receive, or patiently to bear.'

This rebuke from the Admiralty infuriated Richard who just before Christmas set sail for America. Louisa was then expecting their ninth child, but she must have thought it wise that Richard take advantage of the hiatus in the war, to check the plantations. He landed in Charleston on January 13th 1803. Six days later, he applied for the family to become naturalised citizens of America and detailed the names and ages of his wife and their five children. One of the conditions attached to the application was that Richard had to prove his intent to live in the country. It is unlikely that Louisa knew of this.

Only two months after Richard's departure, Louisa wrote a desperate letter to him, which reached him in Charleston. Their only son, Samuel, then fifteen years old, was seriously ill. Richard was 'much alarmed' at the news, but as there was little he could do at so great a distance. Tom Graves, who was always critical of Louisa's childcare, wrote that she would prevent Samuel 'making that figure in the world he might do'. Samuel was often to be found with his nose in a book, and blessed with an astonishing memory he could quote at length passages by both English and Classical authors. When he recovered from his illness, Richard's brothers began to put pressure on Louisa to send the boy to school, which she refused to do.

Richard was back in Exeter at the beginning of July 1803, where, by chance, John bumped into him at the County Meeting. Their relationship was still strained after John's altercation with Louisa and both kept their distance. Nevertheless, John reported to his sisters in Ireland that Richard 'appeared quite well and jolly; his wife was brought to bed of a son some time before his arrival. I hear it is to be christened William Henry Colleton but as it is a common report I cannot vouch for the truth. His eldest son and all his daughters are at home. I hope their father will place them to good schools now he is returned. Hembury Fort is altered and fitted up in great style, but they are now all at Exeter in their town residence on Southernhay'. Richard, against Louisa's wishes, did indeed send Samuel to board at Westminster School in London.

Richard's desire to move the family to America was thwarted, no doubt by Louisa herself. Besides her dislike of travelling by sea, she had no wish to leave England. The building of Colleton Crescent continued apace, and in her husband's absence, she had spared no expense on furnishing Hembury Fort. Locals had watched in awe as carts went through Honiton to the house, carrying suites of furniture upholstered in silk damask, elegant sofa tables, chandeliers with lustres, inlaid satin-wood card tables, ancient sculptures, dining tables and chairs, terrestrial globes and no less than two pianos. Three hundred books, many of which had belonged to Louisa's great-grandfather, were placed on the shelves in the library, and none of which Richard was ever likely to read. Every bedroom had a lofty four-poster mahogany bed, draped with cotton hangings to match the curtains and Grecian sofas were installed in the girls' bedrooms. Looking glasses reflected light onto Axminster and Wilton carpets and polished steel fenders. In the scullery were sets of china, cut-glass drinking glasses, silver and silver-plated tableware: all was set for entertaining on a lavish scale. Louisa also had the gardens landscaped, creating pleasure walks through the park. Streams were dammed up to create ponds, and climbing roses planted under the apple and walnut trees in the orchard.

Despite the great expenditure, the family rarely stayed at Hembury Fort, preferring life in the city. With the approach of winter, John again wrote to his sister Catherine: 'Richard returned from America two months agone. I am told he was offered one hundred and twenty thousand pounds for his American property, which he refused.' The sum Richard had been offered was indicative of the income the plantations were then generating. Since Eli Whitney had invented the cotton gin, which he had patented in 1794, short-staple cotton had become more profitable and planters moved away from soil-depleting tobacco, and indigo, which was being supplied to the British Empire from India. Cotton was all the rage and Devil's Elbow, being on the coast, grew the more valuable sea-island variety. Acres of Fairlawn were also turned over to the crop. There was, it seemed, no shortage of money as John wrote of Richard and Louisa: 'They live quite in style, keep fifteen servants, but I never go to their house. Richard and I are sociable when we meet, that is the most of our intercourse.'

CHAPTER 19

Corrupt Jobs

*

APART from falling out with John Graves, all seemed rosy in Richard and Louisa's household; servants galore, and seemingly no end to the amount of money pouring into their account from America. But after the stately laying of the foundation stone of Colleton Crescent, Louisa ended her memoirs abruptly when only 39 years old, dismissing the rest of her life with this throwaway sentence: 'The years rolled on in the domestic circle unremarked by any events, save sickness, and calamity...'

The first calamity was the death of her baby, William, who was not a year old. He was buried in the graveyard of Buckerell Church on March 18th 1804. Louisa was 'much afflicted' by her son's death. At the end of April, Mrs Admiral wrote to Eliza Simcoe saying that she had seen Richard in Bath: 'He told me, that his wife has not recovered the sudden seizure, & loss of her youngest son: he seemed quite a philosopher on the occasion; he spent a day with Mrs Prideaux; who with her daughter in law, are quite charmed with him, having never met a more agreeable man in their lives; pity that people don't know how to chuse their company properly: for I am convinced every person would be thought charming; by some of their acquaintance; if they were discreet in chusing what circles they should frequent.'

It was while Richard was sauntering about Bath that he received news of his promotion to flag rank, but this was of the 'Yellow'. Although enjoying the title of Rear Admiral and the extra income, he would never fly his flag. 'Yellow' admirals were compulsorily retired the day after their promotion. For Richard, this was the final indignity and disgrace. He returned home to Hembury Fort, and although he had no purpose at sea, he was willing to help with the war effort on land.

With an imminent French invasion feared, General Simcoe, in command of the western 'home guard', began to train his troops in earnest. That winter, with Richard's assistance, Simcoe organised a 'sham fight' to take place around Hembury Fort. Louisa watched the event with her children from the safety of her first-floor sitting-room window as more than four-thousand men and as many as ten-thousand onlookers swept up the hill towards them. The mock battle spun out of control; on the lawns of Hembury Fort there was a 'very sharp attack' and a great fear the soldiers would 'get in earnest'. One volunteer lost his finger, and another, a young boy, lost an eye in the mayhem. General Simcoe had to give orders to the Regulars, who had taken on the part of the French army, to retreat in order to prevent any more injuries.

In the following year of 1805, just days before her forty-second birthday, Louisa was delivered of her tenth and last child, whom they named Octavia. Both Louisa and Richard were initially disappointed at the birth of an eighth daughter, for they had longed for another son. Louisa continued to run a somewhat shambolic household, as Numbers 3 to 9 Colleton Crescent were built. Richard, meanwhile, thought there was a possibility that the British government would grant the Lords Proprietors of the Bahamas additional compensation for the loss of the islands.

The 4th Duke of Atholl had recently been successful in petitioning Parliament for further compensation concerning the family's loss of Sovereignty over the Isle of Man, a small island of 30 miles by 10, off the west coast of England. Since being awarded £70,000 for the Sovereign Rights in 1765, the family had argued over the years that the sum was insufficient. The 4th duke's 'close' friend, the Prime Minister, William Pitt, persuaded Parliament to grant him an allowance of £3,000 a year: the money was to 'come out of the island's revenues'. The Lord Chief Justice of England remarked at the time that he believed the whole transaction was 'one of the most corrupt jobs ever witnessed in Parliament'.

In order for Richard to pursue a case for the Bahamas, on the same basis, he would need support from the other Lords Proprietors. On Christmas Day, the Graveses returned from church to Hembury Fort in driving rain. Richard left the bedlam of the family party, shut himself in the library and wrote to the 6th Duke of Beaufort. The duke would have inherited the Proprietorship of the Bahamas on his father's death in 1803, but for its sale in 1787. Richard argued that they had not been paid enough for the islands and that a company of merchants had offered Louisa £20,000 for Long Island alone. Given that the 4th Duke of Atholl had now been granted even more money, Richard hoped the Proprietors of the Bahamas would be treated in a 'similar fashion'. He ended his letter by asking the Duke of Beaufort if he thought it right to make 'any move respecting them as the object is a considerable one & your Grace best knows how it may be affected'. The duke, who sat in the House of Lords, appears not have been interested in pursuing the matter, as Richard received only a mere acknowledgement of his letter.

General Simcoe might have had enough influence to help Richard and Louisa pursue the government over a further claim to the Bahamas: he had recently been appointed Commander-in-Chief, India. However, before taking up the post, he fell ill whilst on a mission to Portugal, then under threat of invasion by the French. His quarters onboard ship had been freshly painted and it is believed that he was poisoned by fumes from the paint, which contained lead. He was brought back to Exeter, where he died on October 26th 1806.

Louisa had left the matter of the Bahamas to Richard as she was so pre-occupied with the building of Colleton Crescent. Not only did she ensure that the houses were equipped with the latest modern conveniences, but she paid attention to the grounds in front of the curved façade. It was noted that year: 'a fine terrace walk is to be made, which will be near a 100 feet above the bed of the river, from this walk, and from the houses, there is one of the most charming prospects imaginable, the navigable River Ex, the shipping, and crouded quay beneath, whilst the elevated situation protects from the damps of the one, and the noise of the other.'

For all of Richard's failings, he was the one who cared for his brother Tom after he suffered a stroke. He lost the use of one arm, but John wrote to their sisters to say that the 'Hot Bath' at Hembury Fort had given him great relief. He later reported that Tom's daughter, Mary, had told him that Richard 'proved himself a most affectionate brother and friend, sat up with her father and even dressed and undressed him during his illness, and no act of care and attention was omitted by him to her father.' Richard would also no doubt have helped to nurse Octavia, the youngest of his own family, but nothing could prevent her death in early November 1807. She had not reached her third birthday.

John Graves was living at Penrice, his wife's estate in Cornwall, when he wrote to his sister at the beginning of April 1808. His 18-year-old daughter, Mary, had not been well, but he thought that she was getting better. (She would, however, die two years later.) And he wrote of his brother: 'I can say little of Richard living at such a distance from him. I am told his daughters are high bred, they have even taken lessons for getting in and out of a carriage. Sophia, the eldest, has a very fine face, (much like her father) but nothing of a figure. Rather too much of the 'En bon point' though of a truly pleasing temper. Caroline, the second daughter, is a genteel figure, but not handsome. Louisa, the third has a good face, is clumsy and in temperament and the pow'er of the tongue is Mama personified.!!!!!!.'

Samuel, who had been up at Cambridge where he failed to matriculate, seems to have taken after his father, as John added: 'I forgot to tell you amidst the other description relating to the female of Richard's family that I hear his son Samuel is in person no great things, but quite a buck of the age, drives a four-in-hand, and spent for his father the last term at University, thirteen hundred pounds and had nothing to show for it but two gilt bookcases and a few books. This extravagance of debt was incurred exclusive of his yearly allowance from his father. These little anecdotes are not to be mentioned.'

Richard and Samuel had by then left for America as news of the Embargo Act, passed by President Jefferson in late December 1807, had led to Richard offering to take dispatches from the government to Congress. The Embargo Act had been passed as retaliation for, among other grievances, British harassment of American shipping, and the impressing of American seamen into the Royal Navy who were deemed by the British to be British by birth. It was no doubt because the act would have dire financial consequences for Richard and Louisa, as there would be no means of getting their crops out of the country, that Richard felt it worthwhile to attempt any means of conciliation between the two countries. Samuel travelled as his attaché, and they landed in Newport, Rhode Island, in April. From there they went to Washington and delivered the British dispatches to President Jefferson himself. They also met with James Madison, the future president, and 'other gentleman of distinction'. Having been 'most kindly' entertained while in the capital, Richard and Samuel went on to Charleston. The *Carolina Gazette* wrote of Richard, on his arrival: 'This gentleman possesses some landed estate in Carolina, which he has come hither to arrange, in order to guard against impending events.', and that Richard was heading southward, no doubt to Devil's Elbow.

Richard's supposed wealth drew comment from Sir Augustus John Foster, the English Secretary of Legation in Washington. He wrote of the richest landowners of the South, and mentioned that Richard 'had an estate of £3,000 per year in the right of his wife'. This would be nearly a quarter of a million pounds, but with the embargo in place, this revenue was hypothetical. Foster also warned that after June 10th: 'It is mortal to a planter to remain in the country near his rice grounds, and all who can, retire to the city, from whence if they go even for a single day to visit the plantation, it is with imminent risk of life.' It was the habit of the gentlemen of South Carolina, he wrote, to leave for 'the northern states, Ballstown Springs, and other places famed for their mineral waters, in the unhealthy season, and in winter return to Charlestown, 'which is then one of the gayest towns on the continent.'

Indeed, Richard and Samuel left Charleston early that summer of 1808. On their travels they passed through Baltimore, where Samuel met the lovely Madame Bonaparte, Napoleon's former sister-in-law and fell madly in love with her. Elizabeth, née Patterson, was the daughter of the second richest man in Maryland. She was eighteen when she met Jérôme, Napoleon's youngest brother, at a ball.

He was nineteen, on unofficial leave from the French navy, and touring the States. The young Bonaparte was dark and dashing, and the heiress, in addition to her fortune, was noted for her beauty and diaphanous dresses, so in fashion at the time. They had determined to marry and, nervous of Napoleon's likely adverse reaction, the nuptials were hastened. Napoleon was furious when he received the news that they had married on Christmas Eve, 1803, without his consent. He was determined that all his brothers should make politically advantageous matrimonial alliances across Europe.

In 1804, Jérôme and Elizabeth left America for France and were lucky to have survived when their ship was wrecked off the coast of Philadelphia. The following year, they sailed from America in one of her father's ships. Prevented from landing in Lisbon by one of Napoleon's frigates, Jérôme was told that his wife would not be allowed to set foot in France. Napoleon declared the marriage invalid, and offered to grant Elizabeth 'a pension of 60,000 francs during her lifetime, on condition that she will under no circumstance bear my name'. Elizabeth sailed on to England without her husband. On July 7th 1805, she gave birth to their son, Jérôme Napoleon Bonaparte, who would become known as 'Bo'. Although Jérôme continued to protest his love for Elizabeth, he was in debt, and in danger of being banished from France and its territories if he did not consent to the marriage being annulled. Elizabeth returned to Baltimore with her son and ignored Napoleon's stipulation not to use the Bonaparte name. To her great distress, in 1807, Jérôme married a German Princess, Catherina of Wurttemberg, and became King of Westphalia.

Madame Bonaparte, at twenty-two, was two years older than Samuel Graves. She took pleasure in seducing younger men: she flirted and encouraged her many suitors to write her love poems and letters. Samuel was soon dragged away from Baltimore to Philadelphia by his father and, having been too embarrassed to ask Elizabeth to marry him in person before he left, did so by letter. It was probably one of many such letters that Elizabeth received.

On June 8th 1808, Richard wrote to Tom: 'I am here Northward to avoid the summer heats. It is almost intolerable here and as the packet sails Tuesday I cannot let this opportunity pass without writing. The Embargo Laws has prevented my crops reaching England, they are very good ones and would bring if they were now in England £4000 and I hope the present year will not be worse, but the Embargo is ruining me as well as the other planters in Carolina, for if they are not taken off soon two crops will be getting to market at the same time and occasion a glut and lessen their value.'

Richard must have believed that the best course of action was to remain in America in hope that the embargo would be lifted. He and Samuel continued to travel to pass the time and, perhaps remembering the Simcoe's descriptions of their time in Canada, they went to see the dramatic Niagara Falls. They then left for Newport, Rhode Island, from where Richard wrote to an American General of his acquaintance on September 14th. 'I shall plan to leave this place at the end of this month for New York and shall hope to meet you by the 10th or 12th of Octr., at Philadelphia and arrange our movements for the famous city of Baltimore, when we shall enjoy the society of pretty women & partake of hospitality and good cheer.' Samuel was no doubt desperate to get back to Madame Bonaparte, and Richard was clearly not missing Louisa.

However, by the winter of 1808, the tabloid press believed that Richard and Admiral Sir Isaac Coffin had been spying on behalf of the British. Sir Isaac came from a strong loyalist family in Boston, who were themselves descended from one of the ancient landed families of Devon. He was of the same age as Richard, and while serving, had saved on separate occasions, two men from drowning, which caused him lasting injuries. Despite his disabilities, and a court-martial, he had risen to the top echelon of the British navy.

As a reward for his American material losses, Sir Isaac was granted the Magdalen Islands in the Gulf of St Lawrence, and he was visiting the islands at the time. The copy printed in the *Aurora General Advertiser*, under the name of 'Whig', reported: 'False alarm – What if admiral Coffin and admiral Graves, and all the deathful names in the British navy were among us? We will find them in graves and coffins, if they play any of their tory tricks here, and abuse the hospitality they receive, by an ungrateful return.' 'Whig' continued that if England wanted information on 'our harbours, forts, rivers, soundings', etc., then did she not have spies and agents to supply them with information, without sending her admirals to make a voyage on dry land, in disguise, to obtain it?'. There may have been some truth in the accusation that Richard was engaged in espionage; he often sent intelligence to the Admiralty for which, he later complained, he was rarely thanked.

The American embargo was lifted in March 1809, but it was probably the news of Mrs Admiral's death that compelled Richard to return to England. In his absence, she had been re-decorating 15 Lansdown Crescent* and had no doubt died from lead poisoning. In the last letter she wrote to her niece, Eliza, of whom she had recently written was 'too fat to be interesting', Mrs Admiral complained: 'I have been sleeping on two Sophas in the great Drawing Room for this month past and when I shall have the comfort to repose on a Bed again I cannot exactly say. I do sit in my Library again but at the hazard of my health for it stinks of paint like poison.'

Meanwhile, Tom Graves had bagged an heiress, the matronly Miss Blacknell, whom he had been chasing for some nine years. Young Samuel, however, would not be so fortunate. Shortly before he and Richard sailed for England, Madame Bonaparte eventually replied to Samuel's proposal.

---

* Mrs Admiral, who had planted her entire garden in Lansdown Crescent with fruit for her great nieces to enjoy on their visits to Bath, left them her fortune. After her death, the Simcoe girls had some semblance of independence but their mother continued to rule their lives with an iron rod. Elizabeth Simcoe never allowed her daughters to marry, despite the many proposals they received. This was as much because of Mrs Admiral's belief that women should not marry because on marriage their fortunes belonged to their husbands, as had happened to her and Elizabeth. It was only after Elizabeth's death, in 1850 at the age of 88, that Anne, the youngest of her daughters, dared to marry. The Simcoe girls shared another fortune from their mother, and the five eldest, Eliza was then 66, immediately left Wolford Lodge for Bath. They lived together at 11, Royal Crescent until they died.

The envelope was addressed to Richard so that he could first read her refusal. It was with a broken heart and dismay at the thought of a great fortune slipping from his hands that Samuel left America with his father on an American ship, the *Coromandel*. They landed at Hastings, in Sussex on July 12th 1809, having been away for sixteen months.

On their return to Hembury Fort, Louisa quickly learnt of Samuel's romance and subsequent rejection. On the day he arrived back home, Samuel wrote to Madame Bonaparte, once more declaring his love and asking her to reconsider his proposal of marriage. He added that his parents supported his 'fondest wish' and enclosed a somewhat incoherent letter from Louisa, who had written a long scrawl to Elizabeth, diagonally, across several pages. She had clearly lost her head over the thought that her son would marry an American heiress, and such a grand one at that. She bossily wrote, in couched terms, that Madame Bonaparte should not keep her son, 'Bo', in America but return him to Napoleon's fold. There, he would be provided for, 'at least nobly perhaps royally', and advised Elizabeth to divorce Jérôme Bonaparte in America to ensure the offspring of a future marriage would not be deemed illegitimate. Louisa ended by saying that after all the necessary arrangements had been made: 'My husband & myself will accompany our son to meet you at Paris to celebrate Nuptials.' The presumption on Louisa's part that Madame Bonaparte would heed her advice was as preposterous as suggesting a meeting in Paris, whilst Britain was still at war with France.

Madame Bonaparte replied briefly to Louisa, dismissing Samuel's offer of marriage. She wrote that 'neither inclination nor interest can detach me from my son', and added that she felt 'regret at having inspired attachment in Mr Graves'. Although there was no personal note enclosed for Samuel, a year later he wrote to Madame Bonaparte, from Gottenburg in Sweden, to try to resurrect the romance. It is unlikely that Samuel ever received a reply to his last letter to her, but she did keep his, perhaps out of vanity as a testament to the intensity of feelings she inspired in her suitors.

Madame Bonaparte never married again, and had exclaimed: 'I would rather be the wife of Jérôme Bonaparte for an hour than the wife of any other man for a lifetime.'

CHAPTER 20

Trammels of Debt

*

AFTER his return to England, Louisa tried to set Richard to work recruiting bricklayers for Colleton Crescent in Exeter, which was not yet completed. He, however, had business of his own which took him to London. The death of Mrs Admiral had, after twenty-two years, finally released the rest of his inheritance from his uncle. This included land in Nova Scotia, and thanks to Admiral Samuel's first wife, land in the Midlands and Blue Boar Yard, which was a mews just off St James's Street. There were two entrances to it, one for carriages and one for pedestrians, which led into a cobbled yard around which stood several buildings, five coach houses and ten stables. It had been entailed to Samuel, but Richard managed to break this entailment and would, in time sell it for a large sum of money.

Samuel returned from Sweden and entered the Middle Temple to study law. He drove about London in his own barouche, a four-wheeled carriage with a hood, which he rented for £100 a year. While in London, he and his father fell in with Davenport Sedley, the notorious swindler and blackmailer, with predictably disastrous consequences.

Davenport Sedley was an Irish Catholic and a radical to boot. He made a living by selling stories to such radical and anti-government newspapers such as the *Independent Whig* and British *Guardian* and, as often as not though before printing them, offered the principles in the stories the option of buying him off; blackmail in other words. Sedley's main targets were royals, aristocrats and members of the government. By January 1811, both Richard and Samuel were acting as henchmen to Sedley. In their pursuit of scandalous and tawdry information, one victim, himself a profligate hack, described them as 'violent characters'. Louisa, living in Exeter, and having been left to deal with the matter of bricklayers, amongst other concerns, was in total ignorance of the antics in London of her husband and son.

Samuel gave himself a veneer of respectability by obtaining a commission in the West Norfolk Militia, part of the reserve army. He would eventually become a Lieutenant Colonel in this regiment. In peacetime, this would not have been too onerous an occupation as the militia only trained for twenty-eight days a year but as Britain was at war the militia was fully employed on home defence duties. Despite this, Samuel was often in London.

Richard meanwhile still felt so aggrieved at the Admiralty that he published, for public consumption, 'The case of Richard Graves, of the Royal Navy, who was passed over by Lord Spencer, in the Promotion of Flag Officers.' It appeared in January 1812, and was dedicated, in bold, to 'HIS BROTHER OFFICERS', and to the service in general. Richard noted his grievances, beginning in 1790, in a booklet of more than fifty pages. It contained copies of almost every letter that had passed between him and the Admiralty. The thrust of the case was his gross ill-treatment by the Admiralty; that he had only accepted the flag of Admiral of the Yellow under pressure from his friends and that the pension of £400 a year was inadequate as a reward 'for a life, from childhood dedicated to my King and country'. Tom Graves had warned him against publication, but Richard took no notice of him, and neither did the Admiralty of Richard.

He was once more with Samuel, lodging at their usual haunt, Fenton's Hotel on St James's Street, when on April 20th 1812 they strolled to the nearby Thatched Tavern, for a meeting with nearly sixty of their republican cronies. Before he took office, Prime Minister Spencer Percival, as a lawyer, prosecuted Thomas Paine over his book, The *Rights of Man*. The Prime Minister was representative of all Tom and Richard, and those of their political persuasion, loathed about the establishment. Percival would not consider extending the vote beyond the property-owning classes, or allow Catholics to hold public office, these views of course were not restricted to Percival but were held by most 'right thinking men' including the Prince Regent.* At the tavern, Samuel and his father became founder members of the Hampden Club. Through the establishment of branches throughout the country, the club's aim was to call for free elections and thus provide a platform for the lower, middle and working classes to discuss and press for reform. So once again Richard was involving himself in politics. Given that the views he supported were completely against everything the current government and indeed even the opposition Whigs believed in and given that he had never hidden these radical views, it is no wonder that he never received a command in the navy during the war.

---

* Spencer Percival would be shot dead by a madman in the House of Commons less than a month later on May 11th 1812.

Ever headstrong, Richard would have been wiser to concern himself with the family's deteriorating financial affairs, rather than meddle in seditious politics. He was back at Hembury Fort, a few days later, where on the morning of May 4th he took delivery of a strongly worded letter from his brother, Tom. Judging by Richard's reply, Tom again appears to have blamed Louisa and her extravagances for their predicament. After reading it through several times Richard sat down to answer it but, perhaps suffering from recurrent rheumatoid arthritis, he admitted to his brother that he was barely able to hold his pen.

'It is, but too true,' he wrote, 'none but our real friends will tell us our follies, or our faults, and we ought to be thankful to those who do. I know from my earliest recollection I was classed with the foolish and extravagant, yet at this late period of my life, and upon a review, and strict scrutiny of my past conduct except the little foolish happiness incident to a young man moving in a sphere perhaps beyond his pecuniary pretentions, there is no act, on which I can look back with regret. I always made the best appearance on what I had, and till I became a family man I never owed a Guinea to any man living, or ever purchased anything till I had the money to pay for it.' (In fact, Richard often relied on his mother, who presumably had funds of her own, to bail him out in his early days as a Midshipman.)

'When I married we set out with ideas a little elated and a very few months brought me to the end of the remnant of the prize money I had made in the American War – demands became pressing, and not till then did my wife know my real situation – when she did, she met it with that fortitude and superiority of mind, which good sense and virtuous intentions ever dictated. She recommended an immediate break – you remember the result, and we went into a cottage at Gittisham of Eight pounds a year.'

Richard then confessed to Tom, that for several years after this, he lived 'more expensively than what prudence would have dictated'. He continued, 'the sale of some money my wife had in the Funds and the sale by piecemeal, of my wife's scattered property, kept me afloat till we went to America in 1798. I then knew the value of her American possessions which have rose and are rising in value every day. Had I followed the excellent advice my wife often urged I might have lived more economical.

I am happy at this moment to pay a tribute so just to her head and her heart, for even at the time of our greatest difficulties, she was always foremost, in urging my sending assistance to my sisters or to any other part of the family that wanted it. This more particularly bespeaks the goodness of her heart, when I reflect that she married me without any settlement, she threw her fortune into my lap and trusted to my honour, and whatever people may think of her fortune, she has not first and last, in lands and money received here, and lands and Negroes in America given me a sum less than £120,000. This is indisputable, though it does not relieve from my present Temporary embarrassment of which I shall speak next, because my dear Bro'r I wish to satisfy your mind and feelings.'

Not content with having frittered away much of his wife's fortune, Richard also admitted he had borrowed money from his lawyer, Mr Flood, to purchase more land around Hembury Fort. The ease with which he obtained funds, he wrote, increased his greed and he brought land that produced little income, and 'that moth called interest, always eating, and no accrued income arising'. The sum owed Mr Flood had swelled to about £22,000, and he intended to call in mortgages and sell all his outlying parcels of land and his estate at Hawkerland to cover the debt. This, he said, would on his death leave Samuel with an estate producing about £1800 a year. After the debt was paid, Richard would be left with an income of about £1500 a year, exclusive of any income from the plantations in America. He ended the letter by telling Tom that he had been as accurate as he could in relating his financial position.

Although Richard had revealed to Tom the very dire financial situation in which he found himself, he had again not told Louisa. However, the reluctance of local traders to give her credit might have given her some indication of the situation. To add to Richard's predicament, on June 18th, America declared war on Britain. The outbreak of hostilities was a result of many American grievances; trade restrictions, the British Navy impressing merchant seamen, British agitation of the Native Indians, and America's wish to enlarge its territory, principally into Canada. Once again, war would play a major hand in the fate of the Graves family.

Richard was not alone in his financial troubles. On August 14th 1812, Sir James Nassau Colleton, wrote to the Home Secretary, Lord Addington, declaring: 'I and my family are literally in want of every necessary of life, without an income sufficient at these times to support a single individual in any comfort much less a large family, brought up, tho not' in the highest luxuries, yet sufficient to make them feel the present reverse, both in health of body and mind, by abstinence from the actual nourishment of food.' He complained that his insolvency was 'rendered the more poignant & mortifying by holding a rank in life (an old hereditary title) which subjects myself and them to vulgar reproach and the tormenting insolence of our inferiors, the consequence of misfortunes: the original source of which arises from the American Revolution'.

This letter was written from his house in Jermyn Street, which even James Nassau had to admit was 'very unsuitable to me in my present position', but he claimed he had rented the large house so that he could take in 'three of four boarders of rank and fortune', and presumed his lodgers would pay his bills. Until that happened, he was 'at this instant without a shilling to buy as meat and drink, or shoes or stockings, and no means of getting one, as I have nothing to receive out of my official pittance at your Lordship's office to which I formerly belonged, till Christmas next, and that only forty pounds, although I served upwards of three and twenty years, the whole prime of man's life; flattering myself that your Lordship will PAY UP – Yours James Nassau Colleton'.

It was only now, that Louisa, to her horror, learnt of Samuel's involvement with Davenport Sedley, after they were both incarcerated in Newgate on charges of conspiracy to steal bills of exchange, which were letters promising sums of money. Sedley had been arrested and tried for the same crime in 1811, but the evidence disappeared and the prosecution had no case. Amongst Sedley's papers seized on this occasion, were 'fraudulent and swindling transactions practiced upon persons of the first distinction'. Louisa would later refer to Sedley as a 'loathsome toad, of squalid form', who spewed poison, and was, she believed, entirely responsible for Samuel's incarceration. Although Samuel had acted under Sedley's influence, he was more than capable of spewing his own poison.

While in Newgate he and Sedley concocted an article, written under a pseudonym, that appeared in the tabloid *Independent Whig* on August 23rd, composed in the manner of an open letter to the Prince Regent. It harked back to the events surrounding the attempted murder of the Prince Regent's brother, the Duke of Cumberland on May 31st 1810. The duke had been asleep in his apartments in St James's Palace, when his valet, Joseph Sellis, attacked him with a sabre, and with such savagery that as well as other injuries, the Dukes' brain 'could be seen pulsing through one of the wounds'. Sellis was soon found dead in a locked room in the Palace, his throat cut by a razor. The duke survived, but since that night many scurrilous rumours as to the true events that evening had continued to circulate, as no plausible motive for the attack could be discovered. The pseudonymous *Independent Whig* article was clearly sensationalist and was seen as an attempt to blackmail the Duke of Cumberland, so as to stop further scandalous material being printed.

In the absence of a reaction, Samuel and Sedley prepared an article for the following weekend's paper. This duly also appeared under a pseudonym. The duke, they wrote, was hated by both Parliament and the people and the pair again provided 'evidence' as to how Sellis's 'murder' had been covered up. It concluded with an implication that the duke and Sellis had been in a homosexual relationship. The story was to run for some months, expanding with various scenarios: the duke had himself killed Sellis... the duke was a homosexual who had been performing a 'shirt dance' when surprised by Sellis... the duke was sleeping with Sellis's wife when found by Sellis.... the Duke had murdered Sellis when he caught the duke with another man, and other tawdry suggestions. The *Independent Whig* wrote that Francis Place, the foreman of the jury that had swiftly returned a verdict of suicide on Sellis's death, had been part of a government spy ring and had accepted a bribe from the treasury to bring in that verdict to ensure that the duke could not be tried for murder. Place, however, had a spy in Newgate, and discovered that the authors were no less than Sedley and Samuel.

By some means, Samuel was eventually released from Newgate and he arrived at Hembury Fort towards the end of the summer. He was no doubt able to placate his mother and distracted her with his plans to cause a rumpus in the general election that October. He forced a poll in Exeter, when the two principal candidates, John Bastard and Sir Thomas Acland, both large landowners, would have expected to be returned as Members of Parliament, unopposed.

An observer wrote: 'It would be a brave if not foolhardy person who dared to oppose the extended Toryism of Devon during a period of the war when patriotic feeling was high.' Samuel was unabashed and appeared before a political assembly in Exeter. The crowd was at such a pitch, that when he rose to speak, he was greeted with a clamour from the gentlemen and loud 'hisses and groans' from the ladies. According to the *Exeter Flying Post*, Samuel responded to the ladies heckling by saying: 'In the words of Gloster to Lady Anne, "never came poison from so sweeter a place."' In his interminable speech that followed, he advocated the Whig principles of peace, an end to the war, sinecures and taxes.

Richard was to be seen proudly careering around Exeter's surrounding towns and villages with a 'mob' to encourage support for Samuel. Louisa Catherina, then twenty-years-old, joined in the fray and was one of her brother's most vociferous campaigners. While Louisa was often heard expounding her democratic beliefs at the dinner table, for which she had been ridiculed, she did not put her head above the parapet on this occasion. It must have embarrassed her to read the lambasting of both her son and husband in the broadsheets, as the presses ran red-hot during the election. But it was, perhaps, all they deserved.

Samuel lost the poll, garnering only 19 votes. The result did nothing to deter Richard and Samuel from disrupting other elections with the intention of exposing the venality of the contemporary political process. Samuel decided to contest the 'rotten borough of Honiton', considered one of the most corrupt in the kingdom. He was, however, delayed in Taunton and plied with drink, rendering him incapable of reaching Honiton in time to contest the seat. Even though Samuel had failed to reach Honiton, he and Richard wreaked havoc in other elections across England. At Bath, their endeavours ended with a riot.

The sale of Blue Boar Yard, which was completed at the end of 1812 for £13,500, had not covered Richard's debts. And, nor would the sale of Hawkerland, which eventually raised £9,000. At the beginning of 1813, Richard was desperate to pursue any avenue that might bring in extra funds. Without informing Louisa, and without taking legal advice, he had written to the Lords of the Treasury, to ask for their sanction to bring a petition before the House of Commons to state their 'hardship' in the case of the Bahamas. He had claimed they were due further compensation as Louisa's land there, which had personally belonged to her, had been confiscated. Moreover, she had not authorised the sale and she had been a minor at the time of the transactions. He also noted that the Duke of Atholl had received further compensation after the sale of his family's proprietorship of the Isle of Man and, under these circumstances, Richard felt their case should be reconsidered.

That year, the Prime Minister, Lord Liverpool, was inundated with letters from Louisa's immediate family. Not only from Richard, on the subject of the war with America, but from Samuel, complaining of the treatment of his father by the Admiralty, and of his mother's claim for the Bahamas, and also from Sir James Nassau's wife. The baronet was then in Newgate, such were the extent of his debts, and his wife begged Lord Liverpool for financial assistance.

In March 1813, adding to the Graves' woes, the port of Charleston was blockaded by the British, and their 'dear daughter', Carolina, was very unwell. Towards the end of April, Richard told Tom that he and Louisa had taken Carolina, then twenty-two years old, to Clifton to visit the 'Hot Wells', in Wells, which was not far from Bath. They then went on to Bath itself to seek further medical treatment. Richard wrote, 'I have very little to comfort myself from her situation. I think she daily gets weaker and weaker, and I am really broken hearted on her account, as well as on account of her Mother, whose attentions are everlasting and whose own situation from fretting is truly distressing, and I am so situated on her account, that I can't quit this place, however much I wish it, to return to Hembury Fort, till something decisive takes place, and the Author of all being makes his determination.'

Richard was now determined to sell Hembury Fort. He had had an offer from the commissioners for 'Lord Wellington and Lord Nelson', whose role it was to buy land to provide an income assigned by the Government to their heirs, but wrote, 'I have had a letter today upon it, but they do not yet offer up my price.' Nelson had once ridden to Hembury Fort after the Battle of the Nile in 1798 to inspect the house. The nation wanted to present the hero with an estate as they had done for the Duke of Marlborough. He must have been disappointed, knowing of the glories of Blenheim Palace. Also, given his long-standing affair with Lady Hamilton, Nelson may also have thought that Hembury Fort was too close to Exeter, where his wife then lived. John Graves' son was also keen to purchase the house and part of the estate, but he had not yet come of age.

Richard added, 'I am the more fixed in my intention of a sale from a desire of getting rid of all encumbrances and freeing myself from the Trammels of Debt.' However, he wrote, 'The American War has driven me hard, and I can't get sixpence from that country.' He asked Tom, who together with his daughter Mary was looking after his daughter Septima in Louisa's absence, as she was still in Bath with Carolina, to lend him another £200, having borrowed £200 from him the year before.

Carolina, however, seemed to rally and was taken back to Hembury Fort. On her return, Richard immediately went to London to put pressure on the government to bring the war with America, to an end. From his garret room in Fenton's Hotel, he wrote to Lord Liverpool and warned him that the Americans 'have it in their power to do us so much injury'. He insisted the Americans wanted to come to some sort of agreement and were not averse to reconciliation. He added: 'With America in our interests we are able to cope with the rest of the world.'

CHAPTER 21

Impossible

*

RICHARD was probably still in London when the 'amiable' Carolina Victoria, then twenty-two years old, suddenly died at Hembury Fort on July 16th 1813. She would be the fifth of Louisa's children to be buried during her lifetime. It was an era when the 'cure' often killed the patient. If Carolina had been treated with the same drugs as the then also ailing Mary Anne Burges, then it was perhaps not surprising that she did not survive. Mary Anne had always eschewed conventional doctors and relied on homeopathic remedies for her ailments. Amongst other remedies, she took *argentum nitratum*, for the irritated nerves in her face and to calm her unwanted spasms. However, for more than a year she had been following a more brutal regime, taking quantities of henbane, the deadly nightshade, which she commented, made her a 'blockhead'. She admitted to her brother, Sir James Burges: 'The henbane very completely stupefies me, but my face is a good deal easier since I have taken it, so I hope my enemy may again be put to sleep, though there seems little chance of expelling him.' At times, the drug left her so disorientated that she found herself leaving her bed and crawling across the floor of her bedroom, not knowing where she was. Mary Anne had also reluctantly taken arsenic, which she knew might poison her to death, and indeed it did. Less than a month after Carolina was buried, Mary Anne joined her in the graveyard.

The Graves family was back at Buckerell Church on August 26th 1814 to witness the marriage of their eldest daughter, Sophia, to Tristram Ratcliffe. In 1804, he had brought a commission as Captain in the Dorset Militia, boasting that he was the owner of considerable estates and property both in England and Jamaica. But, on the occasion of his marriage to Sophia, it was noted in the *Hampshire Telegraph* and *Naval Chronicle*, on August 30th 1813, that Ratcliff was the 'recent possessor' of his estate, Idsworth Park. However, the new owners, in their absence, employed Ratcliff as steward and he and Sophia were able to continue to live in the house. Ratcliff's estates in Jamaica were then heavily mortgaged, and whether Sophia knew of this, or that he was the father of an illegitimate nine-year-old whom he was obliged by the court to maintain, is unknown.

It was not until October 1813 that the Treasury answered Richard's request for a petition on the Bahamas to be put before Parliament. The reply was not addressed to Richard, but to Louisa.

This was extraordinary, as in the eyes of the law she had no rights over her own property. The Treasury informed her that she had received the same amount as had been paid to the other Lords Proprietors possessing a similar share of the Bahamas. Given the amount of time that had passed since that transaction took place, they could not question the amount paid without very strong grounds for believing an 'Act of Injustice' was committed. The letter, however, did not address Richard's claim that Louisa had not authorised the sale.

Louisa was astonished on receipt of the letter, as Richard had, again, broken her trust by not discussing the matter with her. On October 27th 1813 she wrote to Lord Liverpool and explained that she had not seen Richard's petition before he sent it to the Treasury. She claimed an 'An Act of Injustice' had been committed since she had not signed a power of attorney for Elizabeth Fulford to sell her share of the Bahamas. Moreover, Louisa wrote that Messrs Chamberlayne and White must have threatened her aunt, as they had her, by claiming the islands would be taken anyway, so she might as well accept the money. It was for that reason that Mrs Fulford was induced to sign the document.

A month later, the Treasury replied that they found no grounds for reconsideration. Richard then appeared in person at the Treasury, bearing a letter stating that he was no longer contending redress for a one-sixth share of the Bahamas, but now intended to put in a claim for the Sovereign Rights. But he was later advised that the copy of the deed, given to Louisa by the old employee of Chamberlain and White, would not stand up in court, and retracted the claim. Regardless of this, Louisa was determined that this would not be the end of the matter. She began to build a case the Treasury could not ignore.

In February 1814, the Graveses were in Bath, from where Richard wrote to Lord Liverpool, proposing that the Prime Minister employ his son as an envoy to a meeting in Gothenburg 'to settle the differences between this country and the United States and I should feel much obliged to your Lordship for giving my son that appointment. He will possess a property nearly equal in both America and in England, and on that account must feel anxious to affect a reconciliation without prejudice to either, founded of course on the basis of the instructions he might receive; he has visited the United States and is acquainted with the condition of the Country and the nature of the Government, and with the temper and character of the people; add to these his personal acquaintance with the President and the principal members of the American Government'.

It is bewildering that Richard thought Lord Liverpool would even consider Samuel for such a post. Samuel had, indeed, met the President of the United States; he had also harassed the English Prime Minster for two years, attempted on occasions to blackmail him, and written inflammatory anti-government pamphlets, some under his lightly-veiled pseudonym of 'Ulysses'. And if Lord Liverpool had read the *Morning Chronicle* on February 2nd, he would have seen that Samuel, mistakenly noted as a 'man of fortune', had been found guilty in court of failing to pay his bills to Messrs Houlditch, the coach makers.

Louisa had by now completed her hand-written 'Statement of Claim' of thirty-six pages, which she submitted to the Lords Commissioners of the Treasury. The Treasury put the claim before their solicitor, Mr Litchfield. He queried the fact that Louisa was a minor when transactions were being carried out, and employed John Jones, a most reputable lawyer in Exeter, to find out when Louisa was born. On April 27th 1814, he reported that he could find no record of Louisa's baptism in Exeter but that he had been told it was believed she had been born in South Carolina and that one informant had fixed Louisa as being fifteen when the *Actaeon* was 'burnt' in Charleston harbour. HMS *Actaeon* had grounded and been set on fire on June 28th 1776 in the disastrous attack by the British that summer when Louisa was, in fact, only thirteen.

On May 3rd, Mr Litchfield submitted his findings to the Treasury. He stated it was inconceivable that the other proprietors would each have sold for £2,000 if they had not thought it a fair price, and that not one of them, in the twenty-seven years that had passed since the deed was executed, had 'uttered a murmur against the price which they received'. Using the information given to him by John Jones, he disputed that Louisa had been a minor at the time of the transactions and pointed out that she had contradicted herself by having stated she gave Mrs Fulford a power of attorney in 1785, which she would not have been able to do had she been underage. As to the question of Elizabeth signing the sale deed on Louisa's behalf without the requisite power, Litchfield wrote: 'This act of Mrs Fulford's if it were done without authority is very properly stated to be in fact a forgery and the charge of being privy to that forgery must likewise necessarily attach to the witness Mr Chamberlayne the solicitor for the Treasury and probably to his clerk Mr J Roberts which is likewise more than insinuated by the following passage in the statement viz 'That Mrs Fulford had no authority to sell could not have been unknown to those who conducted the negotiation on the part of the Crown.'

Litchfield also blamed the Graveses for not having taken action earlier on the case. While the deed had been signed by all the Proprietors by March 19th 1787, it was not enrolled in the Court of Chancery until August 16th. He knew that Louisa had married Richard soon after this, and suggested that at the time Richard should have brought his charge against Mrs Fulford and Mr Chamberlayne, which would have prevented the deed being recorded in the Bahamas until the matter had been fully investigated. He also refuted the claim that Mr Chamberlayne had told Louisa that the Government would take the islands – whether she agreed to the sale or not.

However, Litchfield had to concede on one point. He agreed, having read the power of attorney drawn up by Mr Burrows, that it did not give Mrs Fulford the authority to sell the Bahamas. It was, he said, 'impossible to suppose that Mr Chamberlayne could have allowed her to execute under that authority a conveyance of the Bahama property. There must undoubtedly have existed another power either genuine or forged.' As Louisa had pointed out in her claim, 'Common sense will refute the idea of two powers being executed in the same week, to the same person.'

Litchfield had searched through Chamberlayne's papers for the power of attorney used by Mrs Fulford to sign the conveyance, but could not find it. He had, however, found many other papers relating to the transaction, including a draft of a power of attorney to Edmund Rush Wegg and Josiah Tattnall Esq, (the very same men who had sailed with Louisa to the Bahamas in 1785), authorising them to register the documents in the court in the Bahamas. It was, therefore, in his opinion, not impossible that the original deed of sale and the power of attorney were in all probability still in the Bahamas and had not been returned to England. He suggested the Lords of the Treasury write to the Governor of the Bahamas, to find out whether the deed was accompanied by a power of attorney from Louisa to Elizabeth Fulford, and if the 'originals can be traced to return them to this country.'

While the Graveses were consumed by their case, Sir Thomas Graves, Knight of the Bath, had died at Woodbine Hill on March 29th 1814.* It was not until May 8th 1814, that his daughter, Mary, felt strong enough to write to her aunts, Catherine and Isobel, in Ireland to say, 'I have now lost everything in the world.' Since the day her father died, Mary had worn a charming miniature of Tom, which he had painted for his mother when he was a Captain, hanging on a gold chain around her neck.**

Mary mentioned that her stepmother had almost immediately left Woodbine Hill after Tom died, and had gone to London where she intended to stay for at least six weeks. In fact, she would never return. When Lady Graves left Woodbine Hill she took with her the carriage, the horses, all the plate and other valuable pieces of furniture and ornaments from around the house. Mary, in her grief, did not have the will to confront her, but was probably enormously relieved that her stepmother had left.

Richard was back in London that autumn, where he 'daily attended the Treasury' to check the status of their claim for the Bahamas, only to be told repeatedly that the 'board had not yet determined what answer to give'. Richard pressed them: 'It can require no great time to decide whether the Crown has, or has not, a conveyance.' While the Lords Commissioners of the Treasury prevaricated, Richard, overwhelmed by his debts, consequently put Hembury Fort up for sale. The advertisement in the *Exeter Flying Post* on September 22nd 1814 noted, the 'elegant mansion, park and valuable domain of about one thousand and sixty acres of rich fertile land near Honiton Devon', came with a house 'calculated for the residence of a family of distinction'. It was to be auctioned at twelve o'clock on October 22nd in lots, unless previously sold. However, just before the sale, Richard managed to mortgage the property to Messrs Flood and Mules in the expectation that he would eventually be able to pay off his debts.

At the end of October, the Treasury once again rejected the Graves' claim for the Bahamas and ruled that they would not allow the case to

* Margaret Thatcher was a great admirer of Sir Thomas Graves, Knight of the Bath, and during her time as Prime Minister many photographs of her cabinet were taken in front of his portrait which then hung in No. 10 Downing Street.

** This miniature has survived and the glass covering is so scratched that it appears she never took it off.

be reconsidered. The Graveses would not give up and borrowed money in order to obtain legal advice. Richard wrote to Lord Liverpool and made an official application for a copy of the solicitor's report, which they had not seen. This clearly unsettled the Treasury and they sent a letter to Lord Liverpool's secretary: 'If you have not sent your proposed answer to Adml. Graves perhaps you had better not send it now as he has made an official application for a copy of the Solicitors' report.' The Treasury had no option but to give Richard's lawyers a copy and they would be unable to prevent the Graveses from taking their petition to a wider audience.

Richard now had the backing of Peter Moore, a staunch Whig and Member of Parliament. The pig-tailed nabob had made a fortune with the East India Company and was noted for his ability to present Private Member's Bills to Parliament. On Friday, November 18th 1814, when the River Thames was frozen solid, Richard's petition was put before the members of the House of Commons. Moore again claimed that Louisa had been a minor and an 'orphan' when 'offers and threats' had been made to her by the Treasury Solicitors. This was of course untrue: when Chamberlayne had threatened her she was past twenty-one.

Moore asked the House to call for an examination of papers and witnesses, including Richard and Louisa themselves. Richard also stated in this petition that it was not just a case of the private property that Louisa owned, but that of her Sovereign Rights. Their petition was 'ordered to lie on the table', which meant Parliament accepted the petition, but would take no further action. This only served to goad Louisa and she prepared a case presenting all her arguments which she published in 1815 for public consumption.

In this, she alluded to her 'Title Deed' for the Sovereign Rights: 'In 1729, Sir John Colleton purchased the other five-sixths of the Bahama Islands from the other proprietors at a price exceeding £12,000; and from that time, when all the interest of the other proprietors in and to the islands ceased, their attention to them also ceased; and, indeed, even their knowledge of them wholly declined.' Louisa admitted the 'conveyance' could not be found but claimed it was necessary to mention the matter because 'it accounts for the obscurity in which the transactions of the Islands are involved subsequent to that period'.

Louisa would later throw the question of Pitt's honesty over the 'conveyance', in her memoirs: 'Mr Canes, a planter from the island of St Kitts,' she wrote, however, 'tried to get hold of the deed himself, in order to fight a land dispute after a purchaser had reneged on the basis that the Crown's purchase of the soil of the Bahamas could, at a later date, be rendered invalid. For three years, from 1798, Mr Canes 'had applications made for it in the House of Commons, which Mr Pitt always opposed, and having spent five thousand pounds on the matter, he had returned, empty-handed, to St Kitts.'

But at the time, Louisa did take a swipe at the Lords Proprietors of 1787, and suggested that the reason the Proprietors had each accepted £2,000 was because they 'were ignorant of the nature of the property they were required to sell, why they sold without examination, and why for such an immense property they were not only satisfied but deemed themselves fortunate to receive severally the sum of two thousand pounds, which rained upon them like manna on the Israelites, and was received without scruple or reluctance'.

She added that another powerful reason the government should consider her case was that the Scottish Proprietors of the 'Heritable Jurisdictions', which were hereditary feudal powers, were paid £152,000 in 1746, after the Jacobite Rebellion. The Duke of Hamilton received £38,000 of this sum and the Duke of Argyll, £28,000. Louisa wrote that the payment was not for visible property but for 'power, pride, for idea, distinction, custom of living, and habits of thinking, trains of followers, and the Highland dress'. Whilst the government, she wrote, had paid a small fraction of the value for purchase of 'the soil of the Bahama Islands', they had not paid anything for the valuable privileges of the Sovereign Rights. It was all in vain. Parliament once again ignored Richard and Louisa's claims.

CHAPTER 22

Forgery

*

To the Graves' relief, the war with America finally came to an end in the middle of February 1815. But, as the year went on, they came under increasing pressure from Messrs Flood and Mules to clear their debts. To Louisa's distress, Richard sold first her house in Southernhay, and the contents. She then began to fret that Richard's creditors would look to her property in America, and she insisted that she and Richard draw up a series of deeds to prevent this happening.

By the middle of the summer, the *Exeter Flying Post* gave notice that all their possessions at Hembury Fort were to be sold without reserve. This included every animal, carriages, an agate bowl fifteen inches in diameter, musical instruments, their 'rare and valuable books' and pictures 'embracing the works of Correggio; Carlo Dolce, Carracei, Leonardo De Vinci, Titian, Tintaretto, Ruebens, Hughtenburgh, Hemskirk, Mignon, Wovermans, Lonfranc, Vonet, Baptisite, Murillo, N. Poussin, Northcote, Smirke, Gainsborough, Morland, Vanderheyden'. The pictures in this remarkable list, one suspects, were either optimistic attributions or copies, but one or two may have been originals that Louisa salvaged from the Colleton's townhouse in Exeter, and Rill Manor. After these sales, Louisa was left with little more than her clothes, her treasured jewels, which she would never sell to pay any debt, and a few family portraits.

By the beginning of 1816, Hembury Fort, then mortgaged to the hilt, was empty but for a solitary servant employed to prevent it from being ransacked of its marble fireplaces and other fittings. Nevertheless, the proceeds of the sale of six hundred acres of Fairlawn had allowed them to escape again to Bath where they rented an apartment at No. 6, The Circus, one of the grandest addresses in the city. But the funds did not last for long and Richard was declared bankrupt. Louisa wrote, 'the cold blast of penury howled mournfully.' She was now even more desperate to seek compensation for the Bahamas from the British Government, but after Peter Moore re-submitted her claim before Parliament, *The Times* reported on March 16th, that it was again 'Ordered to lie on the Table'.

Louisa was shocked at the outcome. She moaned to everyone, incessantly, about the iniquities of her case and the sale of her house and possessions. This did nothing to endear her to her friends and relations; they had little sympathy and would purposely avoid her company. She had become a dead bore, a death knell in Regency society. When it became known that Louisa would be present at a house party arranged by her daughter Sophia at Idsworth House, many of the guests sent word they would, after all, be unable to attend. One of these was John Graves' son, Joseph, who had been obliged to change his surname to 'Graves Sawle' in order to inherit his mother's estates without encumbrance. Neither he nor his first cousin Mary Graves would have 'any intercourse with that unhappy woman'.

Mary Graves also had reason to feel aggrieved because Richard had not repaid his loans from her father, and she struggled to stay on at Woodbine Hill after his death. Mary felt compelled, in her father's memory and out of kindness, to continue to support her spinster aunts in Ireland. She wrote to them in April 1816: 'Was it not that I feel bound to keep up and inhabit the House my dear Father built for me, I should have little difficulty to retrench my expenses so as to enable me to make up your heavy loss of income. But I cannot live in the Country with less than two maids and one man who waits and works in the garden, & if I had a carriage would drive it, & this is all my present establishment except a poor simple man that has been kept principally out of charity these nine years, & a pair of old Coach Horses I cannot part with, any more than an worn out labourer who has worked about the house since it was built.'

Mary's aunts wished that their niece might have benefited on the death of her childless stepmother, Lady Graves, but she left Mary nothing in her will. 'With the blessing of God,' she told her aunts, 'I hope I shall never be in debt, or so disgrace the principles in which I have been brought up. If everybody was of the same mind in our family I should be able to make your income the same as it was before this unfortunate bankruptcy. I know nothing of my Uncle Richd. but I believe he is in London with his Wife, and that his three daughters with a Governess! are at Mr Ratcliffes.'

The French ports were now opening for business with England, so Richard left for Brussels, as did many other indebted members of the aristocracy and landed gentry. With him went his daughters, Louisa Catherina, aged 24, Septima, 20, and Olivia, 17, all of whom were too old to be incarcerated with a governess. They were delighted to be able to escape the confines of Idsworth House, a dank Elizabethan manor situated in the bottom of a remote valley, for the charming spa city with its ancient ramparts and parks. Louisa remained in England; why she did so is a mystery. It was perhaps to salvage what she could from the wreck, as she had done before. Samuel, it was decided, should leave for America to take over the plantations.

'Desolate is the mansion of Louisa; silent as the dreary tomb are those apartments whence the song and dance late resounded,' Louisa wrote in an address to her daughters, whom she claimed had only left England to 'complete their education'. Louisa was upset that her daughters had chosen to go to Brussels rather than remain with her, 'leaving a widowed wife and childless mother to bewail her hapless destiny.' But she understood why they had chosen to do so, and advised, 'Beware then, unguarded as you now are by maternal solicitude, of the thorns which lurk beneath the rose.' Louisa's warning was not heeded by the feisty and wild Louisa Catherina who, in the absence of her over-protective mother, was 'with child' by the end of the year.

Louisa was furious with Richard for allowing Louisa Catherina to roam un-chaperoned. However, all was resolved on June 16th 1817 when Louisa Catherina left Idsworth House for the nearby Norman church in Chalton. There she was married to a Dutch army officer, the 28-year-old Jacques Louis Dominique van der Smissen. Of stout stature, Jacques was a hardened soldier who had fought for the French in the disastrous Russian campaign of 1812. In 1814, he joined the Dutch army as a major in the Royal Artillery. He was rich and much decorated by the Dutch king for his bravery at the Battle of Waterloo. Louisa was soon taken with the valiant soldier, but unaware that he was not the father of her future grandchild.

Louisa Catherina had become entangled with William, Prince of Orange, heir to the King of the Netherlands. The prince, a tall, good-looking man, who had studied law at Christ Church, Oxford, was notorious for his affairs with both sexes. His marriage in early 1816 to the Grand Duchess Anna Pavlovna of Russia, and the birth of their son, William, in February 1817, had done nothing to curb his sexual appetites. The prince and van der Smissen were 'close', and when Louisa Catherina was expecting the prince's son, it seemed a convenient solution that van der Smissen should marry her. After the wedding, the van der Smissens returned to a castle in the shadows of Kortenberg Abbey, which lay a few miles east from the centre of Brussels, and continued to engage in a *ménage a trois* with the prince. Now that Louisa could no longer trust Richard to ensure Septima and Olivia did not behave like their sister, she, too, travelled to Brussels that summer.

Before Samuel left for South Carolina, needless to say leaving considerable debts behind him, he had used as leverage various deeds that Richard and Louisa had drawn up in 1815 to borrow $40,000 from the London merchants, Davidson and Simpson. Rather than going directly to America, Samuel first went to Nassau where, by some means, he found an original of the power of attorney that had allowed Elizabeth Fulford to sign away Louisa's share of the Bahamas. He painstakingly copied it and sent the facsimile to Brussels.

The document revealed that William Chamberlayne had sworn before the Mayor of London on July 13th 1787 that he was present on April 16th 1785 and 'did see Louisa Carolina Colleton duly sign and seal' the power of attorney that allowed Elizabeth to sell the Bahamas on Louisa's behalf. It was executed in the presence of 'Ann Fulford' and 'William Chamberlayne'. Louisa could clearly see that her own signature was forged on the document, and badly so, as she always signed her full name 'Louisa Carolina Colleton' with a flourish. This document was simply signed 'L.C. Colleton'. Louisa was more astonished to see her mother's signature on the document. Chamberlayne had either forged her plain signature, which was quite possible; or he, and perhaps others, had bribed the vulnerable Ann to sign the document.

It must have been the case that when Elizabeth Fulford signed the final deed for the sale of the 'soil' of the Bahamas on Louisa's behalf at the Guildhall in March 1787, that Chamberlayne had shuffled papers around to ensure that Elizabeth did not at any point see this power of attorney. The only two men present, as stated by the Treasury in a report, were Chamberlayne and his clerk J. Roberts. If Elizabeth had seen the document, even she might have questioned why Ann, who had not seen her daughter for eighteen years and had played no part in her life since Louisa was four years old, would suddenly have been in the same room as her daughter witnessing such a crucial document.

Chamberlayne would not have known, that four days after he had successfully duped Elizabeth Fulford, Louisa signed the power of attorney to Elizabeth, which Joseph Burrows had drawn up. Neither did

Chamberlayne, when adding Ann Fulford as a witness, have any understanding of Louisa's relationship, or lack of it, with her mother.

Louisa was jubilant that she had, at last, the crucial evidence for her case. Richard immediately wrote to Lord Liverpool on July 23rd 1817, telling the Prime Minister that he now had a copy of the power of attorney, and that it was a forgery. He asked that the original deed of sale and the 'pretended power of attorney' be sent home immediately from the Bahamas and he wrote: 'I hereby have the honor to give sufficient notice of my intention to have its production moved for in the House of Commons on the grounds of its forgery and hope to establish a right which has been too long outraged to the great injury of myself and Family no less than to the violation of national justice and faith.'

Shortly after Richard wrote to Lord Liverpool, he and Louisa signed yet another complicated series of deeds which would further put the American lands out of the reach of their creditors. Samuel, now in Charleston, was given Devil's Elbow and Fairlawn. In return, he signed a deed that granted his parents the use of and all the profits from the land in South Carolina. Devil's Elbow was put into a separate trust and titled back to Richard and Louisa for the remainder of their lives. They were to keep possession of nearly three hundred slaves during their lifetimes, after which they would revert to Samuel on the proviso that his sisters, Sophia, Septima, and Olivia were each given six thousand pounds. Richard and Louisa had already drawn up deeds promising this amount to their daughters, Sophia and Louisa Caterina, prior to their marriages. Van der Smissen, no doubt on the back of the loans given to both Richard and Samuel after his marriage to Louisa Caterina, had insisted that a block of land at Fairlawn and a parcel of slaves be earmarked to guarantee Louisa Caterina's share.

For the unmarried Septima and Olivia, the promise of a substantial sum could only help their marriage prospects. Louisa was also mindful that they might well remain spinsters. She could not bear the thought that any of her daughters would be left dependent on their relations for a roof over their head, or their tea and sugar, as Richard's sisters had been for much of their lives. Mary Graves had written miserably on hearing that her young spinster cousin was dying, that she would be better off dead 'as her prospects were so gloomy'.

In late August, Richard received a reply from the Treasury Solicitors answering his demand that the original power of attorney be brought back from the Bahamas to England. He was told: 'Upon a full consideration of the case we see no ground for compliance with Admiral Graves' request.' The Graveses appeared to have lost their case, for without a government order to have the original document returned to England, they had no power to do so themselves.

On September 7th 1817, van der Smissen sent word to Louisa in Brussels that her first grandchild, a son named William, had arrived safely. Louisa, seemingly oblivious to the web in which her daughter was caught, wrote back to her son-in-law to say she could not wait to hold the baby in her arms and asked him that in the meantime to tell Louisa Catherina to kiss the child a thousand times for her. She also castigated her daughter for not listening to her advice on the matter of childbirth. This would no doubt have been sound advice, given that Louisa herself had given birth to ten children. The Prince of Orange, Louisa learnt, was to stand as godfather to the child. Six weeks after William was born, Louisa Catherina and van der Smissen were married once again in the Great Hall in Antwerp, thus validating the marriage in Belgium. The following year, van der Smissen was to be honourably discharged from the army and awarded the title of Baron, to which he added, 'de Cortenbergh'. His motto, admirably, was 'Vestigia nulla retrorsum', which translates from Latin as 'We never go backward'.

CHAPTER 23

Verses on the Cat

*

SAMUEL, meanwhile, had taken up residence in Charleston at 94, The Broad, not far from the landmark St Michaels's Church where Sir James Nassau Colleton had christened his heir, James Roupell, in 1783. As might have been predicted, Samuel soon became 'one of the lads of the village'. He, along with other heirs to great lowland plantations, led slothful and dissolute lives at the expense of their parents. One visitor recorded that as they gambled in their clubs, 'day light often surprises them'. Nevertheless, a local, Dr Irving, wrote of a riot in the theatre shortly after Samuel had arrived in 1817. Samuel, he noted, with all his respect for law and order 'imbibed from his English education', tried to bring order to the theatre as the audience ripped out benches and demolished the chandelier. They could afford to do so, as the price of both cotton and rice were then escalating. Following other planters who were taking advantage of the boom, Samuel quickly purchased fifty-six slaves on credit. Towards the end of the year, he was importing goods into Charleston from Philadelphia; one consignment of claret, paper and ink was for his own consumption.

As Samuel drank all night in the private quarters of the theatre manager, he quite forgot about the delights of Madame Bonaparte. Instead, he set his sights on another heiress, an orphan, the sixteen-year-old Miss Susan McPherson, who had had estates of her own. In addition, she had inherited more than half a million dollars. The impressionable young girl lived with her sister, Elizabeth, and Elizabeth's husband, James Pringle. James was a scion of a notable Charleston family and would later become the mayor of Charleston.

Samuel wrote to the Pringles on March 17th 1818, describing Susan, although probably plain in looks, judging by a portrait of her sister Elizabeth, as the 'most lovely little girl in the world', and told them he would make 'the pleasure of his own life, consist in striving to promote hers'. It is difficult to understand why the Pringles would consider Samuel a suitable husband. His lineage, as a descendant of a Lord Proprietor of the Carolinas, and the boast that he would inherit two notable plantations were perhaps his most appealing virtues, as it was written of him at the time that he was 'careless in his appearance'.

Samuel had a marriage settlement drawn up stating that, after their marriage, Susan's property would be secured on their children, and in default of issue would be left entirely at her disposal. He pledged in a letter to the Pringles: 'I shall also settle the whole property I have in Carolina, on the issue of our marriage, and a jointure to her for life of six thousand dollars a year in addition to her own property. I shall make an additional settlement of property in England; her happiness is very dear to me, and for her, I cannot do enough to satisfy myself.'

Days before Samuel wrote this letter, he had purchased more slaves on credit. The Pringles did not check the validity of Samuel's marriage settlement or his finances, and very shortly after, on April 16th 1818, he and Susan were married. It is likely that Samuel convinced his bride that he had a temporary cash-flow problem, as Susan was 'obliged' to hand over $10,000 to her new husband. A few weeks later, on May 2nd, Samuel sold just over one thousand acres of Fairlawn, in violation of the deed Samuel had signed giving back to his parents the use and profits from Fairlawn for their lifetimes. He also mortgaged Devil's Elbow, which was still legally owned by his parents. It was at this time that Samuel employed Charles Fraser, the talented American miniaturist, to paint two miniatures of him, and one of Susan, at a total cost of $160.*

In November, Samuel unsuccessfully attempted to sell another seven thousand acres of Fairlawn. His failure to do so may have been due to the build-up to the coming financial crisis of 1819. A panic struck the United States: loans were called in, banks failed, the price of land slumped and agricultural prices fell by half.

In February 1819, with her 56th birthday looming, Louisa made an unexpected appearance in Devon. She went to Hembury Fort, which had lain empty, bar one servant since she had left the house four years before. The gardens were overgrown and she wandered alone through the dusty rooms with their shutters closed. Mary mentioned Louisa's visit to Devon in a letter to her aunts, and it appeared that Louisa was showing signs of hysteria and delusion: 'Mrs R.G is now on a visit to Mrs Flood where she came unasked after having been at Exeter planning a new street with some architect. She has found out some rich friend or relation an old

---

* Unfortunately, no trace remains of these portraits.

man worth five millions, as she says, & from whom she expects wonders! But in the meantime is going to London to present her petition to the Parliament about her Bahama claims in which petition she tells the Parliament that she has been long in obscurity. It is now time for her to shine forth, but all this is expressed in such fine language that I cannot repeat it.'

Mary's letter continued: 'As to my Uncle Richd's family I forgot to mention when writing on the other side about Mrs R.G. that she says all of them are going to pay a visit to the Emperor of Russia as he invited them in so pressing a manner that they cannot avoid going. Mrs. R. also says there is some great personage paying his addresses to Septima but she does not know whether she will accept him or nor not. You see they are all far from being objects of pity, as we ignorantly fancied: on the contrary, I dare say they look down on us with compassion or something of that sort, on the other hand I can venture to say that we do not look up at them with envy.' While Louisa was planning to build a new street in Exeter, Mary told her aunts that Richard 'cannot come to England for his debts'.

In August 1819, Richard's nephew, Joseph Graves Sawle, was in Brussels. He had seemingly forgotten his refusal, only three years before, to be in the same house as Louisa, and took the opportunity to visit his family. 'My Uncle Richard', he wrote, 'has a very fine house in the Parc; he and Mrs. R received me with great kindness, Mrs Ratcliff and Septima were at Spa. Madame Van der Smissen [Louisa Catherina] has a house about seven miles from Bruxelles, where she lives with the Baron and her little boy.' Graves Sawle continued, 'She behaves very well,' which may have been a reference to Louisa Catherina's unseemly behaviour before her marriage, 'and appears extremely fond both of her husband and child. I shall say no more of the unmarried ones than that they are in very good health and that everyone seems to be attentive to them, especially the Prince of Orange and the King and Queen, the former of whom asked my Uncle to dinner once, an honour rarely if ever, conferred on an Englishman not in a publick capacity. This I believe as well as their being introduced at Court they owe to Van der Smissen, who was very much esteemed as an officer of merit.' It is to be wondered as to whether Louisa Catherina ever told her parents the reason why the Prince of Orange, and the King and Queen were so 'especially' attentive to the Graves family.

'Septima', John Graves Sawle observed, 'is I believe best liked by the ladies and Olivia by the gentlemen; they seem to be very good-natured and not very fond of dissipation. My poor Uncle seems to be wonderfully broken from what he was. He is still however very much upright but appears to have fretted very much.' Richard had a lot to fret over. Although Devil's Elbow was reputedly producing £9,000 a year from cotton alone, no profits were forthcoming, and none were to be had from Fairlawn. Richard, presumably, kept this from Louisa, as John Graves Sawle said of his aunt: 'Mrs. Richard is better than ever and her age appears to have been advantage to her in soothing her temper and controlling her passions. She is infinitely more pleasant now than she was some years ago. Entre nous her whole ambition now is to be an authoress. I will show you some things she has had printed and you can judge for yourself how far she deserves that title. I think some of the prose pretty and moral.'

Louisa was well known for writing on the backs of old letters when inspired: 'See the scraps of paper fly', she had written, and dedicated her book, *Desultory Thoughts on Various Subjects...*, to her 'beloved children'. The 'trifles' in prose, she explained, were 'Impromptus, to which the burst of feelings gave rise during the painful separation, necessity enforced while my presence was required to business of importance'. The 'trifles', on subjects such as 'Pride', 'Avarice', and 'Dignity', were, she wrote, 'If not marked by burst of genius vivid as the lightening, is, I trust, as delicate as the mimosa of my native land.'

The 'trifles' in prose, were followed by 'Trifles in Verse', and opened with a dedication to Septima in the form of a letter. Louisa writes that she was convinced that when she had been 'dust a hundred years, my compositions will be highly prized'. It is at this point she talks of her 'biographer', whom she added, would no doubt remark: 'that during the eventful period when kingdoms were taken and given with the celerity of magic, this noble lady was during her minority, deprived of her sovereignty; but, being possessed of inexhaustible treasures in the resources of her mind, she retired with dignity from the world, devoting her leisure hours to the muses; the following are verses on the cat.' Her favourite cat was a tortoiseshell, a 'Peerless Pussy, queen of cats', with the improbable name 'Sultana Fidelia'.

The verses, which rightly she thought would be admired, were not only about her cats, and their personification of maternal solicitude. As was the fashion in those Romantic times, they abound with allegories of genies, nymphs and naiads. She writes often of the perils of poverty and the means by which to overcome adversity; subjects which, after all, she had considerable expertise. However, her over-arching themes are of anguish, grief and sorrow, from which, she wrote, she would not be released until death 'chill'd her heart'.

Amidst all this gloom and doom, there was a bright ray of sunshine: Septima became engaged to an 'important personage', Louisa's 2nd cousin, 36-year-old Lieutenant Colonel Sir James Roupell Colleton, the seventh Colleton baronet in succession. The baronet, interestingly, would later refer to Louisa as 'the orphan heiress', and so he, too, was led to believe this was the case.

Unlike his dissolute father who had on two occasions been thrown into Newgate jail for his debts, Sir James Roupell had risen to become one of the most gifted engineers in the British army. He and Septima were married in the house of the British Ambassador at The Hague, Holland, on December 12th 1819. As the marriage was not considered valid in the eyes of English law, they would be married again at St James's Piccadilly, London, on January 6th 1820, 'to obviate any doubts that hereafter arise touching or concerning the validity of the aforesaid marriage.' They then, bizarrely, would marry for a third time, by licence, in front of the same guests, just over a month later. Septima then regaled in the name, 'Septima Sexta Colleton Colleton'. The marriage must have improved Richard's spirits; he was reported to have been in 'high health'.

The bright rays faded when news came from South Carolina that Susan and Samuel's first child, a son, had died in early March 1820, when he was but four days old. The state of Samuel's financial affairs was also causing concern. In June, the Pringles took advice from lawyers as to the legality of Samuel's will, of which they had a copy, and found it littered with discrepancies. The lawyers reported that while Samuel would inherit Fairlawn after his parent's death, he did not own the approximately three hundred slaves on the plantation, nor was Devil's Elbow his to dispose of in his will. Within three days of the lawyers' revelations, Samuel had to borrow £500 to keep his creditors at bay.

Word of Samuel's severe imprudence had finally reached Richard and Louisa, and they at once planned to travel to South Carolina. Although Richard was fearful of being arrested if discovered in England, they sailed on December 13th 1820, from The Downs, bound for New York on the *Indian Chief*, a 'superior coppered' merchant ship of 401 tons which was capable of carrying 65 passengers in steerage. It is probable that they knew the captain, as apart from two servants, they were the only passengers on a ship carrying nothing but ballast. A journey across the Atlantic, as Louisa knew too well, was not for the faint-hearted, and this would be her eighth crossing. The *Indian Chief* sailed in the company of two brigantines for part of the way, which must have been of comfort to her, as was the thought that she would see her beloved son for the first time in four years. With no other passengers on board to amuse Louisa, she contented herself with engaging with the animals and became fond of two pigs, a 'kind-hearted' old boar named Jim and a young pig, 'playful' Joe.

Together the pair wandered the deck grunting in unison; if Joe fell asleep on the deck, the old boy, with 'tenderest care' would recline next to his friend to make him more comfortable. The fate of these hapless pigs inspired her to put pen to paper.

> Cruel Fate doom'd Jim to bleed,
> Joe kindly strove t'avert the deed,
> His furious zeal inspir'd dread,
> In haste th'affrighted butcher fled,
> Alas, poor Jim, he strove in vain,
> To save thee from impending pain

Joe, Louisa wrote, was eventually restrained, and when Jim was dispatched, the old boar fell forlornly on the deck.

As they approached the east coast of America, the temperature plunged. The *New York Post* exclaimed on January 29th 1821, 'Wednesday night last was probably the most uncomfortable and piercing weather ever experienced in this latitude.' The temperature in New York fell to 18°F below freezing, and conditions on board the *Indian Chief* must have been unbearable. They had been at sea for 51 days before the ship entered the all-but-icebound port of New York on February 2nd. Louisa's feet, however, barely touched the ground before the *Indian Chief* left for Charleston. While the wind carried her quickly down the coast, she ran into turbulent seas within sight of the city on the 5th. The *Charleston Daily Courier* reported that the *Indian Chief* took on a pilot, but was still at anchor on February 7th, 'not being able to get in yesterday on account of the heavy sea upon the bar'. It was not until the 9th, that she cleared the bar and sailed into the harbour.

Samuel, meanwhile, was only concerned with race week, 'the culmination of the social season in Charleston.' He had been appointed as a steward to the hallowed Jockey Club of South Carolina in 1818, and that week he had been stewarding at the Washington Course, which was water-logged. Samuel, unaware of his parent's journey from Brussels, was very shocked on their arrival. According to Mary Graves, he had the nerve to say, 'what did they do there as they had no property in that country?' Samuel, Mary wrote, had endeavoured 'to cheat his parents out of the American property, & thinking he had done so, in which luckily he was mistaken.'

Just ten days before Richard and Louisa arrived in New York, an adver-tisement had appeared in the *Charleston City Gazette* announcing an auc-tion on February 18th of nearly 6,000 acres of Fairlawn. By a fluke, Richard and Louisa had arrived just in time to prevent its auction. But learning of the debts then accumulated by Samuel, they were obliged to sell 1800 acres on March 17th. This was the day after Samuel and Susan's daughter, Carolina, was born, and it can only be left to the imagination as to the fraught exchanges that must have taken place over Carolina's cradle.

The Graveses eventually went to Devil's Elbow which, apart from a few acres, Louisa had managed to keep intact since the day she inherited it. She still had no idea of the depths of deception and fraud that her beloved son had sunk to, and was unaware that Samuel had mortgaged the plantation. Devil's Elbow was, however, still functioning, and Richard and Louisa were able to have packed a large consignment of tobacco. They left from Savannah on May 18th, on board the sloop, *Mary*, accom-panied by 'several servants', and after a journey of fourteen hours, arrived back in Charleston.

Only a few days later, on May 21st, Richard and Louisa drew up yet another deed in order to assure their daughters of their promised inher-itances. They put all their slaves into a trust and, after Richard and Louisa's death, Samuel was to inherit them on the proviso that he pay within a year, the sum of £7,000 to Sophia, and £6,000 each to Septima and Olivia. Samuel possessed such charm and charisma that he persuaded his gullible parents of his reformation. And, in an act of monumental stu-pidity, they left Samuel in charge of the remnants of the Colleton estates, believing that he would not sell any more land. Once more, Louisa allowed her heart to rule her head.

No doubt heedful of Sir Augustus Foster's recommendation that no one should stay in Charleston during the hot humid days of the 'sicklie' season, at the end of May, falsely believing they had secured their daughters' inheritance, Richard and Louisa decided to return home. They boarded the *Empress*, bound for New York; this would be Louisa's final 'adieu' to South Carolina. Samuel was no doubt relieved to see the back of his parents.

The *Empress*, carrying a quantity of rice, some of it no doubt from Fairlawn, arrived in New York on June 6th 1821. Five days later, Richard and Louisa sailed for Liverpool on the *Thames*, a ship of 400 tons with 'very superior furnished accommodation', under the captaincy of an old sea- dog, Charles Henry Maxwell. Whilst on board, Louisa, who so often sought solace in animals, became very attached to the captain's little terrier, Thames, who had been born on board the ship.

He, too, inspired Louisa to immortalise him in a poem. After a swift journey, the Graves, under assumed names, arrived in Liverpool, from where they managed to reach Brussels unhindered by their creditors.

CHAPTER 24

A Heap of Dust

*

WHEN Richard and Louisa arrived back in Brussels during the summer of 1821, Louisa soon published a second version of *Desultory Thoughts…*, now containing not only her 'trifles' in prose and verse, but also her story which she had started writing on board her schooner, the *Nancy*, some 36 years before. She began: 'Think not, reader, whoe'er thou art, who in an idle hour castest thine eye over the following lines, that they were written from the vain idea that any circumstance of my life would be deemed worthy the attention or capable of amusing one who, being a stranger to me, must be indifferent to my welfare.'

She now wrote that independent of her title 'Sovereign Proprietress, which from its magnitude includes all lesser titles,' that she was also Baroness of Fairlawn and Landgravine of Colleton. Although, she admits that her titles were 'useless' after the American Revolution and that they lay dormant. The historian, Henry A.M. Smith, in 1900, wrote sneeringly of Louisa that she was not the descendant of a Landgrave, 'but of a Proprietor, and was therefore not a Landgravine; nor is the female heir of a baronet a baroness.' In fact, he was wrong: Louisa was the descendant of a 'Landgrave', and that had titles still been in use, she would indeed have been styled as Baroness of Fairlawn, and Landgravine of Colleton.

Having regaled her reader with tales of her ancestors, Louisa added: 'When I reflect on the exalted rank of my illustrious ancestors, it makes me feel how cruelly I have been crushed, and it overwhelms my spirits even to melancholy.' She probably had even more reason to think the family had been 'crushed'. Sir James Roupell Colleton, perhaps encouraged by Louisa, had pressed the British Government for further compensation for Wadboo. The family had received £900 from the American government for the sale of the plantation, whereby rights, Sir James Roupell claimed the total was near £45,000. Even though he had the backing and support of his friend, the Duke of York, who would later become godfather to his second son, the British government informed Sir James Roupell: 'There are no funds to meet such cases.'

Once again, disturbing news of Samuel's behaviour in South Carolina reached Brussels. Richard and van der Smissen, adamant that Samuel's excesses be curbed for the sake of his sisters, were determined to make a short visit to America. Richard, Louisa, their daughter Olivia, and the van der Smissens temporarily moved to Paris to enable Richard, who would be arrested if he set foot in England, to sail out of a French port. While waiting for a ship, the van der Smissen's second son died, aged eighteen months, and Louisa Catherina begged her husband not to leave her. Richard had to set sail without him. The van der Smissens returned to Brussels, leaving Louisa and Olivia, in Paris, to await Richard's return.

When Richard set sail from Le Havre for New York on February 6th 1822, he did not know that Samuel had advertised the sale of two parts of Fairlawn. The first was the 'Old House' tract of 2144 acres, containing 122 acres of prime 'Tide Rice Land'. It was boasted that some of the land would be well adapted to the 'culture of coton'. The second tract was the 'Stoney Landing Plantation' of 2319 acres, of which 88 were prime rice land. Six weeks later, the Liverpool Packet arrived in New York. Richard at once left for Charleston, where he found that Samuel had sold the 'Old House' tract on February 5th. Unable to deal with his father's unexpected arrival and understandable fury, Samuel at once bolted to his mother in Paris.

Richard was left holding not only reams of sale deeds and loan bonds, but also the sudden responsibility for what was left of the plantations, including the welfare of hundreds of slaves. Moreover, there was the matter of Samuel's naïve wife and her one-year-old daughter, Carolina. Samuel's creditors were taking possession of anything they could seize, including 'six elegant horses and two elegant carriages'. This was only to be the beginning. It could not have been worse for Richard, who had hoped to extract some money from the plantations. Money which he was entitled to under the various deeds he and Louisa had exchanged with their son.

Richard retreated to Devil's Elbow in May 1822 and, in early June, the lawyer J. Hamilton Junior placed a notice in the *Charleston City Gazette* asking Samuel's creditors to meet at the Carolina Coffee House that very day 'on business of importance to themselves'. A few weeks later, one of Samuel's creditors, Thomas Cochran, a land and slave agent, apprehended Samuel's house slave, curiously named Louisa, and delivered her to the sheriff's office. She was to be sold for cash at the beginning of July.

A dishevelled Samuel eventually appeared on Louisa's doorstep in Paris at the end of April. As he had left America so swiftly after his father's arrival, Louisa must have sensed that he had again acted shamelessly, but, as always, she forgave him. Olivia, however, could not forgive her despicable brother, or bear to be in the same house as him, knowing that her inheritance was slipping through his fingers. She went to Brussels to live with the van der Smissens, and was no doubt re-united with her married lover, Henry Jones. After Olivia left Paris, Samuel fleeced his mother for yet more funds in order to travel on to England.

Samuel arrived in Devon where, Mary Graves reported to her aunts, he imposed himself on the Floods for three nights. Christopher Flood, who had for many years acted as Richard's lawyer and agent, had already suffered Louisa's presence uninvited three years before, and now the same with Samuel. It is perhaps indicative of the extent to which the Graveses were disliked, that none of their relations or friends would have them to stay, and only the Floods dared not refuse them. Samuel, Mary wrote, 'talks of living at Hembury Fort next year, but I believe I have as much chance of living there, for I do not find any money is forthcoming to pay the debts. He says his wife is not yet of age, but I suspect she will never be more of age that at present as she was to have been of age I thought before now. He says his wife wishes to remain in America but he wishes to return to Hembury Fort. I think her wish is most likely to be accomplished.'

Mary wrote: 'While he was being entertained by the Floods, Samuel spoke disparagingly of his sisters, except Louisa Catherina, who, according to him, 'was the only one who behaved like a sister to him.' She told her aunts that she believed she could account for this; Louisa Catherina was the only one 'who has got all the fortune she can expect, & the others are fearful their brother will prevent their ever receiving their share, & and are trying to secure it.' Mary could not help but add of Samuel: 'I understand Mr. C.G. drinks quantities of spirits, looks very ill & has been seen drunk of a morning. If so he cannot live many years.'

Mary had always put the blame for Samuel's behaviour squarely on his parents. Some two years before, she had written of a mutual cousin, a young boy, saying that she hoped he would 'not be spoilt, of which I trust there will be no danger, as all his relations must have seen enough of the heart rending evils attending on mistaken kindness and foolish indulgence, especially towards boys'.

Louisa never considered that it may have been her fault, and Richard's, that Samuel behaved as he did. Instead, she put the blame for his misdemeanors on the company that he kept. Her blinkered view of her son would continue almost to the end. In a poem addressed to Samuel's daughter, Carolina, she hoped she would be as good a daughter to her father as Samuel had been to his parents, adding: 'Be thou the comfort of his life, As he has ever been of ours'. Louisa could not, or would not, face the fact that Samuel was, as Mary Graves wrote, 'worthless'. Meanwhile, it had been made clear to Samuel that he was not welcome in Devon, and so he left for New York where he arrived at the end of September 1822.

Louisa's relationship with her three daughters was then already fraught, particularly with Olivia. But after it became more than apparent, not only to Olivia, but to Septima and Louisa Catherina as well, that Louisa had once more indulged Samuel to their detriment, they all but deserted her. Louisa could have been expected at the christening, in Kent, in early September, of Septima's son, Nassau, for whom the 'grand old' Duke of York, the 5th Earl of Rochford and Sophia Ratcliffe stood as godparents. But she did not attend. This was perhaps all the more sad for Louisa, as Septima's first son had died when he was eleven days old, and Nassau was the heir to the Colleton baronetcy. Louisa Catherina, with whom Olivia lived, was expecting her third child, but Louisa did not visit her in Brussels. By the end of the year, Sophia, having never received any of her promised inheritance, was reduced to living with her husband in a small set of rooms in London, paid for by the week.

Adding to Louisa's woes, she now felt entirely abandoned by Richard, who was, by then, 'hopelessly insolvent'. Her desperate letters to him began to stack up in the postmaster's office in Charleston, unanswered, as he remained at Devil's Elbow.

Having received no word from Richard for months, Louisa left Paris for London. She did not know that on her arrival she was being tracked by agents acting for Richard's creditors, who reported that she 'was reduced to the necessity of pawning her jewels, and even her wearing apparel to obtain the necessary means of subsistence'. This was the last sighting of Louisa. According to the press, she died, aged 59, 'near' London on Christmas Day 1822. One can presume that she died while on a coach, or in some roadside inn. Louisa had little more than the clothes she wore.

Perhaps she was on her way to take refuge at Great Fulford, as there was really nowhere else for her to go. She had remained good friends with her first cousin, Baldwin Fulford; invitations to family events flowed between them over the years, and he possessed the generosity of heart to offer her sanctuary. Baldwin had by then several children, and together with his wife, Anna Maria, would no doubt have ensured Louisa had her old bedroom, where the yellow silk curtains had not been replaced since she had left the house in the spring of 1785.

Someone would have had to pay for Louisa's body to be carried from 'near' London to Hembury Fort, and also for the fees incurred as her remains crossed county boundaries. On January 7th 1823, thirteen days after she died, Louisa was buried in the graveyard of St Mary and St Giles Church in Buckerell. No headstone can be found, but some lines from Alexander Pope's 'Elegy to the Memory of an Unfortunate Lady' could well have been written of her:

> So Peaceful rests, without a stone, a name
> What once had beauty, title, wealth and fame,
> How lov'd, how honour'd once, avails thee not
> To whom related, or by whom begot,
> A heap of dust alone remains of thee
> Tis all thou art, and all the proud shall be!

Epilogue

*

PERHAPS it was a blessing that Louisa died when she did, as ill fortune continued to haunt the family. She was not bred for poverty, and after her death, Richard would stumble through one financial crisis to another. He returned to Brussels from South Carolina to deal with his 'deranged affairs', and tried to resurrect Louisa's claim to the Bahamas by writing to the Prime Minister, Lord Liverpool. He received his own letter back with a scrawl in pencil, 'can't be of any service to you.'

In South Carolina, Samuel Graves died six months after his mother, of a heart attack on the evening of his 35th birthday. When the news reached Brussels, Olivia Graves' lover, Henry Jones, at once set sail for America. This was perhaps at Richard's request, as he was unable to travel freely. Jones, who had left his wife by then, was no doubt keen to do anything which might secure Olivia's inheritance. He arrived in New York at the beginning of October but Richard did not land in Savannah until early December 1823, from where he went to Devil's Elbow.

Richard discovered that Samuel had been bombarded with lawsuits in the run-up to his death. The bank had threatened to foreclose on the Devil's Elbow' mortgage, and other creditors clamoured for the sale of the slaves to recover their debts. The tenacious London merchants, Davidson and Simpson, to whom both Richard and Samuel owed large sums of money, also filed a case in Charleston court in June 1824. These dire circumstances drove Richard and Jones back to Brussels.

Van der Smissen, however, was confident that something could be salvaged and insisted that Richard accompany him to Charleston. Louisa Catherina would not be left behind, so together with two of their sons, the party left Le Havre. They arrived in Charleston on Christmas Eve, 1824, but were clearly not welcome. By January 6th 1825, they were all in New York, from where they returned to Brussels. That autumn, Richard wrote to his sisters to complain that he did little more each day than gaze out of the window and, as might have been expected, expressed the hope that he might find a rich heiress or widow.

In 1827, lawyers in Devon were busy selling off all of Louisa's assets. This included 'divers valuable messuages, dwelling houses, rich lands, gardens and pleasure grounds', spread over three parishes. The Colleton's townhouse in Exeter was let on a long lease and somehow escaped the notice of creditors. It was all that was left of Louisa's inheritance. Hembury Fort and the estate were also put up for auction the following year by Christopher Flood and Philip Mules, to whom it was mortgaged.

It was not until June 1828 that the *Charleston Mercury* published Judge Nott's lengthy summing up of the court case bought by Davidson and Simpson against Richard and Samuel, which he admitted was tedious. One of his points was that the Graves's estates in 1817 were valued at $780,000, and that there should surely have been enough money to repay the debt to the merchants, and honour the girls' marriage settlements.

The court cases in Charleston, however, dragged on due to endless appeals by the family, desperate to retain a share of the spoils. In 1829 Samuel's widow, Susan, was repaid the $10,000 she had given him shortly after their marriage. Susan was to marry another wastrel who squandered her inheritance, and on her death, her only child, Carolina, was left $500, and a bond of $9,000, which later proved worthless. Van der Smissen was also paid his dues. After this, both Fairlawn and Devil's Elbow were split into tracts to be sold, and the remaining slaves were to be sold at auction. When Devil's Elbow came up for sale in November 1828, it was decreed by the court in Charleston that Richard would have the month of January 1829, to come and go from Devil's Elbow at will in order to collect his personal possessions. There is no evidence that Richard ever did so.

The sales of what remained of Fairlawn and Devil's Elbow were, however, delayed by a last-ditch attempt to secure Septima's promised inheritance. She and her husband, Sir James Roupell Colleton, sailed for Charleston in 1831. Their case was thrown out of court and they retired to New York, where Sir James appealed to Congress for further compensation over Wadboo. He eventually received the reply, 'no answer whatever'. On December 14th, the night before they were due to set sail for England, Septima, mother of four young children, died of tuberculosis compounded by malaria. The next day, her coffin was carried onto the ship. After weeks at sea, the seventh Lady Colleton was eventually deposited in the family vault in St James's Church, Piccadilly, which, it is reputed, had been built in part with wood grown at Wadboo.

Sir James Roupell never forgave Richard, whom he claimed, in court, had defrauded him. The baronet's bitterness did not end there: he always believed Devil's Elbow, which had been left to his grandfather by his older brother, was his by right. The Graves family to this day, say that 'everyone hated Richard'. He had squandered his inheritance from his uncle, Admiral Samuel Graves, and, by his own admission, had lost Louisa's fortune. Of their daughters, only Louisa Catherina received a share of her mother's estates.

Richard was to linger for another fourteen years after Louisa's death, never finding his rich widow. Instead, he continued to live with the van der Smissens. The hot-blooded baron was exiled from Belgium in 1830 after taking part in the revolution there, and he, Louisa Catherina, and their four sons went to live in Paris. Fortunately, van der Smissen was given a generous allowance by King William of the Netherlands, and Richard was reliant on his son-in-law for 'his daily bread' and roof over his head. So, too, were Olivia, and her 'train', as Mary Graves dismissively referred to her family consisting of her lover, Henry Jones, who was 'perennially broke', and their four illegitimate children. It must have been quite a household with eight of Richard's grandchildren running around.

Richard died aged 78, on March 4th 1836, and was buried in a grand marble and limestone tomb in the Parisian cemetery of Père Lachaise. Even in death, he did not give up his vain pursuit of compensation from the British government for the Bahamas. He wrote in his will that he was entitled to his wife's property, which included the Sovereign Rights to the Bahamas, and noted that proceedings were still pending. Perhaps he had every good reason to persist in his claim, for on June 8th 1828, the Duke of Atholl was granted £417,000, in full and final compensation for the family's Sovereign Rights to the Isle of Man. To his dying day, Richard was also convinced that the treasury solicitors had not only been duplicitous in the sale of the Bahamas in 1787 but that there were still 'monies' invested in the 'Court of Chancery or in some other court or in the hands of trustees or executors or in the Bank of England or in some other bank', which had belonged to Louisa. This may well have been true. Chamberlayne, it was noted at his death, left his son a considerable estate.

Of Richard and Louisa's surviving children, Sophia, who at her mother's death was living in distressed circumstances in Marylebone, had left with her husband, Tristram Ratcliff, in 1824, for Exeter, his plantation in Jamaica, where he had possession of nearly 190 slaves. While Sophia would have had first-hand knowledge of slavery in South Carolina from her mother, she could not have foreseen the horror encountered in Jamaica. The account of an overseer, who had at one point worked at Exeter, described the sexual depravity and barbarism of many of the plantation owners, as fit for hell.

Soon after their arrival in Jamaica, Ratcliff died four days after contracting yellow fever, leaving his indebted estates to his wife. Mary Graves wrote that Sophia was then in a 'deplorable state'. Her estate in England was not worth a hundred pounds a year, and Mary thought that as she 'could receive nothing in this country from her W. Indies property, I do not see what she can do but remain where she is at present where at least she can get food to eat on her own estates while living on them'.

The resilient Sophia remained in Jamaica for six years, then returned to London in 1830. There, she followed in the footsteps of her grandmother, Ann Fulford, when, at the age of 41, she married 26-year-old Maximilian August, Baron von Ketelholdt, at St James's, Westminster. Sophia went back to Jamaica with her husband, a plump Prussian civil servant from an ancient German family, and a year later they had a daughter they named Carolina. In 1865, the year slavery was abolished in America, Baron von Ketelholdt, who sat as a Justice, was brutally murdered during a tax rebellion. Three years later Sophia died, and it was reported that her remains were followed by a 'large body of citizens, anxious to pay a last tribute of respect, not only for the venerable lady just departed, but to the memory of the late baron, who fell victim to the insurrection of October 1865 whilst endeavouring by patience to appease an infuriated mob in a thirst for bloodshed which culminated in the massacre at Morant Bay'.

If Sophia's life had been one of misfortune and high drama, the life of Louisa Catherina, 'her mama personified', would eclipse that of her sister. In 1839, a general amnesty was declared in Belgium and Baron van der Smissen returned to the country. He demanded that the Government restore his titles and also reinstate his half-pay as Lieutenant General. The Belgian Ministry was brought down by failing to reach agreement on van der Smissen's demands. A new Ministry did, however, later restore his titles. But, in April 1840, *The Times* in England reported that the Belgian Government had revoked their earlier decision, and van der Smissen was now 'reduced to the condition of a private citizen, without any functions, civil or military'.

The baron set out to take revenge and planned an attack to overthrow the government on the commemoration day of the coronation of King Leopold I. However, one of the conspirators informed the authorities of the imminent uprising. In October 1841, van der Smissen, Louisa Catherina, their sixteen-year-old son, Ernest, and van der Smissen's brother, Joseph, were, among others, indicted for conspiracy against the state of Belgium and other crimes. *The Times* noted it was the second time van der Smissen had committed treason, and that he would undoubtedly now pay with his life. All of the conspirators were kept in solitary confinement, but, on the 8th, charges were dropped against the young Ernest and he was set free.

In January 1842, a lengthy case commenced in court, and on March 24th the Advocate General declared that even if the prisoners were found guilty and sentenced to death, executions would not take place. On hearing this, van der Smissen and his co-conspirators cried out: 'We want no mercy.' That day the jury deliberated the case for some hours and on their return acquitted van der Smissen's brother, Joseph, and Louisa Catherina, who were asked to leave the courtroom. Louisa Catherina, 'whose grief was intense, exclaimed: "No, I will never quit my husband," and threw herself into his arms. She was allowed to remain. The jury retired again, subsequently returning to the courtroom at seven o'clock in the evening. The verdict was a sentence of death for all four of the remaining men, who were also ordered to pay the costs of the trial. The executions were to be carried out in 'one of the public places in Brussels'.

The Times reported that when the sentence of death was 'passed upon General Van der Smissen and the others, Madame Van der Smissen uttered cries which produced a most painful impression upon all present'. *The Independent of Brussels* reported that 'Madame Van der Smissen accompanied her husband on his return to prison, and remained with him until a late hour'. The *Observateur* speculated that all four of those condemned to death had given notice of their appeal against the sentence and that it was likely the King would 'exercise the prerogative of mercy in their favour'.

While van de Smissen was incarcerated, the authorities allowed his family to visit between ten in the morning and four in the afternoon. He had been feigning illness for some days, which 'afforded a pretext for his wife to prolong her visits'. At 8 o'clock on the evening of November 6th 1842, the family pulled off one of the oldest tricks in the book. The baron, dressed in his wife's clothes, walked out of the jail with their two sons. The next morning, Louisa Catherina was questioned as she was leaving, but explained that she had stayed the night with her ill husband. And with that, she walked out of the jail. Van der Smissen's disappearance was not noticed until three o'clock that afternoon, and by then he had been whisked, by way of Waterloo, across the Dutch border. It was later learned that the jailor did not check whether van der Smissen was in his cell, but hearing a cough, wished him good night. English newspapers revelled in the tale of 'General Van der Smissen's Escape', and the *Examiner* in London, reported on November 12th, 'It seems unaccountable how the keeper could be deceived, the General being a head taller than his wife.'

Soon after, the Magistrates learned that Louisa Catherina and her son, Adolphe, were in Aix-la-Chapelle, just over the border in Germany. The youngest son, Ernest, who had been left behind, was arrested and was 'not permitted to see anyone in prison'. Louisa Catherina and Adolphe were captured and, on November 18th, a vast crowd appeared at the Court of Correctional Police in Brussels to hear the judgment on those culpable of aiding and abetting the baron's escape. The jailor was sent to jail for six months, Louisa Catherina and her boys, Adolphe and Ernest, were sent to jail for just twenty-four hours and ordered to pay the costs of the trial.

Reporters were now, understandably, entranced by tales of the baroness. A press report from Brussels, dated November 20th, stated: 'An anecdote is related to the wife of General Van der Smissen, which if true, is of a rather romantic character. This lady is an English-woman of a somewhat fanciful turn of mind. She is firmly convinced that she shall die on the scaffold, and in her last examination before the *Juges d'Instruction* exclaimed, "I am descended from the illustrious and unfortunate line of the Plantagenets. The sword thirsts for my blood." After the trial and her short imprisonment, Louisa Catherina joined her husband in Prussia. Although she was convinced she would die on the scaffold, Louisa Catherina ended up running a hotel in Hamburg instead.

It was in the city that Olivia Graves and Henry Jones, after a long cohabitation, were finally married in 1845. The wedding took place some five weeks after Henry's wife, Katherine, considered a 'termagant' by some, committed suicide. Upon marriage, Olivia became stepmother to Katherine's sons, who were openly known as the 'Orange Blossoms', as Katherine, too, had had an affair with the Prince of Orange.

It cannot be said for certain as to whether Alfred, the second eldest of Louisa Catherina's sons, was an 'Orange Blossom'. He went on to serve in the Belgian army and reportedly was athletic, impetuous and aggressive; one contemporary said of him that he had 'a heart of gold, a steel arm, a vacuum head'. This could as well have been written of his grand-father, Richard Graves. Alfred was given command of the Belgian Foreign Legion, raised specifically to give support to the beautiful, only daughter of King Leopold I, Carlota, who had married the doomed Maximilian, Emperor of Mexico. While on service in Mexico, Alfred was rumoured to have had an affair with Carlota. It was later widely believed that the result was an illegitimate son, Maxime Wegand, who became commander-in-chief of the French armies in 1940. There is a very striking likeness between Weygand and Alfred, and as Weygand died at the age of 98, he appears to have inherited the Graves family gene for longevity. Weygand, himself, would never be drawn as to his parentage, and always claimed to have been born a foundling. However, as many have commented, Weygand was well-educated and there was no lack of funds for his support. Perhaps the final word on the matter should be left to King Leopold II, who admitted during an interview with the historian, Andre Castelot, that 'Weygand is the son of van der Smissen'.

After the public revelation of another of Alfred's affairs, this time with the only daughter of a fellow officer, Alfred withdrew from his prominent position at the court in Brussels. A few weeks later, on June 16th 1895, he shot himself, aged 72. His three brothers followed suit. William took his own life on June 28th, and the *New York Times* reported that Adolphe, the youngest of the brothers, aged 69, 'blew his brains out with a revolver' on July 15th, in the house next door to Alfred's. In August 1895, the *Huddersfield Chronicle and West Yorkshire Advertiser* reported: 'A telegram from Vichy reports that Baron van der Smissen, a member of a well-known Brussels family, attempted suicide by blowing his brains out on the racecourse, on Friday.' Ernest died of his injuries just more than a year later. These were the tragic ends of Richard and Louisa's grandsons, of whom Richard had written, 'such fine boys, strong and handsome'.

Postscript

*

The Yellow Portrait

Every story should, however, have a happy ending.

IT was only at the end of my 'merry dance' following the tracks of Louisa's story, that I discovered a three-quarter-length portrait of Louisa in her prime, painted shortly after her marriage to Richard Graves in 1787 and also one of Richard, in Captain's uniform, which may have painted in America during the American Revolution.

These portraits were left to Olivia Graves' son, Algernon Jones, who in true Graves fashion had married an heiress, Isaline Hedelhofer. They had one daughter, Annette, who on her marriage to an army officer in 1878, brought with her a dowry of 120,000 francs, and an annuity of a further 20,000 francs. Annette had no children and the portraits of Louisa and Richard went to relations of Annette's mother. By this route, they came into the possession of Hervé Pappillaut des Charbonnerie, a famous resistance fighter in the Second World War, who became the lover of Christian Dior's sister, Catherine. The picture of Louisa hung in pride of place in the Charbonnerie's drawing room in Paris and was later moved to Les Naÿssès, in the South of France, which Catherine Dior inherited from her father. When some of the last possessions of Catherine Dior were sold at auction in 2012, the pictures of Louisa and Richard were amongst them and both were bought by a Parisian dealer. He dispatched Louisa off to auction again, leaving Richard in his stacks.

As Louisa wrote, 'had the hour of my nativity been cast, if the stars deserve any faith, my friends might then have known what a wanderer I was doomed to be.' The same applies to her portrait. Louisa was eventually sold to the Dior conglomerate and sent to Christian Dior's old chateau, La Colle Noire, in the South of France.

Louisa's portrait is known as the 'Yellow portrait' because of the heavy gold silk dress that she is wearing. Her hair, which she described as 'black auburn and very fine, with a slight wave in it', and of which she was so proud, hangs, in defiance of fashion, un-powdered and loose to below waist. Surprisingly, there are many similarities between Louisa's portrait and that of her aunt, Elizabeth Fulford, painted by William Hoare of Bath. They both have their jewels draped from shoulder to waist, and both have twisted pearls on both wrists.

John Graves once wrote that Louisa had appeared at a masquerade 'ornamented with a number of diamonds'. The diamond bandeau on her head and the dark jewels in the portrait, one which clasps her pearls at the centre of her décolletage, and the two which are pinned to the ermine and lace cuffs on her dress, are likely to be those very diamonds mentioned by John – it was, oddly, the fashion at the time to paint the back of diamonds black. Louisa's pearl earrings are also particularly magnificent and can be compared to those once worn by Queen Henrietta Maria, wife of Charles I.

It must have broken Louisa's heart when she had to pawn the jewels at the end of her life; these were the last trappings of her inheritance.

She would though, have been delighted that her portrait did not end up hanging, neglected, in a dark corridor, or languishing in the basement of some gallery or dealer. Instead, Louisa, adorned by her treasures, now graces the Grand Salon of one of the greatest Haute couturiers of the 20th century. A fitting end for the 'little Queen'.

Acknowledgements

*

My thanks to Gerard Molyneaux, (a descendant of Richard Graves' brother, Samuel), for allowing me access to his family papers and portraits.

I thank Todd Gray, an American and yet one of Devon's great historians, who told me that Richard and Louisa were often mentioned in Miss Burges's letters to Elizabeth Simcoe while she was in Canada.

I would like to thank everyone who read early drafts of the book.

My thanks to the family I met on the shores of the River Cooper who led me to the ruins of Fairlawn, and the British Fort. I would never have found them, without their help.

I would like to thank all the staff I met while in libraries and record offices, on both sides of the Atlantic, who, without fail, did their best to help me. These include the Devon Record Office; Plymouth and West Devon Record Office; Cornwall Record Office; West Sussex Record Office; Somerset Record Office; Gloucestershire Record Office; Badminton Muniments; House of Lords Record Office; British Library; Bodleian Library; Public Record Office; London Metropolitan Archives; Maryland Historical Society; South Carolina Historical Society; South Carolina Department of Archives and History; Department of Archives, Nassau, Bahamas; Caird Library, National Maritime Museum; National Art Library Archives, Victoria and Albert Museum.

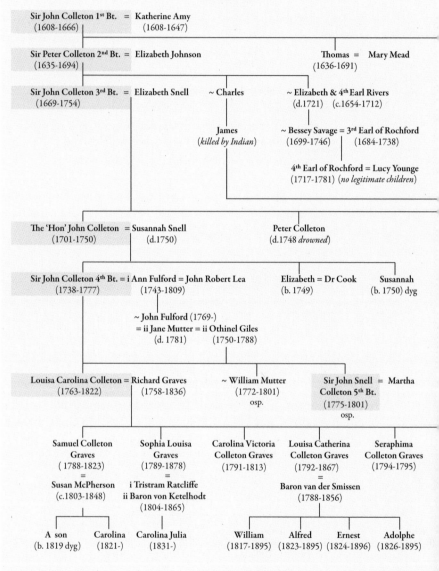

— COLLETON —
FAMILY TREE
(simplified)

Sir John Colleton 1ˢᵗ Bt. = Katherine Amy
(1608-1666)   (1608-1647)

Sir Peter Colleton 2ⁿᵈ Bt. = Elizabeth Johnson   Thomas = Mary Mead
(1635-1694)   (1636-1691)

Sir John Colleton 3ʳᵈ Bt. = Elizabeth Snell   ~ Charles   ~ Elizabeth & 4ᵗʰ Earl Rivers
(1669-1754)   (d.1721)   (c.1654-1712)

James   ~ Bessey Savage = 3ʳᵈ Earl of Rochford
(*killed by Indian*)   (1699-1746)   (1684-1738)

4ᵗʰ Earl of Rochford = Lucy Younge
(1717-1781) (*no legitimate children*)

The 'Hon' John Colleton = Susannah Snell   Peter Colleton
(1701-1750)   (d.1750)   (d.1748 *drowned*)

Sir John Colleton 4ᵗʰ Bt. = i Ann Fulford = John Robert Lea   Elizabeth = Dr Cook   Susannah
(1738-1777)   (1743-1809)   (b. 1749)   (b. 1750) dyg

~ John Fulford (1769-)
= ii Jane Mutter = ii Othinel Giles
(d. 1781)   (1750-1788)

Louisa Carolina Colleton = Richard Graves   ~ William Mutter   Sir John Snell = Martha
(1763-1822)   (1758-1836)   (1772-1801)   Colleton 5ᵗʰ Bt.
osp.   (1775-1801)
osp.

Samuel Colleton Graves	Sophia Louisa Graves	Carolina Victoria Colleton Graves	Louisa Catherina Colleton Graves	Seraphima Colleton Graves
(1788-1823)	(1789-1878)	(1791-1813)	(1792-1867)	(1794-1795)
=	=			
Susan McPherson	i Tristram Ratcliffe		Baron van der Smissen	
(c.1803-1848)	ii Baron von Ketelhodt		(1788-1856)	
	(1804-1865)			

A son   Carolina   Carolina Julia   William   Alfred   Ernest   Adolphe
(b. 1819 dyg)   (1821-)   (1831-)   (1817-1895) (1823-1895) (1824-1896) (1826-1895)

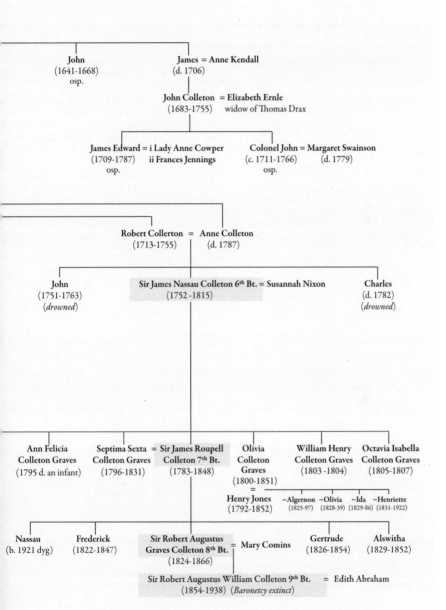

John
(1641-1668)
osp.

James = Anne Kendall
(d. 1706)

John Colleton = Elizabeth Ernle
(1683-1755)   widow of Thomas Drax

James Edward = i Lady Anne Cowper
(1709-1787)   ii Frances Jennings
osp.

Colonel John = Margaret Swainson
(c. 1711-1766)   (d. 1779)
osp.

Robert Collerton = Anne Colleton
(1713-1755)   (d. 1787)

John
(1751-1763)
(*drowned*)

Sir James Nassau Colleton 6th Bt. = Susannah Nixon
(1752-1815)

Charles
(d. 1782)
(*drowned*)

Ann Felicia
Colleton Graves
(1795 d. an infant)

Septima Sexta = Sir James Roupell
Colleton Graves   Colleton 7th Bt.
(1796-1831)   (1783-1848)

Olivia
Colleton
Graves
(1800-1851)
=
Henry Jones
(1792-1852)

William Henry
Colleton Graves
(1803-1804)

Octavia Isabella
Colleton Graves
(1805-1807)

~Algernon ~Olivia   ~Ida   ~Henriette
(1825-97) (1828-39) (1829-86) (1831-1922)

Nassau
(b. 1921 dyg)

Frederick
(1822-1847)

Sir Robert Augustus
Graves Colleton 8th Bt. = Mary Comins
(1824-1866)

Gertrude
(1826-1854)

Alswitha
(1829-1852)

Sir Robert Augustus William Colleton 9th Bt.   = Edith Abraham
(1854-1938) (*Baronetcy extinct*)

— GRAVES —
FAMILY TREE
(simplified)

James Graves (Colonel in King William III's army) = Maria Herdman
(c. 1654 - c. 1689)

Samuel Graves = Jane Moore (said to be nearly a hundred years old)
(1674-1727)

Rev. John Graves = Jane Hodson	Admiral Samuel Graves = i Elizabeth Sedgewick
of Castle Dawson, Ireland *m. 1739*	of Hembury Fort (1729-1767)
(1711-1776)* (1713–1784)	(1713-1787) = ii Margaret Spinckes
	osp. 1727-1808)

Rear-Admiral	Rear-Admiral	Rear-Admiral
Samuel Graves	John Graves	Sir Thomas Graves, K.B.
(1741-1802)	(1743-1811)	(c. 1747-1814)
=	=	=
Catherine	Elizabeth	i Bridget Bacon (d.1795)
Fetherstonhaugh	Sawle	
(1763-1816)	(1748-1819)	Mary (1772-1860)
		=
		ii Miss Blacknell

| Mary | Sir Joseph Graves Sawle | = Dorothea |
| (1789-1810) | (1793-1865) | Prideaux- Brune |

* The Rev. John Graves and his wife supposedly had fifteen children but due to the poor condition of the Parish Records in Castle Dawson, Magherafelt, Northern Ireland, it is hard to be accurate.

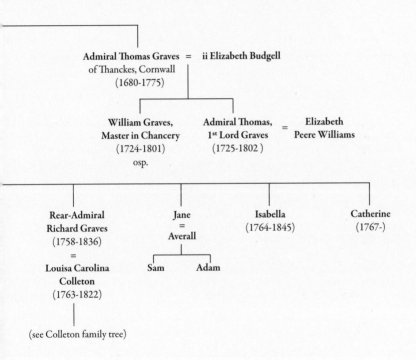

Admiral Thomas Graves = ii Elizabeth Budgell
of Thanckes, Cornwall
(1680-1775)

William Graves,
Master in Chancery
(1724-1801)
osp.

Admiral Thomas, = Elizabeth
1st Lord Graves   Peere Williams
(1725-1802)

Rear-Admiral
Richard Graves
(1758-1836)
=
Louisa Carolina
Colleton
(1763-1822)

Jane
=
Averall

Isabella
(1764-1845)

Catherine
(1767-)

Sam   Adam

(see Colleton family tree)

Select Bibliography

*

Albury, Paul, *The Story of the Bahamas*, (Macmillan, 1975)

Anzilotti, Cara, *In the Affairs of the World: Women, Patriarchy, and Power in Colonial South Carolina*, (Praeger, 2002)

Attmore, William; Rodman, Lida Tunstall, (ed.), *Journal of a Tour to North Carolina, 1787*, (University of North Carolina, 1922)

Barnes, G. R. (ed.) and Owen, J. H., (ed.), *The Private Papers of John, Earl of Sandwich*, Vol. I, August 1770-March 1778 (Navy Records Society, 1932)

Beacock Fryer, Mary, *Elizabeth Postuma Simcoe: A Biography* (Dundurn, 1989)

Borik, Carl P., *A Gallant Defence: The Siege of Charleston, 1780* (University of South Carolina Press, 2012)

Bourguignon-Frasseto, Claude, *Betsy Bonaparte: The Belle of Baltimore*, (Maryland Historical Society, 2003)

Bray, Mrs Anna Eliza, *The Borders of the Tamar and the Tavy: Their Natural History, Manner, Customs, Superstitions, Scenery, Antiquities, Eminent Persons, Etc.*, Vol. II (W. Kent and Company, Devon, 1879)

Bryan, Evelyn McDaniel Frazier, *Colleton County, S.C. A History of the First 160 Years, 1670 – 1830*, (Florentine Press, 1993)

Buchanan, J. E., *The Colleton Family and the Early History of South Carolina and Barbados: 1646-1775* (University of Edinburgh, 1989)

Buchanan, John, *The Road to Guilford Courthouse: the American Revolution in the Carolinas*, (John Wiley and Sons, 1997)

Campbell, Barry, *The Badminton Tradition*, (Michael Joseph Ltd, 1978)

Cann and Bush, *Exmouth History*, Vol. III (Exmouth Library)

Catesby, Mark, *The Natural History of Carolina, Florida, and the Bahama Islands*, Vol. II (1743)

Charnock, John, *Biographia Navalis*, Vol. IV (1795)

Chesnutt, David R. (ed.) and Taylor, C. James, (ed.), *The Papers of Henry Laurens*, Vol. XVI (University of South Carolina Press, 2003)

Cheves, Langdon, *Cases at Law, Argued and Determined in the Court of Appeals of South Carolina*, Vol. I (A. S. Johnston, 1840)

Clarke, James Stanier (ed.) and McArthur, John, (ed.), *The Naval Chronicle*, Volume VIII (Cambridge University Press, 2010)

Coker, Kathryn Roe, *The South Carolina Historical Magazine*, Vol. 96, No. 2 (South Carolina Historical Society, 1995)

Craton, Michael, *A History of the Bahamas*, (San Salvador Press, 1983)

Craton, Michael and Saunders, Gail, *Islanders in the Stream, A History of the Bahamian People*, Vol. One (University of Georgia Press, 1999)

Crawford, Michael J. (ed.), *Naval Documents of the American Revolution*, Vol. X, 1777 (Naval History and Heritage Command, 1996)

Cross, Russell J., *Historic Ramblin's Through Berkeley*, (Berkeley County Historical Society, 2002)

Didier, Eugène Lemoine, *The Life and Letters of Madame Bonaparte*, (C. Scribner's Sons, 1879)

Dunn, Richard S., S*ugar and Slaves, The Rise of the Planter Class in the English West Indies, 1624-1713*, (University of North Carolina Press, 1972)

Easterby, J. H., (ed.), *Wadboo Barony: The Fate as Told in Colleton Family Papers, 1773-1793*, (University of South Carolina Press, 1952)

Edgar, Walter B., *Partisans and Redcoats: The Southern Conflict that Turned the Tide of the American Revolution*, (Harper Collins, 2003)

Edgar, Walter B., *South Carolina, a History*, (Univ. of South Carolina 1998)

Everitt, W., *Memorials of Exmouth*, (Exmouth, 1855)

Ford, Timothy, (notes by Barnwell, Joseph W.), *Diary of Timothy Ford, 1785-1786*, (The South Carolina Historical and Genealogical Magazine, Vol. XIII, October 1912)

Foster, Sir Augustus John, Bart., *Jeffersonian America, Notes on the United States of America Collected in the Years 1805-6-7 and 11-12*, (The Huntington Library, California, 1954)

Fraser, Walter J., Jr., *Charleston! Charleston! The History of a Southern City*, (University of South Carolina Press, 1991)

Ganzi, Kurt, *Victorian Vocalists*, (Routledge, 2017)

Gillespie, Joanna Bowen, *The Life and Times of Martha Laurens Ramsay, 1759-1811*, (University of South Carolina Press, 2001)

Graves, Louisa Carolina, *Desultory Thoughts, on various subjects, by Louisa Carolina, wife of Rear Admiral Richard Graves of Hembury Fort, Devonshire, and daughter of Sir John Colleton, Baronet. Born Baroness of Fairlawn, Landgravine of Colleton and Sovereign Proprietress of the Isles of Bahama*, (The British Press, Brussels, 1821)

Gray, Todd, *East Devon: The Traveller's Tales*, (Mint Press, Exeter, 2000)

Grieg, James (ed.), *Joseph Farington*, Vol. V, January 9, 1805 to December 21, 1809 (George H. Doran Company, 1924)

Harvey, Hazel, *Exeter Past,* (Phillmore & Co Ltd, 1996)

Hirschfeld, Fritz, *George Washington and Slavery: A Documentary Portrayal,* (University of Missouri Press, 1997)

Holcomb, Brent, *South Carolina Naturalisations,* 1783-1850, State Records, Misc. Records 0-3, 713-4 (Genealogical Pub. Co, Baltimore, 1985)

Huger-Smith, Alice and Huger Smith, D.E., *The Dwelling Houses of Charleston, South Carolina,* (J.B. Lippincott, 1917)

Irving, John Beaufain, *A Day on Cooper River,* (A. E. Miller, South Carolina, 1842)

Johnson, Joseph, *Traditions and Reminiscences Chiefly of the American Revolution,* (Walker and James, University of California, 1851)

Johnson, William, *Sketches of the Life and Correspondence of Nathanael Greene: Major General of the Armies of the United States, in the War of the Revolution,* Volume 2 (published by the author, 1822)

Kinvig, R. H., *The Isle of Man: A Social, Cultural and Political History,* (Liverpool University Press, 1975)

Leiding, Harriette Kershaw, *Historic Houses of South Carolina,* (J. B. Lippincott Company, 1921)

Ligon, Richard, *A true & exact History of the Island of Barbadoes,* (Peter Parker, 1657)

Masefield, John, *Sea Life in Nelson's Time,* (Methuen & Co., 1905)

McCalman, Iain, *Radical Underworld, Prophets, Revolutionaries, and Pornographers in London, 1795-1840,* (Cambridge University Press Archive, 1988)

McCandless, Peter, *Slavery, Disease and Suffering in the Southern Lowcountry,* (Cambridge University Press, 2011)

McCrady, Edward, *The History of South Carolina in the Revolution 1775-1780,* (Macmillan, 1901)

McCrady, Edward, *The History of South Carolina in the Revolution 1780-1783,* (Macmillan, 1901)

McCrady, Edward, *The History of South Carolina under the Royal Government 1719-1776,* (Macmillan, 1901)

Moore, A., *The Annals of Gallantry: Or, The Conjugal monitor: Being a Collection of Curious and Important Trials for Divorces, and Actions of Crim. Con. During the Present Reign,* Vol. 11 and Vol. 154 (Sold by M. Jones, 1814-15)

Murray, Venetia, *High Society: A Social History of the Regency Period, 1788-1830,* (Viking, 1998)

Nicolas, Sir Nicholas Harris, (with notes by Colburn, H.), *The Dispatches and Letters of Vice Admiral Lord Viscount Nelson,* (Henry Colborn, 1846)

Nova Scotia Historical Society, *Collections of the Nova Scotia Historical Society*, Vol XX, (Wm. Macnab & Son, Halifax, N.S., 1912)

Olsen, Kirstin, *Daily Life in the 18th Century England*, (Greenwood Publishing Group, 1999)

Orvin, Maxwell Clayton, *Historic Berkeley County, South Carolina, 1671-1900*, (M. C. Orvin, 1973)

Pinkney, Elise (ed.) and Zahniser, Marvin R., (ed.), *The Letterbook of Eliza Lucas Pinkney, 1739 -1762*, (University of South Carolina Press, 1997)

Ravenel, Henry Edward of Spartanburg, S. C., *A History and Genealogy of the Huguenot Family of Ravenel, of South Carolina*, (Franklin Printing and Publishing Company, 1898)

Reid, Dr Bill, *A South Carolina Baronet's Revenge*, (Southern Visions, Vol. I, No. I, South Carolina Historical Society, Colleton 30-4)

Riley, Sandra, *Homeward Bound, A History of the Bahama Islands to 1850, with a Definitive Study of Abaco in the American Loyalist Plantation Period*, (Island Research, 1983)

Riley, William, *Riley's Law Cases, Exclusive of Those Published in 3d Hill's Law Reports,* (McCarter & Dawson, 1860)

Rodger, N.A.M., *The Command of the Ocean: A Naval History of Britain, 1649-1815*, (Penguin, 2006)

Rodger, N.A.M., *The Insatiable Earl, The Life of John Montagu, Fourth Earl of Sandwich 1718 – 1792*, (Harper Collins, 1993)

Rogers, George C., (ed.), *The Papers of Henry Laurens, Vol. 8, 1771- 1773*, (South Carolina Historical Society, 1980)

Rogers, George C., Jr., *Charleston in the Age of the Pinckneys*, (University of Oklahoma Press, 1969)

Rogers, George C., Jr., *The History of Beaufort County, South Carolina*, Volume 1, 1514 - 1861, (University of South Carolina Press, 1996)

Rowland, Lawrence Sanders; Moore, Alexander; Rogers, George. C.; Wise, Stephen R. and Spieler, Gerhard, *The History of Beaufort County, South Carolina: 1514-1861*, (University of South Carolina Press, 1996)

Ryan, Richard, *Biographia Hibernica: A Biographical Dictionary of the Worthies of Ireland, from the Earliest Period to the Present Time*, (J. Warren, 1821)

Scott-Stokes, Charity, (ed.) and Lumb, Alan, (ed.), *Sir Henry Francis Drake, (1723-1794); Letters from the Country, Letters from the City*, (Devon and Cornwall Record Society, The Boydell Press, 2019)

Severens, Martha R.; Charles L. Wyrick, Jr., (ed.), *The Miniature Portrait Collection of the Carolina Art Association*, (Carolina Art Association, 1984)

Siebert, Wilbur Henry, *Loyalists in East Florida, 1774-1785*, Vol. I (Florida State Historical Society, 1929)

Sirmans, M. Eugene, *The South Carolina Royal Council, 1720-1763*, (Omohundro Institute of Early American History and Culture, 1961)

Smith, David Bonner, (ed.), *Letters of the Admiral of the Fleet The Earl of St Vincent*, Vol. 1, (Navy Records Society, 1937)

Smith, Henry A. M., *The Baronies of South Carolina*, (The South Carolina Historical and Genealogical Magazine, 1917)

Smith, Henry A. M., *The Baronies of South Carolina*, (South Carolina Historical Society, 1931)

Smith, Henry A. M., *The Colleton Family in South Carolina*, (The South Carolina Historical and Genealogical Magazine, Vol. 1, No. 4, 1900)

Stamp, Alfred Edward, *Admissions to Trinity College*, (Macmillan, 1911-16)

Sugden, Dr. John, Nelson, *The Sword of Albion*, (Bodley Head, 2012)

Travis, John. F., *The Rise of the Devon Seaside Resorts, 1750-1900*, (University of Exeter Press, 1993)

Vickery, Amanda, *The Gentleman's Daughter: Women's Lives in Georgian England*, (Yale University Press, 2003)

Weir, Robert M., *Colonial South Carolina: A History*, (University of South Carolina Press, 1997)

Wells, Louisa Susannah, *The Journal of a Voyage from Charlestown, South Carolina, to London*, (New York Historical Society,1906)

White, Charles, *The Belgic Revolution of 1830*, (Whittaker and Co., 1835)

Wickwire, Franklin and Mary, *Cornwallis, The American Adventure*, (Houghton Mifflin, 1970)

Willcox, William B., (ed.), *The American Rebellion: Sir Henry Clinton's Narrative of his Campaigns, 1775-1782*, (Yale University Press, 1954)

Index

*

INDEX

Weygand, GeneraL, Maxime, 215
Willan, Reverend, 103, 109, 110, 129
Wilson, Lieutenant John, 69, 71
Wolford Lodge, 101, 115, 116, 118, 120, 121, 152

Woodbine Hill, 111, 115, 187, 191
Wylly, Captain Alexander, 86

Yamasee Indians, 15, 16